# Phenomenal Difference

# Phenomenal Difference

## A Philosophy of Black British Art

Leon Wainwright

LIVERPOOL UNIVERSITY PRESS

First published in 2017 by
Liverpool University Press
4 Cambridge Street
Liverpool
L69 7ZU



British Library Cataloguing-in-Publication data
A British Library CIP record is available

ISBN 978-1-78138-312-4 hardback
ISBN 978-1-78138-417-6 paperback

Typeset by Carnegie Book Production, Lancaster
Printed and bound by CPI Group (UK) Ltd, Croydon CR0 4YY

# Contents


*List of illustrations*     vii
*Acknowledgements*     xi

Introduction     1

1 Representation     19

2 Affective relations     37

3 Placing the past     53

4 The body and perception     70

5 Equivalence     109

6 Reversibility     132

7 Intertwining     158

8 Art and mediation     172

Conclusion: The phenomenal as practice     193

*Bibliography*     207
*Index*     222

# List of illustrations


1  Keith Piper, *The Fictions of Science*, 1996, still image from video. Image used with permission.  3

2  Manjeet Lamba, *Arrival*, 1992, watercolour. Image used with permission.  19

3  Permindar Kaur, *Arrival*, 1991, glass and steel, 168 x 114 x 152 cm. Image used with permission.  21

4  Permindar Kaur, *Arrival* (detail), 1991, glass and steel, 168 x 114 x 152 cm. Image used with permission.  22

5  Sonia Boyce, *Big Women's Talk*, 1984, pastel and ink on paper, 148 x 155 cm. Private collection. © Sonia Boyce. All rights reserved, DACS 2016.  58

6  Sonia Boyce, *She Ain't Holding Them Up, She's Holding On (Some English Rose)*, 1986, crayon, chalk, pastel and ink on paper, 216 x 99 cm. Middlesbrough Collection at Middlesbrough Institute of Modern Art. © Sonia Boyce. All rights reserved, DACS 2016.  59

7  Keith Piper, *A Ship Called Jesus: The Ghosts of Christendom*, 1991, first part of the installation, mixed media with computer montage on timber. Installation: Ikon Gallery, Birmingham. Image used with permission.  62

8  Keith Piper, *A Ship Called Jesus: Onward Christian Soldiers*, 1991, second part of the installation, mixed media with computer montage on timber. Installation: Ikon Gallery, Birmingham. Image used with permission.  63

9  Johannes Phokela, *Mortal Diptych Surmounted by Cameo Emblems*, 1997, oil and mixed media, each panel 198 x 168 cm. Courtesy of the artist.  76

10  Aubrey Williams, *Quartet no. 5, Opus 92*, 1981, from his
*Shostakovich* series (1969–81), oil on canvas, 132 x 208 cm, private
collection.    79

11  Said Adrus and Bhajan Hunjan, *Trespassing*, 1993, paint on
wood, 31 x 31 x 1 cm. Photograph by Bhajan Hunjan.    80

12  Vanley Burke, *Outside George Street Church*, 1972, monochrome
photograph. Image used with permission.    82

13  Vanley Burke, *The March*, 1977, monochrome photograph.
Image used with permission.    83

14  Vanley Burke, *Church Meeting*, c.1980, monochrome photograph.
Image used with permission.    84

15  Vanley Burke, *Portrait of a Woman*, c.1980, monochrome
photograph. Image used with permission.    85

16  Shanti Thomas, *The Traveller*, 1988/1989, pastel on paper,
141 x 132 cm. Image used with permission.    87

17  Juginder Lamba, *The Cry*, 1993, wood and metal,
213 x 152 x 107 cm. Wilberforce House, Hull.    88

18  Juginder Lamba, *Pod Four, Phase II*, 1994, oak wood,
30 x 33 x 48 cm. Image used with permission.    90

19  Juginder Lamba, *Local Marriage*, 1998, lime wood,
126 x 46 x 44 cm. Image used with permission.    91

20  Juginder Lamba, *Tree*, 1995, walnut wood, 186 x 44 x 40 cm.
Image used with permission.    92

21  Mona Hatoum, *Corps étranger*, 1994, video installation with
cylindrical wooden structure, video projector, video player,
amplifier and four speakers, 350 x 300 x 300 cm. © Mona Hatoum.
Photo © Philippe Migeat. Courtesy Centre Pompidou, Paris.    97

22  Mona Hatoum, *Baid Ghanam (Sheep's Testicle) (Jerusalem)*, 1996,
C-type print, 18 x 26 cm. © Mona Hatoum. Courtesy White
Cube.    99

23  Mona Hatoum, *Rous Ghanam (Sheep Heads) (Jerusalem)*, 1996,
C-print, 18 x 26 cm. © Mona Hatoum. Courtesy White Cube.    100

24  Mona Hatoum, *Kroush (Tripe) (Jerusalem)*, 1996, C-print,
20 x 29 cm. © Mona Hatoum. Courtesy White Cube.    100

25  Mona Hatoum, *Recollection*, 1995, hair balls, strands of hair
    hung from the ceiling, wooden loom with woven hair, table,
    dimensions variable, installation. © Mona Hatoum. Photo ©
    Fotostudio Eshof. Courtesy Beguinage St Elisabeth, Kortrijk,
    Belgium and White Cube.                                         103

26  Mona Hatoum, *Recollection* (detail), 1995, hair balls, strands of
    hair hung from the ceiling, wooden loom with woven hair, table,
    dimensions variable, installation. © Mona Hatoum. Photo ©
    Fotostudio Eshof. Courtesy Beguinage St Elisabeth, Kortrijk,
    Belgium and White Cube.                                         104

27  Sonia Boyce, *Afro Blanket*, 1994, 37 afro wigs, installation view
    at the South Bank Centre. © Sonia Boyce. All rights reserved,
    DACS 2016.                                                      106

28  Mona Hatoum, *Measures of Distance*, 1988, colour video with
    sound, duration 15 minutes. A Western Front video production,
    Vancouver, 1988. © Mona Hatoum. Courtesy White Cube.            112

29  Yeu-Lai Mo, from the *Food Jars* series, 1998, curry sauce,
    lard, oil, water, carved carrots and radishes. Image used with
    permission.                                                     121

30  Yeu-Lai Mo, *Foodscape: Tank 3*, 2000, lard, hundred-year-old
    eggs (preserved duck eggs), water, seaweed, lily bulbs, fine
    vermicelli noodles. Image used with permission.                 122

31  Chila Burman, *For Tune*, 2000, cibachrome and mixed media,
    91 x 64 cm. © Chila Burman. All rights reserved, DACS 2016.     135

32  Sonia Khurana, *Breath 1*, 1998, single-channel video projection,
    colour, silent, 5 minutes, looped. © Sonia Khurana.            140

33  Sonia Khurana, *I'm Tied to My Mother's Womb with a Very Long
    Chord*, 1998, two-channel video diptych (stacked screens), colour
    and sound, 5 minutes, looped. © Sonia Khurana.                 143

34  Sonia Khurana, *Lone Women Don't Lie*, 1999, single-channel
    video (vertical screen), black and white, 3 minutes 20 seconds,
    looped. © Sonia Khurana.                                        145

35  Sonia Khurana, *Anhad: the 'Original' Sound*, 1998, duratrans
    print photograph on lightbox and video projection, black and
    white, silent, 3 minutes, looped. © Sonia Khurana.             147

36 Sonia Khurana, *The Waters, Forgotten of the Foot: Part I, Juggler*, 1998, single-channel video, black and white, silent, 7 minutes, looped. © Sonia Khurana. 148

37 Sonia Khurana, *The Waters, Forgotten of the Foot: Part II, Big Sleep*, 1999, video diptych (stacked screens), black and white, with sound, 5 minutes, looped. © Sonia Khurana. 149

38 Sonia Khurana, *Zoetrope*, 1999, photographed simulated performance, on painted wood and metal kinetic object, 165 cm. Courtesy Kiran Nadar Museum of Art, New Delhi. © Sonia Khurana. 150

39 Mona Hatoum, *Jardin Public*, 1993, painted wrought iron, wax and pubic hair, 89 x 40 x 49 cm. © Mona Hatoum. Photo © Edward Woodman. Courtesy White Cube. 161

40 Sonia Boyce, *Talking Presence*, 1988, mixed media on photographic paper, 165 x 122 cm. © Sonia Boyce. All Rights Reserved, DACS 2016. 163

41 *Alien Nation*, cover of the exhibition catalogue, 2006. ICA/inIVA publication. 175

42 Hew Locke, *Hemmed in Two* (Victoria and Albert Museum version), 2000, cardboard, acrylic, marker pen, wood, found objects, height 4 m, length 7.5 m, width 6 m. Photo by the artist. © Hew Locke. All rights reserved, DACS 2016. 177

43 Hew Locke, *Golden Horde*, 2006, mixed media including plastic, metal, textile and wood, maximum height 273 cm, length 253 cm, width 200 cm. Photo: Marcus Leith. © Hew Locke. All rights reserved, DACS 2016. 178

44 Mario Ybarra Jr, *Brown and Proud*, 2006, mixed media. Photo: Marcus Leith. Image used with permission. 179

45 Kori Newkirk, *Merk*, 2006, pony beads, artificial hair extensions, aluminium and dye, approx. 239 x 183 x 3 cm. Courtesy of the artist. Photo: Marcus Leith. 181

46 Henna Nadeem, *People*, 2006, digital montage, 32 x 36 cm. Courtesy of the artist. 183

# Acknowledgements

This book was a long time in the making and over its years of development it has benefitted from being shared with numerous audiences and readers in diverse settings, and from numerous institutional contexts, here in the United Kingdom and abroad. Working across a range of archives and collections – chiefly those at Tate Britain, Goldsmiths College London, the Institute for International Visual Arts (Iniva), and the African and Asian Visual Artists Archives – progress on the book began while teaching at the School of Oriental and African Studies at the University of London, where I would present various accounts and versions of the topic. I taught from the material there as well as at Middlesex University and the University of Sussex, where I held posts in departments of visual culture studies and art history. I remain grateful to all those I have taught who have shaped my thinking, and it has been gratifying to see so many of them – notably Benedict Burbridge, Lucy Bayley, Anjalie Dalal-Clayton, Beccy Kennedy, Polly Savage and Giulia Paoletti – having taken up the impulse to attend to contemporary art in their distinguished teaching, scholarship and curating. I have been very fortunate for the opportunity to share ideas from the book over the years in ever-widening circles of staff and students: the groups marshalled by Whitney Davis at the University of California in Berkeley during my fellowship, at Yale University during another fellowship at the Center for British Art, Manchester Metropolitan University, the material culture seminar at University College London, the University of the West Indies at St Augustine in Trinidad and Tobago, the Institute of Commonwealth Studies in London, the University of Newcastle and at the Aga Khan University in Karachi. An invitation from the John Hope Franklin Center and the Department of Art, Art History and Visual Studies at Duke University (extended by Richard J. Powell, Ian Baucom, Sonia Boyce, David A. Bailey and others), and a generous commission to contribute to the award-winning *Shades of Black* anthology, allowed me to explore my provisionally formed thoughts among a formidable set of artists, curators and thinkers, including Lubaina Himid, Judith Wilson, Dawoud Bey, Sutapa Biswas, Kobena Mercer, Zineb Sedira, Keith Piper, Susan Pui San Lok, Isaac Julien and Sandy Nairne. Their contributions to this field have remained in view when formulating a corresponding philosophy and I hope that they feel this is a fitting response to our discussions. Towards the end of the process of preparing the book, I presented parts of it at the University of Bristol, the University of Edinburgh, Chelsea College of Arts, Tate Britain and Loughborough University, and consequently I remain indebted to Paul Gilroy, Elizabeth Robles, Jeremy Melius, Allison Young, Dot Price, Zehra Jumabhoy, Marlene Smith, Marsha Meskimmon, Paul Goodwin and Pratap Rughani.

The very first people to suggest that this book should be published were Chris Pinney, Tania Tribe, John Picton and the late Jean Fisher, whose compliments on the work I noted and have cherished. Whenever I was reticent to speak about the progress I was making, it was advice from the late Stuart Hall ('too much self-abnegation, Wainwright!') that I tried to take on board. Indeed, Hall's direction and personal encouragement gave me the confidence to participate more fully in the black British art community, and I have enjoyed that social dimension of the research the most. There have been so many similar demonstrations of openness and support for this particular line of work that I can barely signal them here. Among the milestones are: being brought onto the editorial board of the journal *Third Text* by Rasheed Araeen; when Gilane Tawadros implored me to break my silence on exhibition curating and review her *Alien Nation* show; working behind the scenes at the first *Africa Pavilion* at the Venice Biennale, together with Olu Oguibe, Salah Hassan and Yinka Shonibare; striking up lasting professional friendships with Margherita Sprio, Pauline de Souza, Roger Malbert, Barbara Walker and Kay Dickinson; benefitting from the extensive networks of Gasworks and the Triangle Trust, thanks to Alessio Antoniolli and Robert Loder; curating the first nationally funded retrospective of the art of Aubrey Williams, together with Reyahn King at the Walker Art Gallery, National Museums Liverpool; establishing, with Alnoor Mitha, the curatorial laboratory of the Asia Triennial Manchester; and contributing to cultural diversity programming at Tate Britain together with Vicky Walsh, Andrew Dewdney and David Dibosa. I am deeply grateful to the Leverhulme Trust for its generous support through the personal award of a Philip Leverhulme Prize (PLP-2012-077: History of Art), which followed a Leverhulme Early Career Fellowship.

A contribution from the Central Research Fund of the University of London proved to be invaluable, alongside the support of colleagues at the University of Sussex, The Open University and Colgate University in New York (enabled through my inaugural appointment to the endowed Kindler Chair in Global Contemporary Art). The book had expert input at the various production stages by Elena Trivelli, Liam Baldwin, Kevin Parker, Gen Doy, Sophie Orlando, Celeste-Marie Bernier and the superb editorial staff at Liverpool University Press and Carnegie Book Production, not to mention the editors and anonymous peer reviewers of this book series. I will remain forever grateful to the many artists who spent time with me discussing their projects, and those among them who have lent their kind permission for the reproduction of illustrations. Finally, I extend heartfelt thanks to all my family – two new members, Robin and Luca, came along just as I was finalising the manuscript – and above all, to Anna, for her love and the sheer mettle she shows in helping to hold all of this complex picture together.

# Introduction

This book offers a detailed philosophical account of art by individuals of black and Asian backgrounds who have worked in Britain at one time or another over the past four decades. It explores a vivid range of intimate, bodily encounters with art, involving the senses, perception and the emotions, and so emphasises the affective relations between works of art, their viewers and the world at hand. Black British artists have for a long time worked in ways that complicate and unsettle the more familiar frameworks of critical theory that have been applied to understanding their art and from which their art-making has in part drawn. As such, this book projects what may become the future basis for seeing black British art, by tackling the historical over-reliance upon such key terms as identity politics, representation, cultural difference, ethnicity and diversity, showing how cultural theory may be rethought and reinvigorated with the benefit of an 'ontological turn'. Consequently, this book presents a detailed case for recognising the role of black British art and artists in shaping a more layered and contemporary account of aesthetics as a field of social practice. It takes the distinctive approach of showing that works of art do not simply have continuing relevance for advanced theoretical thought, but are themselves a sort of philosophy.

By the time I began research on this book in 1997, the chief vocabulary of cultural criticism associated with black British art was already quite established in academic discourse, and its appeal was widening into more accessible and popular sorts of writing. Travelling through Verona airport a few summers later, I came across a work of science fiction by the Australian writer Greg Egan entitled *Diaspora* (Egan, 1997), translated into Italian. I found it equally remarkable that the book took the word 'diaspora' for its title and that I had found it when killing time at an airport, on a carousel of books destined for travellers' laps. But, of course, what more apt place to find *Diaspora* than at a nodal point of modernity and geographical movement such as an airport? A machine for channelling migration and processing the need for connectedness among communities on the move; on the flipside, it is also an organ of restriction, discrimination and 'security'.[1] Evidently, the widening arc of circulation for the term 'diaspora' is itself an example of a diaspora-redolent uprooting, dispersal and localisation. The concept is demonstrably both moveable and adaptive to contexts beyond academia (and much beyond Anglophone publishing), compelling in its metaphors for how cultures flourish and continue following their sometimes violent displacement. The discourse surrounding diaspora culture leaves a wide margin for the imagination too. Egan's *romanzo di fantascienza* is a tale of exodus, travel and (post)human adaptation in outer space, a biotechnological leap into the void where relationships are worked out in a yet unexplored, extraterrestrial distant future (the year 2975 CE).[2]

Just as the specialist term diaspora was finding new discursive sites in the late 1990s, not least in the science-fiction publishing mainstream, its centrality for black British art was beginning to slip and shift. In the same year that Egan's *Diaspora* was published, the British artist Keith Piper assembled a series of digital compositions that he entitled *The Fictions of Science* (fig. 1). One of its montages enlarges Piper's own face, putting a ruler to his cheek, clamped in place to measure the distance between his left nostril and his ear. This was an artist's response to a certain problem: how to explode a myth – by drawing attention to the fiction of its claims – surrounding the vaunted disinterestedness and boasted objectivity of scientific thought and practice. The primary operative fictions here are the findings of racial science, and by fabricating and parodying the somewhat clinical morphology of his own anonymised head, Piper had pressed art into a field of politics. Yet while Piper focused on science itself as a fiction, his work set me thinking about an artist's standpoint on the production of knowledge in another, adjacent manifestation of epistemic thought: the social sciences, more specifically, the domain of cultural theory and its rubric for an analysis of difference, migration, exile and hybridity.

Deploying the diaspora concept has been dynamic and politically worthwhile, helping to think through, and to dignify, the histories and

---

1   On this latter issue of airports, territory and mobility, focusing on responses from contemporary artists, see Jim (2014).

2   Egan has also written, ostensibly much outside the 'hard-sf' genre, on the plight of asylum claimants held at Australia's immigration detention centres, in his 'The Razor Wire Looking Glass' (2003). Published at http://www.gregegan.net/ESSAYS/ RAZOR/RazorWire.html (accessed 8 February 2016).

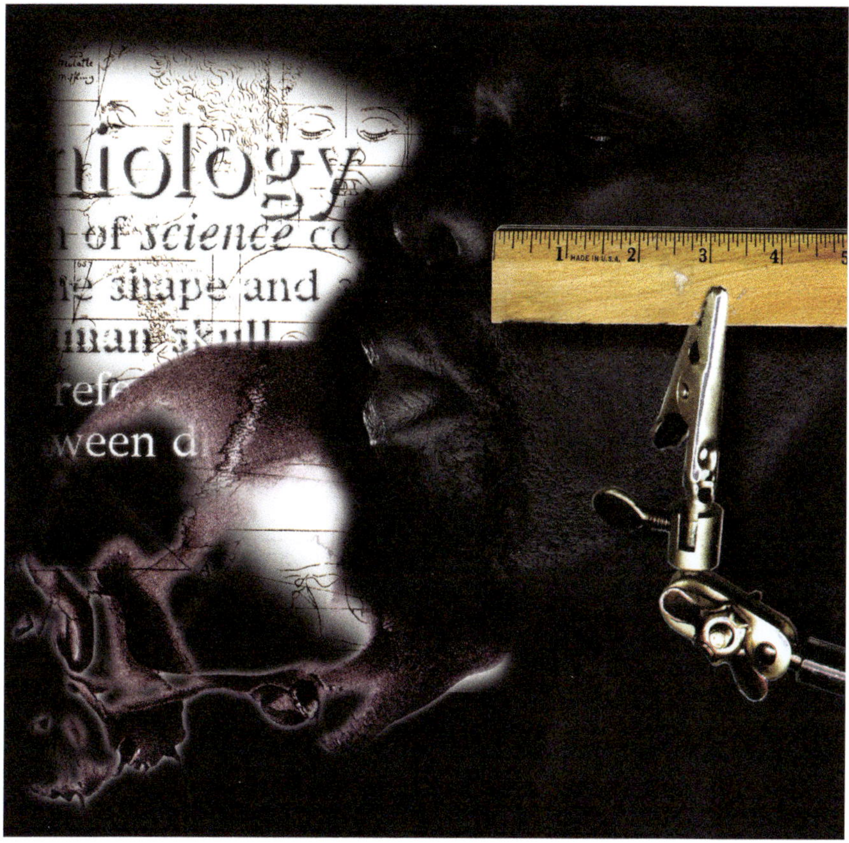


Figure 1: Keith Piper, *The Fictions of Science*, 1996, still image from video. Image used with permission.

contemporary experiences of African, Asian and Caribbean people and their descendants in Britain. It is vital for elucidating the psychic and discursively intricate workings of modern subjectivity under conditions of displacement and cultural transmission. It has helped to establish a debate on national cultural identities and how they may be disrupted or countered by black British subjects. But that interest has also risked their art being allocated a separate and even a rather precarious place in the field of attention to contemporary British art. The study of black British art has drawn upon just a handful of theoretical paradigms. It has inspired writing that by some accounts strains to move in step with developments in art practice itself, which exceed the present scope of concerns with the cultural politics of 'race', ethnicity and nationhood.

The very language of definition and conceptualisation that was devised to assist this art and to lend its artists agency seems to have helped in creating some of its own barriers to thinking about art's wider and more lasting value.

Perhaps far too much is shared between critical theory and the ruler and crocodile clip of anatomical itemisation pictured by Piper. This art is less likely to be overlooked by scholars of culture than unduly encumbered by the terms and tactics that were devised to understand and celebrate its significance. While such art has played a role in resisting the marginalisation and exclusion of diaspora communities from a nation-space such as Britain, the danger of reducing art to its discursive content is considerable. There is nothing to be gained from abstracting aesthetic experience and translating it into a single critical lexicon. And if black British art may have largely secured its entry in a historical record of national culture, it may have simultaneously lost its place in a more contemporary and diversifying humanities.

Suffice it to say that Keith Piper's intervention against an initially Victorian fascination for the lumps, bumps and proportions of the human head is a signature piece for an extended problematising of cultural analysis in the field of diaspora and black British art. The philosopher Maurice Merleau-Ponty famously noted that 'science manipulates things and gives up living in them' (1964a: 159), and 'objective thought is unaware of the subject of perception' (1962: 207). In breaking away from such abstractions of scientific thinking, works such as Piper's *Fictions of Science*, along with much other art featured here, set the tone against a stultifying (social) science fiction in favour of a more emancipated mode of philosophy.

## Uncomfortable paradigms

Before engaging with the possibilities offered by philosophy, it is important to uncover how black British art has become confined to demonstrating the 'language, textuality and signification' paradigm (Hall, 1996c: 271) of post-structuralist thought and subjected to what Barbara Stafford has called the 'ruling metaphor of reading' (1995: 6). This metaphor seems to suggest that encounters with art are made by a mind somehow removed from its body, so that training our attention too closely on art's significations alone may lose a sense of its broader, perceptual virtues. The reader of art takes visual objects as displaced spaces where meaning is constructed in complex, simultaneously arbitrary and conventional ways, but nonetheless always diminishing the power of materialisation by rendering it secondary to language. The main motivation for taking art to be an encoded medium of communication – for rendering the visible legible – is one of trying to remove the element of chance, the ambiguity, discontinuity and sheer messiness of the imagination: ultimately, to try to clear up any doubt about the social value that art may have. Despite a general postmodern and postcolonial shift towards analysis of cultural indeterminacy, fluid identities and cultures 'in-between', such commentary has been quite frustrated in its efforts. Where it has tried to refuse fixed categories of cultural experience, it has nonetheless contended with the misunderstandings and pressures that circumscribe black British art. The most potent among these is the myth that such art subsists in an entirely separate sphere of cultural production or is accessible only by way of a particular route map or method.

This book speaks back to such outlooks on black British art, taking issue with an emphasis on the significations of difference that such artworks are presupposed to offer. I have identified elsewhere how this tendency has an impact on how such artists are framed and studied in the university and art school curriculum (Wainwright, 2010). Plainly they occupy a place well outside the main thrust of attention to modern and contemporary art and aesthetics, serving instead in the compromised role of a pedagogical resource with which to explore the recent histories of British multiculturalism, struggles to decolonise art history and so on. Black British artworks are often diminished in status, pushed back on to a grainy backdrop illustrating a surrounding nation fitfully working away at its race relations, such artworks being deployed as an idealised emblem of inclusivity and 'tolerance'. At the same time, commentary has pointed to their potential for assaulting an ideology of 'British culture', while blithely ignoring how art and artists have already seriously undermined its hegemonic structure. A side effect within this economy of images is that artists in the notional 'community' of black British practitioners come to be interchanged all too easily with one another, since there is little to attune commentary to the discrepancies of vision that animate the diversity among artworks.

The problem stems from a general overdetermining choice about what is to be identified as cultural material in the first place. Indeed, I suspect that black British artworks are at a loss from a too narrow view of 'the cultural' and 'the historical'. They sit in a far less plurivocal or differentiated intellectual space than they deserve, with little room left to wonder about the alternatives. What expressly *philosophical* frames may come into use that would accord with the political desire for social agency that has been vested in the production of black British art? This book is an extended meditation on that question. It asks whether the current epistemology of art has not brought some adverse political consequences, and gauges the extent to which intellectual work on black British art has succumbed to a worrying degree of conformity. Might such art be seen with new eyes or according to new currents of curiosity and attention beyond those of cultural and historical contextualism?

The title *Phenomenal Difference* refers to making a difference to this field by working otherwise from the familiarly existing terminologies and research methods around black British art, by taking up phenomenological approaches as the starting point for such a transformation. The debate pivots on the original conceptualisations that may be found to bring us into an intimately perceptual relation with artworks, and reconnects to the creative ambitions of numerous black British artists who emerged at the end of the twentieth century, and those still practising today.


## Presence

What would happen if, as I propose, understanding of this art – as a visual register of language and textuality – were put at least momentarily to one side? One answer is that we are left with the *presence* of artworks themselves – in David Summers's words, 'that which is not simply before us but which "stands out" and concerns us, that to which we are in a sense subject' (1996: 6; cf. Maniura and Shepherd, 2006). To explore such a presence is important and timely for apprehending the art of black Britain. Indeed, black British artists can be meaningfully approached in terms of what David Freedberg has located as 'the effectiveness, efficacy and vitality of images themselves' (1989: xvii). This makes for a direct, perceptual and bodily embrace of artworks, showing how they have brought their viewers and makers into distinctive moments and modes of engagement. Focusing on the materiality and immediacy of artworks then becomes a way of seeing how their viewers enjoy complex encounters that are fundamentally aesthetic in character.

What follows in this volume is a search for the means to appreciate art and artists of African, Caribbean and Asian backgrounds in Britain both *within and without* the standard models of cultural analysis. Certainly this means looking at art that has circulated within a vigorously contested cultural context: that of the struggle for belonging and nationality in Britain in the face of marginalisation, exclusion and racism, and more particularly, the rights of black British artists to belong and to be remembered and represented in canonical histories of art. But the value of art extends beyond what it may reveal about contexts of production and circulation, and so it is surprising that, for all the repeating theorisation of the 'relative autonomy' of contemporary art, hardly noticed are areas in the current exegeses of black British artworks that may unwittingly weaken its sovereign status. Black Britain's cultural politics of representation needs less reiteration than 'transposition' into a fresh understanding that is attentive to artworks and can augment their criticality. This is a fruitful arena of philosophical inquiry, its very starting point being the aim to reverse art's reduction to a theme of critical discourse, while seeking to build respectfully on the remains of a long-running campaign to take this art seriously and keep it open to intellectual scrutiny.

## Perception

I began the research for this book by talking to black British artists about the interconnected histories, ambitions and disciplinary locations of their art. Perhaps because I am from the first generation of scholars whose training in postcolonial and critical theory came to be so central, I was not always well prepared for their responses. Many of those I spoke with would suggest that their material history – the art they had assiduously produced – had actually been buried under the weight of the same cultural analysis that ostensibly promotes black British art. Others would highlight, more simply, the gap between their visual practice and the record of debates about Britain's so-called 'black arts sector'. They saw that gap as a challenge to go further and apply the tools of black and diaspora cultural criticism to previously overlooked, uncharted artworks and artists.

A smaller set of artists took the longer view, suggesting that academic thought was so many steps behind the actually unfolding history of art. Art itself points the way for new intellectual work of a kind that neither the academy nor the wider world of exhibition curating had yet fully countenanced. If only we took the time to review artworks with the appropriate individual attention, setting them apart from the general background of analytical 'noise'. It was a crucial instant for me when the range of artists' voices that I had heard came to persuade me of one thing: to stop disavowing my primarily *perceptual* relationships with their art and to take licence to begin embracing them. At which point, what moved to the middle of my vision was the multilayered experience of art, the rich interplay of thought and deed which so motivates artists, and which they can be so effusive about. I then could see why artists had felt the need to hold on to the right to make art. Based on my dialogues with artists, I resolved to find out how such a primarily phenomenological interest can reassert that sense of self and purpose (thereby unburdening a growing weight of disappointment), and to show why it is now high time to give black British art its pointedly philosophical due.

## Labelling

The same considerations about recognition extend to the naming of these artists, honouring personal choices made within the vortices of historical consciousness, art and politics. There are several contested terms used in my text that are pertinent to fraught issues of labelling and identification. These deserve to be customarily marked with inverted commas, but I have kept these to a minimum for the sake of clarity and to avoid testing the reader's patience. Rather than hide behind typographical devices, however (or casually suggest that we read such terms as if 'under erasure'), I have tried to tackle matters of disagreement more openly. There is a convention for grouping all diasporas in Britain (African, South Asian, Caribbean, Middle Eastern, East Asian and so on) under the term *black*, which was long ago established by authors in the field of black British cultural studies (see, for example, Gilroy, 1993a; Mercer, 1994). I have taken up this usage as a shorthand, and to indicate how this book has some of its roots in work in that area. But whether or not this conventional tactic of naming serves to bring actual political or social advantages for the individuals described is the very issue up for debate; and the same question could be asked about the effectiveness of identification with the diaspora concept.

Distinguishing this volume is its use of the terms black and diaspora to indicate only those individuals who have conceded to such descriptors (of course reserving the right to change their minds at any time). Obviously this has been hard to judge in some cases, and I took care over what artists were comfortable with in the course of our conversations, or what they have declared to be their associations through showing and presenting their works, organising, supporting or writing about themselves and other artists, giving permission for reproduction of their works and so on. This is less easy than it sounds and in such idiosyncratic circumstances there are no guarantees of appropriateness or accuracy. Artists of Caribbean and African descent may in fact be less keen to pass under the black or diaspora label than those who identify with South Asian, Chinese or Middle Eastern backgrounds, especially if this means that their artistic interests will be undermined or circumscribed by critical attention to ethnicity and cultural differences.[3] And a generalised feeling of fatigue, and then of dismay, if not suspicion, has also formed towards the *black British* label. Understandably, many artists feel that the designation brings reductionist or anachronistic patterns of identification, akin to where certain American artists and thinkers have gone in the effort to move 'beyond black representational space' (English, 2007). In response, a chief aim of this book is to problematise such a proclivity and to respect the currents that make this such a sensitive terrain. It shows that a consideration of 'race' or ethnicity is not something we should leap to in trying to understand this art.

## Origins and the phenomenal

The alternative conceptual compass for this book, which orients my entire discussion, is the *phenomenal*. The phenomenal has a special part to play in understanding since it cannot be isolated merely as a theme of black British artists' practices, but is actually relevant to all of their artworks. Nor is the phenomenal something that we can expect simply to find *in* their works (nor as a meaning somehow 'behind' their art); rather it *is* their works, they are phenomena. Phenomena, or 'that which appears to us', are issues of perceptual and phenomenal experience relative to diaspora artists and their art which pinpoint the presence of artworks themselves, the depositions of material they have left behind, which discloses their histories in a particular and immediate way. This is not a separable or singular 'black British experience' (to which such art unproblematically corresponds), nor a cultural 'background' or 'inheritance', or any other euphemism for art as a representative sample or artefact of a static and bounded culture. Instead, black British art

---

3 The ground of this discussion, understandably, does not stay still. Dilip Hiro noted in 1992, specifically in relation to Asian Britons, that the term 'Asian' was the most appropriate label despite understanding Asians as 'politically black' given that they are racially 'disadvantaged and oppressed' (1992: viii). According to R. Victoria Arana, artists with a background in 'India, the Middle East, and other places' have been unsympathetic to the black label (2009: x).

itself is the primary visible and physical foundation for a material analysis whose deeper history is marked by Heidegger's sense of the work of art's 'origin' ('The question concerning the origin of the work of art asks about its essential source', writes Heidegger, reprinted in Krell, 1978: 143), yet in a quite different way from our more everyday use of the term.[4] It is pressing to consider perception as the means to apprehend the phenomenal in its primacy, through a philosophy of concrete experience that identifies the importance of origins through the lived body. The lead is offered by Merleau-Ponty,[5] especially the theme typified in his comment that 'Perception is not a science of the world, it is not even an act, a deliberate taking up of a position; it is the background from which all acts stand out, and is presupposed by them' (1962: x–xi). What emerges are the contours of a vividly corporeal understanding of works by black British artists, suggesting a critical sense of the intimate and entwined relationships between the phenomenal value and the representational capacity of their art.

## Artworks themselves

Any successful illustration of the purpose of such a phenomena-centred analysis largely depends upon being able to convey what it does. Part of my task is to avoid all constructions and impositions placed upon the experience of black British art in advance, which in this case would apply primarily to the theoretical character of the existing perspectives on them. Adopting such an attitude raises awareness of any prejudicial influence that might issue from the conceptual language and assumptions that have structured this field, avoiding any easy complicity with its terms, theoretical claims and pronouncements. Crucially, this is not directed by a struggle somehow to dis-embed the authority of those accounts, as would be the case for a mundane interventionism in which a single critical paradigm is displaced in favour of another. Instead, by moving

4  I should point out at the same time my sense of ambivalence and caution towards Heidegger, which is widely shared: 'Heidegger's unrelieved world-historical gloom falls within the kind of late-Hegelian totalization I have tried to avoid on principle, and, dangerous as the modern world has been and remains, and acute as Heidegger's critique of it has been, it still offers positive choices we must learn to make in terms of the values rooted in a revised being-in-the-world' (Summers, 2003: 19; cf. Boeztkes and Vinegar, 2014).

5  Merleau-Ponty first names the project of a 'phenomenology of origins' in the preface to his book, *Phenomenology of Perception* (1962: xviii).

through the steps and stages of phenomenological thought, my aim is to augment the distinctive character of critical work on black British artists, namely by returning to artworks themselves.

Such an attitude of avoidance can only be adopted provisionally, it should be noted, and only as a philosophical procedure. The already circulating theoretical schemes applied to diaspora artists have held a role in the production of these artists' experiences, and so cannot simply be avoided unproblematically, as if there were some essential division to be made between how their works have been theorised and some other, more pressing reality. Indeed, such theoretical interests are writ large in the diverse views and opinions of those who populate the histories of black British art – the artists, critics, curators, arts organisers, archivists – and in the informed perspectives of many others. This book is designed to evaluate those established discourses of explanation while undergirding them with a more phenomenal understanding. This requires an ontological distinction to be made between theoretical discourse and black British art: a wavy line that allows us to recognise the linguistic and the material without overlooking their interactions and overlaps, and moreover the intellectual difficulties that their coexistence may pose.

Any desire to account for the social significance of black British artists must first face up to that material or thingly element of their histories – the artworks themselves – and the question of how they might be grasped through perception, as physical deposits that vie for primacy within the wider social imaginary. This direct inquiry into the material nature of art has the character of setting aside plainly social questions until a later stage of analysis – the exact pattern of the philosophical arc running through this book. Although drawing into view the notion that artworks present a codification of meanings (and are socially mediating by virtue of that ability to signify), a contrastingly phenomenal-styled account tackles in greater detail how these works exist for us perceptually. In other words, I consider how black British art discloses a rich phenomenal experience which must be levelled with assumptions about its roles as social or cultural media. This is an argument best made by turning to artworks through rich description, a detailed review of precisely *how* black British artists have created their works, how the complex fabric of this art enables the marking of cultural meanings in an intersubjective mode.

While it is commonly recognised that cultural life in general consists of various significations of experience (through which diverse realities come to be articulated, commented upon and understood), by comparison, the accompanying *experience of signification* is less often considered. Experience is transposed into signification, and vice versa, a relationship that consists through black British art being a field of practices. This art may be conceived as phenomenally present, indeed it may have *presence* as such,[6] and this attitude takes art to be a primary locus and the foundation for social questions about black British artists from the starting point of their art. Using such an intellectual aperture launches a debate about the oppositions and interactions between a phenomenal analysis and a more critically positioned account of black British art as a site of visual representation. The current approaches taken in studies of diaspora culture in Britain are based on the cardinal concepts of signification and discourse, and draw on theoretical terms generally operative in the discipline of cultural studies. There, scholars tend to explore the realm of 'natural language', or 'the discrete instrumentality and systematic objectification of experience abstracted from experience for general use' (Sobchack, 1992: 12), that is, a kind of both everyday and scientific use of language which circumvents experience itself through abstraction. Quite crucially, phenomenology opposes the view that these are the grounds for inquiry into embodied experience, and instead devotes attention to the processes of existence *before* the imposition of such systematic explanation. Focusing on the phenomenal gives way to an understanding that is not permitted by critical attitudes and helps in grasping the dynamic perceptual concerns of diaspora artists. The phenomenal relations made possible by their artworks are in turn levelled with the realities faced by black British artists.

The chapters of this book deal sequentially with these issues and problems. They show why it has become urgent to consider phenomenological themes across a range of visual works made by black British artists, including sculpture, installation, photography, video and digital art, painting and drawing. Chapters 1 and 2 ('Representation' and 'Affective relations') dynamically and graphically state the purpose of the book, from the starting point of vivid descriptions of signature artworks by Permindar Kaur and Manjeet Lamba. Lamba's watercolour entitled *Arrival* pairs a colonial Briton with an elderly Indian man, contrasting the former's calfskin shoes and signs of imperial power with the homespun cloth and

---

6 In doing so, I take up the combined sense from David Summers's definition of presence: '*Praesens* is a participial form of *praeesse*, "to be before," which it means in two senses: the first is simple, spatial, prepositional location; the second involves precedence or command, being higher in rank, more important than' (1996: 6).

respectful comportment of the latter, in a play of asymmetry and opposites. Kaur's installation, also entitled *Arrival*, is an entirely non-indexical rendering of potentially similar themes, loosened from such a reading by its aesthetic exploration of two clusters of steel arrows, spiked rods driven into the wooden floor of a gallery, topped with fragile, hand-cut glass containers. In their divergent creative approaches – and high potential to trigger a critical reading of their convergent meanings – these works serve to underscore the case for a careful philosophical treatment of this art. The tools for such work can be found in Heideggerian and Merleau-Pontian thought, assisted by ideas from more recent thinkers such as Jacques Rancière, Zygmunt Bauman, Hal Foster, Rasheed Araeen, Alfred Gell and Jean Fisher, as well as by black and Asian artists, curators and critics who have been integral to shaping the British context. With their contributions in view, these chapters launch a discussion of the dynamic interaction between phenomenological and critical approaches that forms this book's theoretical architecture.

Chapter 3 ('Placing the past') explores the consequent shape of an alternative theorisation of this art, in which artworks operate as both signs and things in a productive 'making present' of diaspora historical consciousness. It shows how artists have looked to the past as a strategy for inscribing themselves in the present and for contesting their contemporary circumstances. This discloses a range of experiences that phenomenological initiatives may equip us to understand more fully. A case study of Keith Piper's installation *A Ship Called Jesus* becomes the focus for overlapping concerns with personal memory and post-memory, for the intersecting histories of the black Church, plantation slavery and group resistance through image-making. Memories of childhood, elicited in Sonia Boyce's celebrated pastel drawings – often mistaken for painted portraits – are cardinal to forms of visual efficacy that allow the celebration of individual and shared histories. Through them, these artists have practised a form of 'visual historiography' that touches on both personal and collective pasts – whether historically 'evidential', imagined or fictive. My close descriptions of these works in this chapter recommend the primacy of a distinctively 'phenomenal' response to the central question of how to grasp the emotional and perceptual dynamics of this art.

Chapters 4 and 5 ('The body and perception' and 'Equivalence') pursue a phenomenal analysis along several specific avenues, by thinking about the body (e.g. the 'body image') in the making and experience of a range of visual works. These chapters examine the perceptual relations between vision, colour and touch, showing how black British artists have treated hair, hairpieces, body parts, both animal and human, medical collections, preserved food and a spectrum of other ephemera. Chapter 4 features Vanley Burke's black-and-white photographs of ecstatic bodies in charismatic worship, locked in the drudgery of manual work or exploding in protest at a street march; *The Traveller* by Shanti Thomas, her mother and child wrapped in diamond-blue cloth, breathing sooty air at a train station; Juginder Lamba's water-smoothed wooden assemblage *The Cry* and his toiled-over *Pod* series of organic vessels and filaments; Mona Hatoum's endoscopic journeys around her own body; Zarina Bhimji's *Vulnerable and Sticky*, disgorged brains on silk; and Sonia Boyce's *Afro Blanket*, a curly patchwork carpet of scalps. The analysis is set in motion by an account of the South African painter Johannes Phokela, recounting his technique during an interview in the studio he used when domiciled in London, and his unfinished painting *Mortal Diptych Surmounted by Cameo Emblems*, a response to Rubens and a litany of Flemish masters. 'I felt like a surgeon making it', he told me: 'I laid the canvas horizontally and bled paint through the slashes from behind'. This attention to the body, tactility, texture and sight is germane to these artists' otherwise critical artistic interests and, as I will show, it results in a special aesthetic fabric that interweaves vision and touch.

The discussion in Chapter 5 pursues such processes further by showing how Asian British artists have sometimes used image–text relationships in languages other than English to represent themselves in distinction from their African and Afro-Caribbean diaspora peers. I expand in particular on the significance of the language that accompanies Bhimji's discarded hair clippings, dropped on to soft white muslin, and her appropriated Mughal miniatures in the work *Live for Sharam, Die for Izzat*, a photo and text series; and Yeu-Lai Mo's jars of cooking ingredients – black fungi, bean sprouts, radishes and raw eggs. Mo's series of works '*begins* with an obsession', as she told me, of her intriguing layered and undulating landscapes of gravy and noodles, and opens up an important emotional field. Building on this account of the overlapping of the senses, these two chapters draw on a long history of philosophical debate about the inseparability of perceptual experiences from 'making sense' as such. This should be of particular interest to historians of art who are seeking to entwine Cartesian models with more sensory registers of inquiry.[7] With the benefit of detailed descriptions of

---

7  For instance, the sort of scholars who have paid attention to the work of Peter de Hooch (see Bernstein, 2003).

individual artworks, chapters 4 and 5 debate the phenomenological idea of 'equivalence' (suggested in the early work of Maurice Merleau-Ponty), in order to suggest an identifiable scheme for embracing the perceptual along with the linguistic parities of such art.

Chapters 6 and 7 ('Reversibility' and 'Interwining') advance the argument in order to deal with the analytic of 'reversibility' and 'interwining'. Such terms are suggested in the posthumously published work of Merleau-Ponty, and this chronological development in his thought bequeaths a structure to the book and its contribution to a philosophy of the experiential relations of black British art. Specifically, these chapters show how artists have established through art-making what the anthropologist Alfred Gell had called 'personhood'. This process is evaluated and cross-examined by describing artworks that both disclose the presence of their makers – their bodily proximity to the image, for instance – and have a certain 'presence' of their own. Examples of such phenomena in Chapter 6 include Chila Kumari Burman's colour-saturated cibachrome photographs, procedures based on intimate items from her wardrobe and garden; and Sonia Khurana's videos and performances, her hypnotic screen projection *Breath* and her celebrated *Bird* sequence, in which she presents her nude, voluptuous body in a moment of failed flight; and the nuzzling and kissing of her own face, made possible in the split monitors of *Lone Women Don't Lie*. Chapter 7 features Mona Hatoum's *Jardin Public*: the animation of steel furniture through the introduction of organic, hairy matter; and Sonia Boyce's bare lovers against a London skyline, her graphic *Talking Presence*. The result is a detailed, interlinked debate that grounds such exemplary artworks in a philosophical discourse about their presence and efficacy, and discloses their status as worldly phenomena that demand serious perceptual attention.

Chapter 8, 'Art and mediation', and the book's Conclusion, 'The phenomenal as practice', explain how all these close analyses bring the entire field of black British cultural studies on to fresh and original ground. I estimate the potential impact of the book upon current scholarly attitudes as well as the political climate in which artists live and work. A focus on the concept of 'mediation' allows me to raise the issue of how to examine the public display of art, and draws together works made by black British practitioners with several by individuals from outside the United Kingdom who have been shown alongside them. And by thinking about phenomenology as offering another 'theory of practice' – in which artworks are analysed as a mode of social agency through the materialising of 'affect' – irreversible shifts can be made in current knowledge about black British art and political representation.

Chapter 8 leads with a discussion of *Alien Nation*, a touring exhibition which was among the last of its kind in Britain, commissioned when public funding for the promotion of 'cultural diversity' had not yet suffered the significant cuts that followed the global economic crisis that erupted in the last decade. What made it significant was how the exhibition attempted to hold a mirror to the expectations – indeed, the burden of representation – placed on artists of diverse backgrounds, through which state arts policies are articulated to the wider political agenda of 'social inclusion'. While such art was in part treated as a medium of communication (through the paradigm of 'art as media', still promoted inter alia in the field of writing on black British culture) because of its shared interest in artworks and film, it nonetheless allowed visitors to experience the specificities of this art, through complex three-dimensional and site-specific installations. I alight on this development to explain why particular scrutiny of the 'art–media' coupling is urgently needed in the arena of black British art, in an effort to remove the obstacles to a more considered exploration of these artworks, one that centres on their intellectual contribution and historical significance.

Contemporary artists of many ethnic and creative backgrounds (addressed in this chapter are Hew Locke, Henna Nadeem and Kori Newkirk) have worked on aesthetic projects that promote in-depth interrogation of any monolithic conception of the aesthetic means and motivations of contemporary art. Even so, such artworks have been presented in curatorial projects that focus on an understanding of black and diaspora subjectivity that hastens a minimising of the role of art to that of messaging and visual communication alone. Although such conceptualisations of diaspora culture and identity have at times worked in favour of black British artists, as circumstances have altered with lessening public support for them, the problems and legacies of these older critical frameworks have come into clearer view.

The Conclusion sets out these issues in summary, going on to discuss what such art seems now to need: a radical rethinking about its value, through a newly positioned, expressly philosophical response. The close descriptions given in the chapters of this book show up the necessity and the measures to be taken for considering simultaneously the complex perceptual and emotional as well as intellectual, historical and social relations that pertain to the art of British subjects of a range of marginalised ethnicities. The book closes by revisiting Rasheed Araeen's historical criticisms about the failure of historiography and exhibition curation to recognise the value of this art beyond a limited lexicon. It is a point developed by the sociologist Zygmunt Bauman's insights about the militant assertion of cultural identities in globalised, metropolitan cultures, which I take up with contributions from Rancière, Latour and other thinkers.

## Phenomenology at work

I would suggest trying to challenge the prevailing critical preoccupation that sees black British artworks as markers of ethnicity, as discursive and signifying, by engaging with the processes of correlating and mobilising subjective experience through a broader, sensible world of aesthetic materiality. Such art should be embraced for the way that its artists locate themselves within the British artistic milieu, and shared aesthetic and philosophical traditions, in an effort to transcend the legacies of marginalisation and exclusion. Recognising this while building on critical commentary requires a carefully approached form of 'strategic phenomenology' (Wainwright, 2003) that is focused on diaspora culture. I name this approach as such since the aims and the results of this book are far from a 'pure' phenomenology, but rather a transformative turn to attend to art's phenomenal presence, putting phenomenology to work, pressing it into better service. A firmer sense of the skein of relations between artists, art audiences and artworks themselves comes simultaneously with a view of art's critical and phenomenal presence: its embodiment of values, its social agency and cultural politics, and its sensual and affective power.

As such, this book approaches creative work by black British artists in order to understand how their art objects offer multiple sites in which language, signification and discourse intertwine with vision, touch and the perceptual. It is an understanding intended to enhance considerably our sense of this art as important historical and material depositions which problematise the primary allocation of art to the conditions and discourse of difference. There is a need for a firmer and balanced sense of how diaspora artists' practices are perceptually present in the first place (how they have *presence* as such), while at the same time being culturally specific and contingent. This is at least one possibility for understanding the 'peculiar relations between persons and "things"', as Alfred Gell put it (1998: 9) in the setting of the art of several diasporas in contemporary Britain, re-examining them through what has come be called the 'new materialism'. These theoretical pathways lead to a space of debate about the political need to assess and assert such relations, which asks, in the special case of black British art, what we might want such accounts to deliver. This book's resolutions, such as there are, point to how such original approaches to art practice and diaspora culture can reverberate outwards, issuing first from a context of topical particularity in the black British milieu before making a wider phenomenal difference.

# Chapter 1

# Representation

Manjeet Lamba's watercolour piece *Arrival* of 1992 (fig. 2) shows a young Englishman with calfskin shoes, a wing collar and meticulously pressed linen. His hair has been carefully trimmed and treated, a lick of cream to keep it in place. Across from him, slumped in a scrapingly low chair, is an elderly Indian, male, tailored in 'the cloth of his kind', a crumpled badge of what in colonial language might betoken

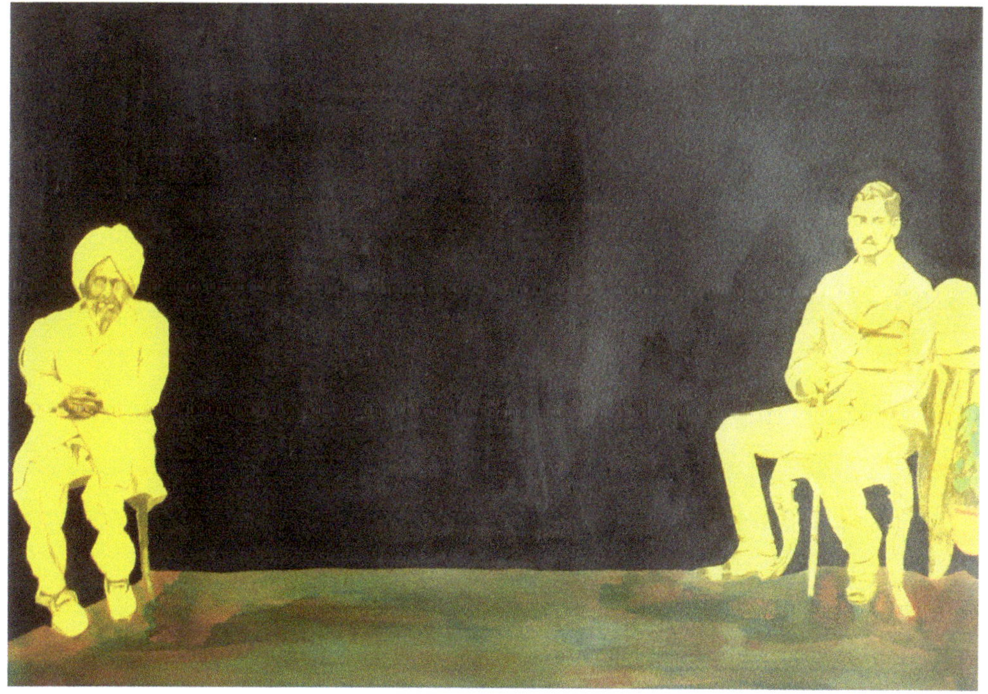

Figure 2: Manjeet Lamba, *Arrival*, 1992, watercolour. Image used with permission.

'Asiatic peoples'. One to the other, these two postured bodies are curiosities thrown together by circumstance and yet mutually fashioned: they are 'opposites paired in a structure of domination and subordination' (Chakrabarty, 2001: 178). Their cloth and cane and leather trappings are signs to unravel, a puzzle of visual syntax that dwells on their sameness of sex, and their differences in age and colour. Buckled under the weight of empire and conspicuous to colonial inspection, the bearded Indian is voiceless, his companion's steady stare fixing him as a sign of his country and peoples, in an ambivalent projection of imperialist reverie and malaise.

Permindar Kaur's sculpture and installation work of 1991 (figs 3 and 4), also entitled *Arrival,* has a pivotal link through its title to Lamba's piece, and it can be shown to accord with the same network of references to collectivities, their displacement and encounter. Kaur's *Arrival* is a cluster of glass and metal structures, ten transparent geometrical shapes supported, yet at the same time incised, by dark arrows of steel. These rods point upwards, precariously driven into the wooden floor of the artist's studio, their spiked heads visible through the faces of variously fashioned glass containers. Double-pointed, the rods spring reed-like and are grouped to left and right, forming a corridor comprising the stiff ranks of a regimental parade. As steel and glass, these various parts are the building materials of the modern architectural movement, components of a reworked kit. At the floor plane, these sharpened points are balanced by symmetry, stationed, oriented and in position. Winking light from their rectangular faces, at their uppermost plane, the glass shapes are crowded, sitting unevenly on metal mounts. The tips of the rods are danger points, guarded by the fragility of glass.

Pursuing this line of interpretation further, Manjeet Lamba's watercolour *Arrival* would be understood as a structuring device for thinking through mutual histories of empire and migratory movement. Its features, once made readable through description, refer to moments of colonial encounter and dialectic; an encounter of two human units, linked by virtue of their contemporaneity and coexistence, yet detached and distanced through racial and cultural difference. By juxtaposing these works it is clear that they each involve the encounter of one 'body' in relation to another: be it the actual gendered figures in Lamba's drawing, or else the two arrangements of spiked rods in Kaur's installation. Such a distinction inflects upon the title of the works too – arrival at a moment of cultural and historical encounter between British and South Asian

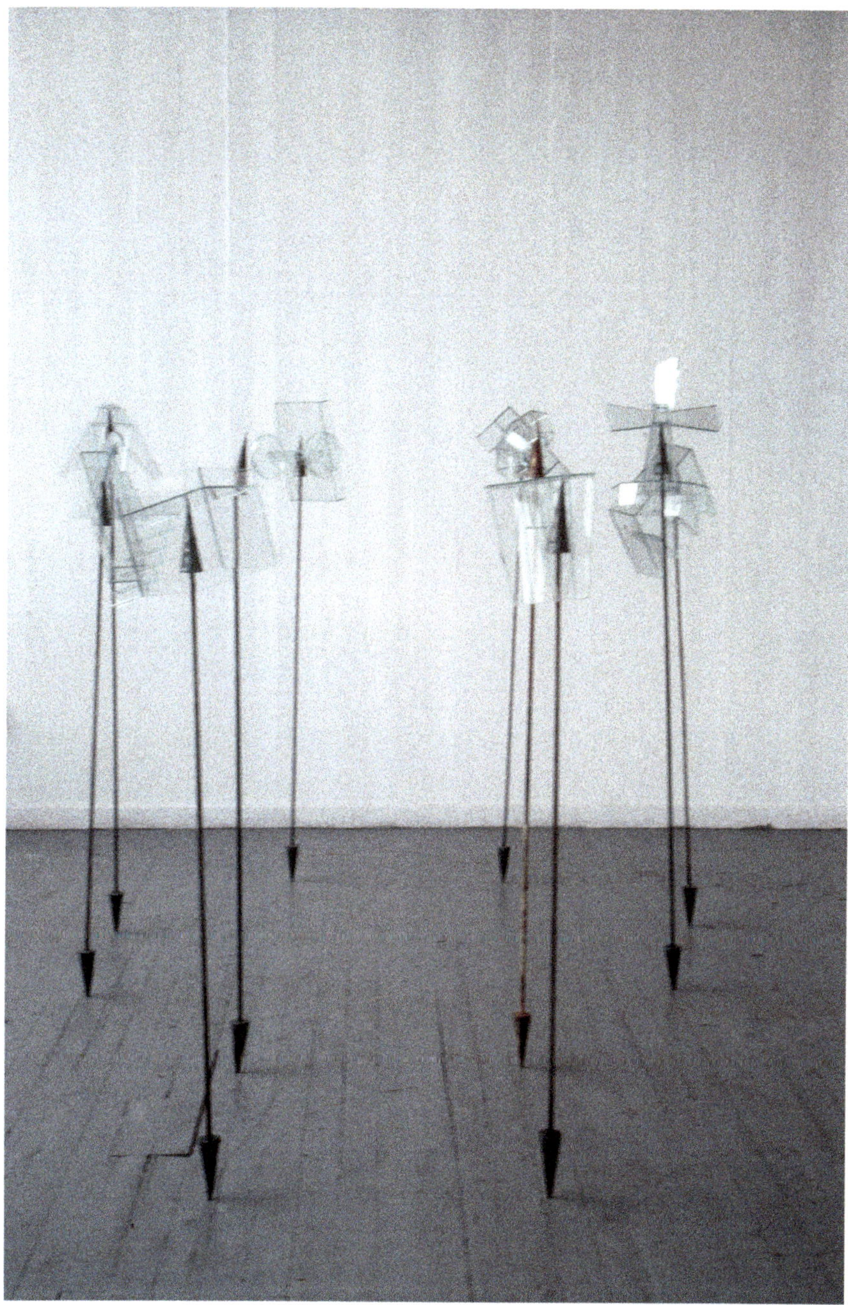

Figure 3: Permindar Kaur, *Arrival*, 1991, glass and steel, 168 x 114 x 152 cm. Image used with permission.

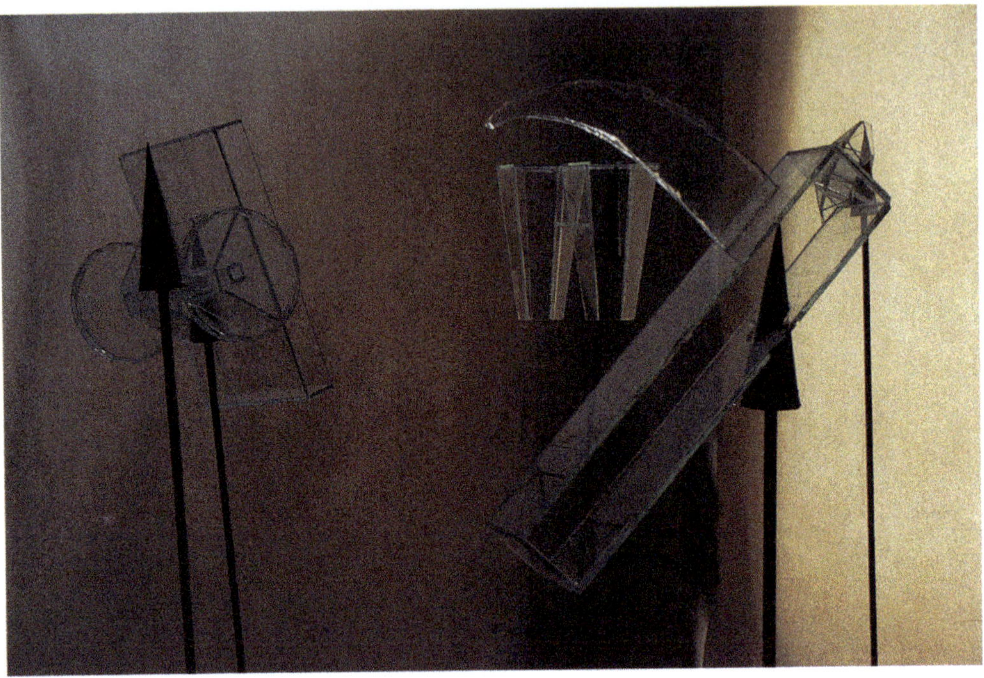

Figure 4: Permindar Kaur, *Arrival* (detail), 1991, glass and steel, 168 x 114 x 152 cm. Image used with permission.

subjects, or else a more material point of tense non-resolution, a floating and difficult impasse.

I have opened this chapter in this way in order to focus discussion on how this now familiar approach to analysing black British art has come about – the formation of a critical discourse on this art, and its subsequent assimilation within art history (which I have signalled here by characteristically juxtaposing two artworks). As I will argue, however, this generally uncontroversial analytical approach may itself have become something of an obstacle for developing a more directly philosophical engagement with black British art. And it may also be a problem for satisfying the critical aims that have oriented cultural commentary in this field since its inception. Accordingly, while showing how there has long been a preoccupation with the struggles over cultural representation, what follows is an outline of the relative gains and losses of the established species of approaches, and the stakes involved in drawing attention to its intellectual structure. Most importantly, it hints at what would happen if we chose to try to change and reorient it. Overall, the discussion paves the way for this book to answer the question: What positive difference could be made through allowing philosophy to enter the domain of criticism on black British art?

## Diaspora and vision

Artists of the African, Asian and Caribbean diasporas in Britain amassed a rich record of making and displaying art in the second half of the twentieth century, along an avenue of achievement that runs into the present day. Theirs is a history of asserting themselves as artistic subjects, often ebullient cultural activists, and distinct personalities in Britain's social and political life and in British and international art networks. They began to appear in growing numbers in Britain during the early 1980s, first achieving commercial and critical success in an art environment and gallery network with a heavy focus of activity in London.[1] During the same decade, and the early 1990s, it was common for many of these artists to group together for the purpose of exhibiting their works and to bring to the fore the issues and difficulties involved in establishing the public display of such art – struggles at the levels of education, resources and critical reception (see, for instance, Araeen, 2004; Chambers, 2014; Hylton, 2007; Owusu, 1988).

This narrative of making and displaying art has been elaborated through a remarkable and detailed mass of critical writing, and subjected to a fertile process of frequent revision. Whether inspired or written by artists themselves, such commentaries and responses to exhibitions, polemical and historical overviews, documentary and archiving projects, public lectures and other channels comprise an important textual record. An analytical and critically reflexive field, attentive to the need for a politics of modern and contemporary art that relates to Britain's broader, lived realities, such writing has also seen a recent renewal of interest within the academy.[2] This has tended to sustain the concentration of

---

1 A skeletal list of the more notable exhibitions here includes *Black Art an' Done* (Wolverhampton Art Gallery, 1981), *5 Black Women Artists* (Africa Centre, London, 1983), *The Other Story* (Hayward Gallery, London 1989) and the many events that took place at the Black Art Gallery, London. For a more complete outline, see Bailey et al. (2005) and Keen and Ward (1996).

2 There is a narrative to be heard here of art and artists in their troubled relationships with public institutions (see Chambers, 2014). Some recent research projects based within universities include *Making Histories Visible* (University of Central Lancashire),

effort from previous decades to show how artists produce their works out of a diverse range of experiences that come from living in diaspora communities in Britain, having sought to identify themselves primarily through the sphere of public culture. This has engaged historiography of the emergence in Britain of artworks and artists as cultural agents, and engendered various new strands of narrative that plot the recent history of art among black British people, drawing out the memories and voices of artists and participants in this history, while pressing in particular for fresh attention to art practices themselves.

The more specific objective of much existing discussion of black British artworks is to serve an invitation to trace out a role for art production for those cultural communities that occupy the spaces of diaspora following histories of migration and movement. The diaspora term in particular plays a key role in the interpretation of this art, helping to declare what is shared by those whose presence in Britain is integral to the long process of colonialisation and decolonisation that so animated the twentieth century. In turn, artworks have been employed to serve more general claims about the historical and cultural value of excluded or marginalised communities within modernity, presenting to theorists certain analytic possibilities for 'deepen[ing] our understanding of the critical and creative role of estrangement and displacement in the story of modernism and modern art as a whole' (Mercer, 2008: 6). Here the analytic of diaspora has helped in 'opening up a deep historical perspective on black experiences of Western modernity' (Mercer 1994: 246). It has remained the key to all commentary concerned with such exclusions from dominant histories of art. This is the locus of 'modernity's phantoms – that is, the disturbances and lingering presences, or presences of absence in the orders of visual appearance, through which current social formations manifest the symptomatic traces and uncanny signs of modernity's history of violence and exclusions' (Demos, 2013). In this way, black British art has been conceived as a set of practices consisting of performed identities and identifications; a productive relationship between difference, discontinuity and a desire to generate cultural narratives. These are in fact the key terms of an approach

a catalogue of letters and reviews, posters and publicity from black artists' exhibitions and events, surveyed from the 1980s to the present day; and *Black Artists and Modernism* (University of the Arts, London and Middlesex University), which includes a database of works by black British artists held in public collections throughout the United Kingdom. See also my own bibliography of such sources (Wainwright, 2005).

to black British art that has a genealogy of uses in the context of post-war anti-racism, and the concomitant elevation of the 'vision' and the 'visibility' of black British art and artists through scholarship. A range of individuals have been assembled and interpreted according to a framework that focuses on the visual languages that artworks employ – in film-making, photography, performance, painting, installation and so on – as well as artists' more broadly based involvements in exhibition curating, publishing, writing and criticism, policymaking, archiving, arts organising, promotion and activism.

The diaspora concept has an unfolding, adaptive set of uses that can be surveyed over the last few decades (Gates, 2010; Mirzoeff, 2000; Gilroy, 1993a; Mercer, 1988). In what most commentators would probably recognise as the more post-structuralist application of the term, diaspora intersects the diverse histories of migration, what might be indexed in the skin tone and physiognomy of the body (a discourse of 'race'), as well as markers of heritage, tradition and historical origins, class, gender and sexuality.[3] The term's political or strategic value is also suggested by some notably divergent uses, and shows its greatest political and intellectual potential when it ceases to be clear in what sense and to what ends it is being used. However, that more elusive and often critically pliable character of the diaspora concept needs to be evaluated quite carefully. While at particular moments it has been useful for political manoeuvring and in debates around multiculturalism, where it has been strategically deployed with important analytical possibilities, the term also brings limitations. Thinkers in Britain have rationalised attention to aesthetics by way of their interest in diaspora subjectivities, and the issues this raises regarding how to see black British art beyond the analytic of diaspora and a framework of representation need to be examined closely.


## Contingency and difference

Some of the most detailed polemical and theoretical claims upon black British artists' practices in the later twentieth century are offered in

3   A widely cited definition of diaspora experience, which would typically bring this breadth into view, is Stuart Hall's sense in which diaspora experience 'is defined not by essence or purity, but by the recognition of a necessary heterogeneity and diversity; by a conception of "identity" which lives with and through, not despite difference; by hybridity. Diaspora identities are those which are constantly producing and reproducing themselves anew, through transformation and difference' (1990: 235–236).

Kobena Mercer's interest in 'positions in black cultural studies' (1994). Explaining the implications of seeing black artists as agents engaged in wider struggles against racial exclusion and marginalisation, Mercer takes the view that too much attention has been given to inadvertently piling a 'burden of representation' on to black artists through the critical politicisation of their practices. As he suggests, this 'tends to overlook certain contradictions arising from the gap between the categories and criteria of its critical framework and the actual aesthetic principles operative in black art works themselves' (1994: 236). In response, Mercer has set about juxtaposing the term 'diaspora aesthetic' (cf. Gilroy, 1993b; 1988a; Hall, 1990; 1996c: 220; Mercer, 2009; 1992) against a discussion of 'actual aesthetic principles', and tried to straddle both categories. He registers agreement with Paul Gilroy's sense that a 'dynamic volatile force' issues from the diasporic and particularly transnational character of black expressive culture. At the same time, Mercer sees black visual practice as a 'politically overdetermined site of ideological struggle' (1994: 237), whereby black arts criticism faces the difficulty of trying to break with the tendency 'of making value judgements that are ultimately moral, rather than aesthetic, in character' (1994: 239).

Two areas of concern, the 'social responsibility of the artist' and the need to be true to the 'authenticity' of black cultural forms – each addressed in Eddie Chambers's writings on what he has called 'black arts activity' (Chambers, 1998; 2012; 2014; Clarke and Tawadros, 1999) – are underpinned by such moral judgements. Chambers argues that critics should recognise a 'separate' field of black aesthetics in the work of a set of British artists of diaspora backgrounds, and he decries a lack of public awareness about such artists – the philistinism of white journalists and academics in failing to make more art historical-styled observations about the spate of 'black art' exhibitions that took place during the 1980s. But Chambers leaves aside the matter of what such an aesthetics might look like, instead offering evidence of art's emergence from the social inequalities experienced by black artists.

A response to the pervasive rhetoric of the American Black Arts Movement, which became a source of inspiration for Chambers and many of his contemporaries during the 1980s (Ratnam, 1999a), can be found in Paul Gilroy's notes on the exclusionary uses of the trope of 'authenticity' in connection with blackness – 'none of us enjoys a monopoly on black authenticity' (1988b: 44). Indeed, Chambers's refusal to explore the visual peculiarities of 'black art' as an issue of primarily aesthetic response is symptomatic of the difficulties surrounding cultural identification. Mercer, by contrast, in a search for uncluttered ground on which to establish the interpretative issues around debating an art of diaspora, dismisses racial distinctions altogether, seeing no basis in the 'political fiction of race' for a viable account of difference. This allows him to tackle the conceptual polarities of the notion of white versus black audiences, and 'overground/underground institutions' (1994: 244), and to broach the difficulties of throwing off the 'burden of representation' heaped on to black culture. More clearly than any other writer in this area, Mercer acknowledges the degree to which understanding the aesthetic dimension of diaspora artists' works has been beset historically by such predominantly ideological preoccupations. Nonetheless, he above all encourages interest in the political economy of aesthetic value: 'what is needed is an historical account of how the distinctive values of our diaspora traditions have been materially produced' (Mercer, 1994: 246). This is what the art historian Gen Doy, in her treatment of 'black visual culture', describes as a 'materialist framework which attempts to understand both theory and artworks as being rooted in their economic, historical and social context' (2000: 236). This sense of being 'rooted' is endorsed by a hermeneutic method that has 'a contextual and conjectural orientation to the contingent and worldly circumstances in which aesthetic experience is integrated into everyday diaspora life' (Mercer, 1994: 246; cf. Fisher, 2003). In other words, what each promotes is the project of accounting for materiality and aesthetics – but only insofar as that may enlarge on the politics of representation and the contingencies of difference.

## Signification and aesthetics

Contrary, then, to what all their preparatory work and declaration of methodological frameworks could anticipate, little room remains for a purposefully aesthetic philosophy of the art of diaspora. This does not reflect any particular failing by the thinkers involved but can probably be explained by the methodological constraints that can emerge when mobilising around their political commitments. For all the careful clearing of ground for a 'materially produced' sense of aesthetics (Mercer, 1994: 246), the actual sense of aesthetics that surfaces is heavily subject to the workings of cultural semiosis, gravitating to the study of how individual artworks are 'made to mean' (Hall, 1982). Here visual meaning is conceived as a representational system analogous to language, wherein signs 'stand for or represent to other people our concepts, ideas and feelings' (Hall, 1997: 1), emphasising art's 'signifying' or loosely semiotic functions. This honours a commitment to materialism of the Marxian variety by integrating thought on sign systems and actual practices of representation, rationalising their relationships by addressing them within a so-called 'circuit of culture', a common space in which difference and power intervene between participants and thereby define a given cultural setting (Hall, 1997: 11). The approach elevates the role of the dialogical, since it is through communication that cultural production, consumption and regulation take place, interweaving processes of identity formation for the individuals who participate in this 'circuit'. References to the 'dialogical' in such writing suggest the use of Bakhtin, as acknowledged by Hall (Morley and Chen, 1996), and integrated by Mercer (1994), yet without acknowledgement of his source. Hall's model of a 'circuit of culture' that is common or shared is evident in Mercer's position that 'oppressor and oppressed inhabit the same discursive universe, with finite symbolic resources that are nevertheless articulated into a potentially infinite range of representations within the social imaginary' (1994: 255).

But if that 'social imaginary' only consists of 'symbolic resources' – forms of language, visual or otherwise – then that makes it more difficult (but not impossible) to perceive a phenomenal world beyond the structuring and dialogic domain of culture. The problem this raises for contemporary thought is how to contend with this state of affairs by philosophical means in the effort to make that world intelligible. Describing 'the struggles of the sign inscribed in the artistic text of the black diaspora' (Mercer, 1994: 255) can result in subtending aesthetic analysis within a critical method of visual interpretation, with the consequence of losing the aesthetic dimension and traducing it to a component of culture, another 'site' of meaning.

Through identifying the benefits of the existing theoretical work on black British art and artists, it becomes easier to see its limits. It is understandable why, for Hall, Mercer, Gilroy and others, the emphasis on power and difference within the model of diaspora culture has endowed cultural criticism with its strategic capacity – adopting a signifying framework for assigning meaning to visual performances and objects while keeping a dynamics of power very much within view. When the term 'diaspora aesthetic' first surfaced in their writings (Gilroy, 1988a; 1993b; Hall, 1990; 1996c: 220; Mercer, 1992; 2009), it did so in service of the need to register how diaspora identity or subjectivity is visually articulated, rather than offering a direct contribution to aesthetic analysis. Terms such as 'diaspora aesthetics' and the ideas that have punctuated accounts of black visual culture are harnessed to an agenda that became politically effective by insisting on the value of semiotic criticality. Indeed, taking up the 'diaspora aesthetic' as a discursive category has required considerable effort, invention and indeed repetition, in the effort to try to control and fix that idea. It is also clear, however, that the terms diaspora and aesthetics can pull quite forcefully apart. We need only consider the formal differences between works of art such as Lamba's and Kaur's, with their shared title *Arrival*, to see that even at the height of 'black art' in Britain there was no single or unified aesthetic.

It is admirable that this framework for writing on black British art has lasted for so long, with its aim of marshalling together not so *many* artworks but quite so *various*. It has held on to declarations of the 'diversity' of black British artists in order to sustain a politics of difference, yet at the same time, out of necessity to its founding objectives, it elided the dissimilarities among such artists and artworks. Somewhat regardless of difference, we might say, the discourse identified one and all according to a common category, arranged under the rhetorical sign of diaspora culture. But that signifying framework has fallen short of reaching a deeper aesthetic analysis wherein a semiotic-like model for art interpretation is but one element.

## Disciplinary specificity

Such limitations raise the question of why commentators on black British art have held on to post-structuralist and cultural studies approaches whose intellectual agenda hardly prioritises visual analysis. In the first decades of its inception, cultural studies followed an interventionist drive that was all the more powerful for not being shared across all other disciplines in the humanities, and allied itself most closely with sociology. The setting for such work has been significant: choosing to address black British art by way of the social sciences, into which cultural studies became enfolded, may have lent its conclusions more authority, given the nature of received ideas about 'hard' versus 'soft' disciplines. Such thinkers were not simply trying to score points in favour of cultural studies itself, in a sort of disciplinary chauvinism; nor were they unaware of similar art historical interests around visual discourse and social distinction, somewhat more closely attuned to analysing actual works of art. Nonetheless, here was the route map or alibi by which disciplines more traditionally focused on art – art history – or on aesthetics – philosophy – have tended to isolate black British art as a special topic, disconnected from the mainland of their interests.

More specifically, the emphasis on cultural politics and the signifying model for understanding black British art has set considerable limits on how to appreciate its contribution to aesthetic problems in a more philosophical domain. Perhaps thinkers in this field have assumed that any methodological model that differs from their own only subscribes to a *universal* aesthetic – belief in an aesthetic that transcends social and historical situatedness. There are many more options on the table, however, than an unreconstructed ideology of aesthetics which cannot countenance its own implication in changing and specific discourses and their institutions. Despite attempts to integrate 'aesthetic experience ... into everyday diaspora life', to quote Mercer again (1994: 246), there is still much to say about the specifically phenomenal reality in which material, ideological and aesthetic worlds are gathered within the scope of black British art.

Clearly I am not taking issue here with established interest in the concept of diaspora. There is no need to dispute the term's wide applicability, but only what happens to artworks when diaspora cultural criticism comes to be the sole intellectual architecture available to their conditions of reception. The field of writing on black British art shows an overwhelming bias toward evaluating the textuality of black visual objects, whereby they are construed as signifiers, named as cultural products, transformed and translated into signs and representations. Black artists are regarded above all as practitioners in the field of 'signification', and black cultural forms show 'a "syncretic" dynamic ... disarticulating given signs and re-articulating their symbolic meaning' (Mercer, 1988: 57). Art-making forms a diverse set of visual reminders of the very dialogic nature of diaspora identification: forms of assemblage and performance, negotiation with 'otherness', belonging and unbelonging, nationality, 'race' and ethnicity. Predominating here is the very emphasis on *cultural* production, on the idea that works of art are registers or indexes of 'black culture', a term that replays continually and is indivisible from that of 'art'. Black culture produces its objects, and in their turn they serve to reproduce and maintain that culture, doing so by virtue of what they represent *of* it, and *to* it. As Stuart Hall would suggest of cultural identity, for example, it is 'not the rediscovery but the *production* of identity' that is the very fabric of black art-making (Hall, 1990). From this viewpoint, the objects of black artists are media, in the sense of mediating cultural relationships and meanings (Hall, 1988), and are variously channels or units of communication, bundles of signifiers and textualities. By virtue of these objects sharing a 'signifying' relationship with culture, at one and the same moment they instantiate the originating events that gave rise to them, while permitting those exigencies to be reproduced and constructed, their histories retold.

## After the critical decade

These politics of diaspora have proved germane to understanding many of the pathways and compulsions of Britain's visual artists. Contemporary art practice entered an especially intense period of thought and activity during the 1980s, which is still being felt and contemplated. Equipped with the emerging and diversifying visual media of that time, and with a sense of their own political directedness and social positioning, black artists would become conspicuous by their strident embrace of visual critique, provocation and activism. If the 1980s may have seemed somewhat short-lived for some,[4] nonetheless at the end of what became known as the 'critical decade' for black culture (Bailey and Hall, 1992a; Julien and Mercer, 1988), a historical precedent had been set for black British art-making as an overtly 'critical' practice. Although by that time they had amassed a great deal of complex and remarkable visual art, and were active in a range of professional capacities, still the entry of these artists into public life was generally undervalued, the importance of their contributions to Britain's history of art vastly overshadowed by extended attention to their white contemporaries.

It would be unfair to lay any blame here on the very scholarship that aimed to elevate the importance of such art and to galvanise artists and transform the attitudes of art audiences, building a transformative discursive space for creativity in contemporary Britain. That said, towards the end of the twentieth century, black artists began to find themselves feeling unsure about a reputation that went before them, put in place by such criticism. Black British art seemed almost exclusively governed by the drive to make visual texts that held the goal of representation centrally in view, and by what appeared to be a predominance of interest in revisionism and opposition (see Araeen, 1989b; 1991; 1994).

---

4 Eddie Chambers (1998), for instance, argues that the properly 'critical' period ended in 1986.

An impasse had been reached for artists who felt encumbered with matters of cultural identity and its politics, which dominated their art's reception.

In the 1990s such artists were not helped by the celebration in the broadcast media of 'young' black artists, and rituals of acceptance and commendation in the granting of prestigious newcomer awards such as the Turner Prize.[5] For those keenly aware of the slowness of more profound changes in attitude within the country's art institutions, the success of those prize winners simply offered another case in point of the need for critical thought and practice (Chambers, 2012; Ratnam, 1999b). Since acclaimed work by black British artists seemed playful and politically vacuous – and therefore had a more popular appeal – such prize giving and commendations in no way confirmed the ability of British audiences at large to accept or understand 'different' art practices or creative subjectivities.

On the contrary, the rate of adaptation by art institutions and their absorption of criticism from detractors suggested little more than an agile capacity to construct and 'manage' cultural difference itself. Kobena Mercer aptly called this 'multicultural managerialism' (2000: 234), writing:

> To the extent that the postcolonial vocabulary, characterized by such terms as 'diaspora', 'ethnicity' and 'hybridity', has displaced an earlier discourse of assimilation, adaptation and integration, we have witnessed a massive social transformation which has generated, in the Western metropolis, what could now be called a condition of *multicultural normalization*. (2000: 234; see also Hall and Maharaj, 2001: 46)

That art historians too have played their part is suggested by the similar representational demands on artists from the African continent, which John Picton describes as 'the Jack-in-the-Box syndrome: the artist is thrust in a certain category, ready to jump out and dance only when the art historian springs the catch' (1999: 119). The general feeling since the late 1990s is that the ground of art's reception and the language of acceptance around black British artists may indeed have shifted, but many of the same issues – around the difference that such creativity can make – have remained.

---

5  I am thinking here, for instance, of the 1998 prizewinner, painter Chris Ofili, and the 1999 winner, film-maker Steve McQueen.

The subsequent situation for black British artists can best be understood by reference to such attitudes and persistent tendencies. The more developed historical and theoretical writing hailing their importance has dealt largely with bringing to light how identifications with various cultural narratives, as well as social, gendered, sexualised, racialised and political practices and identities, are bearing on these artists' visual output (see, for example, Chambers, 2014; Doy, 2000; Mercer, 1994; Gilroy, 1993b; Araeen, 1989a). In so doing, the stress has been on the very constructedness of black identities and cultures, the key role of visual practices as performative sites of identification. By way of a Foucauldian 'theory of discursive practice', the subject of culture remains conceptualised through processes of identification in which identity is always strategic and positional (Hall, 1996d). This view is largely commensurate with theoretically inflected attitudes among black artists themselves which favour the making of visual commentaries that narrativise the self. Artists have brought to the fore the way in which identity is never unified but always about becoming: fractured, constituted within representation and subject to change.

Black cultural studies has been important for making these artistic directions clear, unsettling many of the sureties of conventional arts and humanities scholarship, particularly with regard to the epistemological tendency of 'othering' black subjectivities. The general intention has been to make sure that it is no longer analytically or politically necessary to subscribe to the notion of an 'essential' black subject (see Hall, 1988; Bailey and Hall, 1992b). Nor is it desirable to find 'traces of ethnicity' in contemporary artworks – such that an art historian may be able to 'attribute' the formal properties of such works to the authorial black artist (as if to restate in the black British context a retrograde methodology pioneered by Wölfflin in 1932; see also Araeen, 1991). Artists who invoke 'otherness', indeed, are thought only ever to do so strategically or ironically, with the aim of upsetting the expectation of a visible 'difference' in their work. At the same time, however, critical commentary has been rather less able to explain the limits of this aim, and to evaluate whether it has been successfully met, other than to gesture generally towards the role of art's audiences (see Mercer, 2000; Fisher, 1994; 1996; 1997).

## Difference as fetish

In the present day, identifying with the category 'black British art' has become far more elective on the part of any individual artist, and this right needs to be upheld. A better understanding of such artists seems to require that we give up grouping them together, as if to accord with what Cornel West once termed the 'new cultural politics of difference'.[6] Although West's proposal has offered much potential for political progress, such an orientation for cultural commentary detracts from aspects of black British art that *do not* signify difference as part of a cultural politics – of ethnicity, identity or 'race'. It is obvious that an actual theory of art falls outside the preferred rubric of black cultural studies, and that is a very real shortcoming, politically and intellectually.

Calibrating art theory in line with the dynamics of cultural politics is an approach that has not weathered well in the changing institutional, policy and market situations for art and artists. Despite some finessing of models of visual representation and difference, the normativity of such approaches has served only to cement the sense that ethnic difference is the only or 'all-purpose defining social parameter' (Picton, 2001: 73) when trying to understand works of art. Parameters of difference in the arts present particular institutional problems too. Kobena Mercer has pointed out that ideas of diversity, heterogeneity and hybridity in the Western metropolis during the 1990s were accommodated under conditions in which 'the subversive potential once invested in notions of hybridity has been subject to pre-millenial downsizing' (Mercer, 2000: 235).[7] Critiques of art world organisations and markets (for example, Fisher, 1997; Papastergiadis, 1995) show up 'a major area of complicity between the demand for minority representation and the adaptation to diversity that the global marketplace seems happy to make' (Mercer, 2000: 235). Critical analysis of the cultural politics of difference and representation, it is plain to see, has not been enough to alter the 'everyday relationships

6   'Distinctive features of the new cultural politics of difference are to trash the monolithic and homogeneous in the name of diversity, multiplicity, and heterogeneity; to reject the abstract, general, and universal in light of the concrete, specific and particular; and to historicize, contextualize, and pluralize by highlighting the contingent, provisional, variable, tentative, shifting, and changing' (West, 1990).

7   By 'downsizing', Mercer indicates the systematic absorption and circumscription of initiatives towards diversity by public and other institutions, a meaning given special inflection by this borrowing of vocabulary from the corporate ethos of productivity and efficiency.

of power' in which the hegemonic idea of a homogeneous Western culture persists, even as it modifies itself to 'accommodate' diversity. As the historian Dipesh Chakrabarty has written, with a focus on Europe: 'Analysis does not make it go away' (2001: 178).[8]

Jean Fisher has remarked that it is crucial that we see 'cultural marginality no longer as a problem of *invisibility* but one of an *excessive* visibility in terms of a reading of cultural difference that is too easily marketable' (1996: 35). Difference has been fetishised in art world contexts, and black cultural studies has played an unintended role in permitting such misrecognition of this art. The 'normalisation' and 'excess' of difference has come to colour relations among artists, the marketplace, art's public institutions and scholars of this art. Consequently, the habit of privileging difference, identity and ethnicity as the basis for the historicality of artworks has to be questioned quite carefully. We need to stop producing a species of prose that returns the same results and instead engage with a new mode of thought about art that is even more reflective in its purpose.

## Aesthetics and social practice

I would not question or downplay the seriousness or very real basis of the motives, perspectives and agents that constitute the changing field of black cultural politics. But these outlooks need to be bracketed for a moment as we undertake the sort of investigation of black British art that might point to conclusions that are generalisable for philosophy. The point is not to search for alternative meanings in such artworks – to come up with inventive 'rereadings' of them – but to strike an altogether different attitude towards the bearing of philosophy upon this field, accepting that it too has the simultaneous status of a social practice. The time has come to exploit a more diverse and open range of philosophical options, while remaining mindful of the established vocabularies and frameworks. There is also a clear necessity for black British art to draw attention from a wider community of interests than has historically surrounded it. That should take it out of the separate, if complementary discourse on British art into

8  That quote in full: 'Liberal-minded scholars would immediately protest that any idea of a homogeneous, uncontested "Europe" dissolves under analysis. True, but just as the phenomenon of Orientalism does not disappear simply because some of us have now attained a critical awareness of it, similarly a certain version of "Europe," reified and celebrated in the phenomenal world of everyday relationships of power as the scene of the birth of the modern, continues to dominate the discourse of history. Analysis does not make it go away' (Chakrabarty, 2001: 178).

which it has fallen. It should at the same time try to avoid the equally problematic *translocal* notions of blackness or diaspora and their reputation for supposedly transcending the specificities of place and historical context altogether – such as I have identified with the Americocentrism of prevailing critical views about art of the African diaspora (Wainwright, 2011).

The model of diaspora cultural formation has come to be used without pause for thought about whether black British artists' works really should be made to fit in with its particularistic sense of difference. In the theorists' attempt to link visual practices with discursive cultural identifications (and thereby highlight the visual as a discursive field), what happens is that perceptual dimensions of artworks that are not so neatly locatable within the milieu of cultural difference go unrecognised and remain invisible. This falls short, ironically, of the customary theoretical aim of delivering a more just outcome for this art through a process of intellectual recognition.

It has long been acknowledged that stressing the politicisation of black art practices 'tends to overlook certain contradictions arising from the gap between the categories and criteria of its critical framework and the actual aesthetic principles operative in black art works themselves' (Mercer, 1994: 236). Even so, such *a priori* categorisations, which separate the perceptual or aesthetic complexities of black art objects from their social and political importance, seem to have hampered the development of a philosophy of this art. Black British artists have often felt circumscribed – their ambitions and interests utterly traduced – by the focus on cultural difference among commentators, funders and audiences.[9] We need to face this problem seriously and try to remove any further harm from ethnicising or racialising discourse. This needs to go further than throwing off what Mercer once called the 'burden of representation' heaped upon the art of black Britain (sometimes by such artists themselves), or else trying to pretend that art practices are not representational. Rather than seek to obliterate the problem of representation itself, philosophy should strive to accommodate a theory of representation and find innovative ways of working through the discursive contexts for black British art without seeing them as a burden.

9 Jean Fisher has written of 'the relation between art from the black or non-European artist and the Western art system … where the greater the work's visibility in terms of racial or ethnic context the less it is able to speak as an individual utterance. The galleries and museums have responded to the demand to end cultural marginality simply by exhibiting more non-European artists, albeit on a selective and representative basis, provided that they demonstrate appropriate signs of cultural difference' (1996: 33).

# Chapter 2

# Affective relations

The art and artists of the first and second generations of migrants to Britain, coming mostly from its former empire, stand at a point of convergence between institutional interests – between cultural criticism and theory, public policy, curating and arts programming. The policy dimension in particular has had a bearing on intellectual work in a way that is salutary for the future development of a philosophy of this art. Policies of multiculturalism were put in place in the visual arts in Britain in the last decades of the twentieth century, designed to ensure the institutional 'inclusion' of artists of diaspora backgrounds by representing a heterogeneous national community assembled under the rubric of 'cultural diversity' (see Hylton, 2007, especially chapters 4 and 6). Recently, such policies have faced strong criticism for insisting on racial differences as the basis for understanding art production and reception, and for administering state support. They have been charged with elevating 'race' as the chief parameter for making sense of works of art by black and Asian British artists, and with overlooking the actual diversity among such practices, while obscuring their deeper historical relation to British art of the canonical 'mainstream' (Araeen, 2000b; Hylton, 2013; Mirza, 2006).

While it is clear that state arts policy and flows of funding in Britain's art scene have been formative in the institutional and economic nexus of black and Asian artists' careers, excessive attention to such forces has obscured the extent to which artworks themselves have embodied interests that may transcend such circumstances. Works of art by individuals who were the subject of attention from policies of diversification in the arts, when approached with the necessary philosophical care, show a surprising disconnect from the terms of their official promotion. This was the case even when the politics of representation – and a theory of representation – were at their most fiercely argued and intensely worked. Black British artworks could still be differentiated as phenomena from their surrounding critical context, having developed their own aesthetic agendas within and despite institutional pressures – from the academy, from public arts funding bodies, from the infrastructures of art exhibiting, curating, publication. While critical theory of the 1980s and 1990s always emphasised the agency of artists, there has been little reflection on whether the terms of analysis and the arbiters of value in which and through which black British art was evaluated and promoted could in turn limit that aim. Cultural commentary generated to illuminate and support such artists was not out of step with the decisive and principal creative currents in artists' actual projects, nor were these in any way antagonistic – most often they were in tune and worked to a shared purpose. At the same time, there was a rather too close similarity between such commentary on black British artists and the official language of state arts policy, cultural programming and public display, with the all too easy appropriation of the critical terms of black British art. That development has shown that a critical conceptualisation of this art can have expedient uses well outside the community of diaspora artistic practitioners, organisers and thinkers who launched it, and sometimes against that same community's interests.

Greater self-reflection on how such art ought to be understood – its 'visibility' in scholarship as much as in public exhibitions – can assist the philosophy of black British art to recognise past disappointments and equip it to imagine further-reaching alternatives. As this chapter will show, the aesthetic complexity of black British art has proved difficult to elucidate fully, given that cultural criticism in the main has not girded its approaches with the properly phenomenological attitude that could uncover and compare the perceptual endeavours of black British artists. Current expansion in the study of aesthetics has led to particular interest in the emotional purchase of contemporary art. The intimate, affective relationships that might be struck with works by black British artists have philosophical importance that might be weighed against existing attention to art's cognitive uses in the more familiar ground of cultural criticism. The objecthood and immediacy of this art is the basis for its endurance in a contested cultural field, and the challenge ahead for the black British milieu is to embrace the advantages brought by the expanding possibilities offered by contemporary philosophy.

## Content and form

Maurice Berger's writing on artistic 'minimalism' has become seminal for showing how to reinstall a sense of the political in the aesthetic, and the aesthetic in the political. Citing Hans Haacke, Mary Kelly, Robert Morris and Adrian Piper as examples, Berger asks:

> What aspects of these artists' minimalism – the more direct address to the spectator, the employment of reductivist forms and gestures, the rethinking of pedestals, classical staging, and other distancing devices, the use of factory-fabricated forms, industrial materials, and everyday movements and street clothes – would engender or support political content? (1997: 4)

Berger declares his objective as an attempt 'to deal with the relationship between ideology and form', and commits to a dichotomous project focused on form versus content. This leads him to weigh up these two terms of evaluation as if they were distinctly opposable categories, before going in pursuit of things to meet their criteria, and to fit and fill his binaries.

It is not unusual to find writers on black British art taking a broadly similar approach to Berger's, where they have held the methodological purpose of undertaking semiotic or 'signifying' readings of artworks. A form–content pairing has persisted in accounts of black British art as a medium saturated with a codified surplus of meaning. The pattern can be seen in some genre-making literature: histories of artistic motifs across the black Atlantic world (Gilroy, 1993a: 1993b; Mercer, 1994; Chandler, 1997); semiotic-like accounts of art by black women (Gupta, 1995; Tawadros, 1995; 1996; 1997); key writings on this art by Stuart Hall (for example, Hall, 1992a; 1992b; 2006; Hall and Sealy, 2001); the bulk of artists' monographs (most notably Baucom et al., 2004; Dempsey et al., 1998; Gupta, 1995; Malik, 1998; Sealy, 1993), and so on. Such writing shares much with the larger body of semiotically derived modes of attention in cultural studies and art history (Bal and Bryson, 1991; Preziosi, 1998; du Gay et al., 1997; Hall, 1997; Panofsky, 1972) and is subject to the very same critiques they have faced. That visual form is subsumed to content in critical theory, making content the dominant of the pair, is one of the bases for the objections that have been levelled at structuralism (see MacCormack and Strathern, 1980), and at post-structuralism for its adherence to dichotomies even when claiming to be doing differently. Heirs to the Saussurian legacy, among whom Stuart Hall would count himself (see Hall, 1997), concede that there is such a thing as meaningful form, which is therefore open to a semiotic-like decoding. But they tend to decide in advance what manner of form is to be privileged with meaning. Much adjudication over what sorts of visual experiences are beyond the sphere of legitimate attention when asking social questions – precisely which phenomena to dispense with for not lending themselves to an account of signs and codification – has resulted in cultural criticism that disregards much material that it cannot countenance to be meaningful and in that sense 'cultural' at all.

The concept of 're-presentation', promoted by Hall as a tool for clarifying the cultural dynamics of black British art, helps to enlarge on the purpose of a signifying approach. It highlights the innovative reuse of formal elements by artists – theoretical tropes, signifiers of sexuality, markers of history and so on – which become sites for the reinscription of meanings in a way that suggests that the making and reception of artworks (described as 'visual practices') constitute acts of contestation, negotiation and resistance. The balance of interest here is not, however, on the production of new *form* emerging from such practices, so much as an unfolding process of enunciation and the production of meaning along a chain of signifiers. While not pretending to be a total theory of art, by this logic, art is counted among the many sites for the ongoing generation of meaning within the communicative circuits of culture.

Engaging a more properly philosophical account of black British art requires a deliberate break from this style of commentary, putting aside the functional allure of the form–content binary and tackling head-on its persistence in post-structuralism. It clarifies physical relationships to actual artworks without disavowing the role of language in the cultural field, seeking instead to interrelate these while taking greater care over dichotomous thinking. This means exploring at the level of perception and the human body, while discussing aesthetics more on the basis of phenomenological particulars. On the question of the relationships between political meaning and aesthetic experience, a greater degree of parity can then emerge, granting access more directly to the existential dimensions and ambiguities rather than simply the semiotic ambivalence that black British artworks present.

## Perceptual primacy

Much like Jacques Lacan, I recommend the view that subjects exist on the basis of their desires, rather than that coherent subjects are primary and the presence of desire can be elicited from them. This order of things (desire creating a subject, rather than a subject creating desire) presents an important code of understanding upon which the remaining chapters of this book proceed. It answers a question of what and how significance is to be given to the aesthetic drives of artists who are otherwise primarily, if not exclusively, known for their cultural politics. For although they are politically engaged in order to assert themselves as human subjects, it is also fair to argue that the basis for that creative subjectivity rests on the very facticity of their art in an aesthetic realm.

It is a view that derives from Merleau-Ponty's manner of posing the origin of the subject as an ontological question within the terms of perception (Merleau-Ponty, 1962; 1968; Vasseleu, 1998, 27). If social dynamics and values work through perception rather than through detachment from it (Merleau-Ponty, 1968; Danto, 1988), then here is a phenomenal primacy that cultural theorisation has to take more seriously. But somehow seeking to accommodate the ontology of black British artists' works within the existing theoretical frameworks, and trying simply to include or assimilate the phenomenal, would fail to understand that primacy. These are art objects positioned discursively by a cultural theory of identification, difference and diaspora, the cultural politics that are constructive of their histories. That particular historical sense of them cannot be heightened or underscored by the phenomenal, since the phenomenal does not have the status of being a generative theme or signifying trope, to take it for yet another historicising figure (another trope or framework of 'explanation') would be a mistake. That said, a better sense of the perceptual presence, efficacy and originary status of black British art, and an understanding of these artists as embodied subjects, has a responsibility to reason with its discursive effects, while questioning the normativity of cultural theory in the present context.

In parallel, returning the gaze onto the cultural theorist puts under scrutiny and into some doubt the professional gains to be had by continuing to ignore the intellectual possibilities that lie beyond theoretical attention to the cultural politics of identity and representation. The theoretical work of trying to 're-present' an analytical object (black artworks, in this case) has regrettably drawn the assumption that black thinkers and artists have a kind of pre-awareness or special sensitivity to the encoded meanings of black cultural 'texts' and 'products'. There are contexts in which black British artists and thinkers have been required to negotiate the role of 'speaking for' black or diaspora interests in the main, and that requirement should be resisted. Trying to represent black visual culture as if from the perspective of what Olu Oguibe has called an 'intimate insider' (1999: 326) ignores the complexities of difference. Stuart Hall promoted the view that black people are individually differently inserted into situations of power and that we should therefore be wary of positing a common black essence, a 'shared black experience' (Hall, 1980c; Morley and Chen, 1996: 25–130). Critical thought is itself an example of the work of 're-presentation' (Hall, 1980a) and establishes relationships of difference between its participants, problematising the idea that they 'belong' to one or other racial or ethnic community. The notion of 're-presentation' has special value for helping to counter the assumption that a scholar who identifies as black may capture the voices, passions and intentionalities of black British art and artists without mediation. But questioning the authority of a 'representative' speaking subject is not quite the same as questioning the authority of cultural criticism itself. Indeed, problematising the idea of a 'shared black experience' may even be a requirement for the assertion of cultural criticism's epistemic force.

But none of these, albeit careful, considerations have met with the realisation that the very emphasis in black cultural criticism on relations of representation – with or without a hyphen – leaves viewers of black British art to somewhat circumambulate art objects themselves. A set of discursive objects are brought to the fore by a theory of visual meaning, but the physical objects in the hands of black British artists have a materiality to which regimes of representation only partially adhere. Black British art has textures and colours that no scheme of discursive inquiry has yet felt the need to fully apprehend. There is no danger of post-structuralism losing sight of such objects if Ernesto Laclau's assurance still stands, that '[to recognise] the discursive character of an object does not, by any means, imply putting its *existence* into question' (1990: 100). Still, given the common balance of emphasis in black cultural criticism, there is cause for concern that a prescription has been made about *how* art objects exist, by subtracting the crucially existential dimension from an appreciation of their critical effectiveness.

Viewers of black British art seem to be at risk of becoming so far detached from its material existence that they are unable to see it outside the prevailing analytical scheme. Ensuring that this sort of passivity, this perceptual numbness, does not set in requires specific attention to how black British artworks are always the foundation for *affective relations*. These artworks may be a register or deposit of social relations, but their potential to relate to the social is a matter of perception as much as it is about meaning. We ought to recognise that art operates in a phenomenal world of which it is a part and to which it belongs; that art makes possible that which would otherwise be impossible, through imagining and opening up a world of relations and experience. These are basic appeals to the sovereignty and power of art, loosened from the strictures of cultural explanation.

A distinctive philosophy of the phenomenal experience of black artists' objects has to tackle these issues directly. It has also to exceed the limits of existing studies on diaspora culture in Britain, dispensing with its now orthodox structure. It should help to properly fulfil the ambition set by art historians in Britain to show up 'the links between aesthetics and politics, historical consciousness and affective sensation', such as T. J. Demos (2012: 24) has detected in cinematic works by Zarina Bhimji – an approach that shares much with the recent critique of cultural theory in its 'turn to affect' (Wolff, 2012; Leys, 2011; Venn, 2009; Hemmings, 2005). And it takes heart from accomplished philosophical work on the 'relevance of immediatist phenomenology – or *aesthesis* – to black aesthetics' in the United States (Taylor, 2016: 26), in the effort to show that the material presence and phenomenal *fullness* of this art has hitherto remained undisclosed in scholarly work on black Britain. Although in the British setting it was often claimed that 'black cultural politics insists upon the ascendancy of a broader aesthetic and political project' (Tawadros, 1996: 274), the weight has been unmistakably on the latter, as perhaps one might expect of a self-consciously political mode of cultural criticism. This is a very real problem of disparity that the adoption of a phenomenal analysis can address head-on.

Not all writing on black visual culture has seen itself as especially politically led, nor has it found in black British art a discrete cultural politics of difference. But the phenomenal presence of this art will remain very difficult to elucidate without the benefit of an explicitly philosophical treatment. In order to become open to their presence, encounters with art objects need to enjoy a degree of independence from the exegetical drives of black cultural criticism. That is to say, we would do well to find some distance from the idea suggested in Benjamin's early enigmatic essay from 1917, 'On Perception in Itself', that 'perception is reading/ Only that appearing in the surface is readable... / Surface that is configuration – absolute continuity' (quoted in Caygill, 1998: 3).

By persisting with the same notion that 'perception is reading', black cultural criticism has become complicit in flattening out the aesthetic field, losing sight rather of what may be essential about this art. The point is put most succinctly by Merleau-Ponty: 'Looking for the world's essence is not looking for what it is as an idea once it has been reduced to a theme of discourse; it is looking for what it is a fact for us, before any thematization' (1962: xv).

I recommend embracing the phenomenal as a means for rescuing black British art from being reduced to a discussion of meaning alone, and from the dominance of modelling art linguistically. Since she or he is beset by a desire to abandon the 'already-existing' or 'original' (Hall, 1982: 64), for the cultural interpreter, the prospect of grasping the value of perception and a phenomenology of origins has drifted from view. The situation seems to call for a mistrust of the tendency encouraged by Hall's notion of 're-presentation', as much as in Benjamin, to 'construct perception out of the perceived, to construct our contact with the world out of what it has taught us about the world' (Merleau-Ponty, 1968: 156). As Jean Fisher put it, most writing in this area has tended to suggest that 'art is more a cultural product than a dynamic process or complex set of immanent and sensuous relations' (1996: 33). By contrast, while her work does not explicitly deal with phenomenology (nor solely with black British art), in 'Some Thoughts on Contaminations', Fisher does advocate that:

> Visual art remains a materially based process and functions on the level of *affect* not semiotics alone – i.e., a synaesthetic relation is established between work and viewer that is in excess of visuality. It involves rather enigmatic sensations such as the vibrations of rhythm and spatiality, a sense of scale and volume, of touch and smell, of lightness, stillness, silence or noise, all of which resonate with the body and its reminiscences and operate on the level of 'sense' not 'meaning'. (2003: 253)[1]

---

1 Fisher prefers an art criticism of 'the dynamic encounter between the work and the viewer/writer. That is, what the work does ... as an affective machine or event capable of compelling a new trajectory of thought has been of more concern than an artist's putative intentions, biography or genealogy' (2003: 13). The trajectory she may have in mind is represented in Marks (2000; 2002) and Stafford (1995). Fisher continues: 'In effect, the work has to engage the viewer as a participant not an observer ... Thus, the experience of art [is] ... a suspension of knowledge and reason, an encounter with something that has no prior referent ... an experience of the re-embodiment of language through sensation outside discourse as its instrumental form' (2003: 13).

## Efficacy

What, then, is the strong sense in which works by black British artists succeed in touching upon and giving rise to those relations of an 'immanent and sensuous' kind? To appreciate what makes this visual art so engaging and individual works so unique requires turning to such specific issues. Visual art is not only a form of making statements and representation, but is an ambiguous, dynamic and historically vital perceptual sphere. From along the avenue offered by such interest, it might then be possible to deal closely with how that experience is articulated to the more established lines of critical inquiry.

A different rendering of black British art might explore more fully the idea of its efficacy, a term with an elastic usefulness for philosophy. On the one hand, it provides a focus for social questions and observations about critical patterns; the relation of artworks to political struggle, for instance, or the signifying and assembling of cultural affinities and communities. Such preoccupations fall within the scope of a consideration of how material objects become invested with value through practices of public exhibition or everyday contexts of display and visibility. On the other hand are the material, existential applications for efficacy, which invariably overlap with social considerations but at the same time retain their distinction. Bringing efficacy into play can point to black British art as enabling and illuminating relations that pertain between artworks, their artists and ourselves as viewers.

I am thus attentive to exploring the role lent by efficacy in helping to describe a specifically *perceptual* realm, from which social questions are temporarily suspended until the further, later stage of analysis in this book. Through attention to perception, efficacy has the virtue of ushering in an inquiry into processes of visual and tactile experience, the ways in which artworks serve to affect us bodily, and what here in general I have called the *phenomenal difference* of black British art.

Asking questions around efficacy can assist, therefore, with taking stock of directly critical concerns, yet broadens out into further areas of thought. I here set out the emerging possibilities of thinking through what lies at the heart of the history of black British art as a site of opportunity for in-depth intellectual work. Less the outcome or 'products' of black culture than an affective presence, such art objects take up places in the world; indeed they occupy and dwell in those places, commanding and energising perception. This view pays tribute as much to Heidegger's notion of how the world is 'set up' (*aufstellt*) through the art object (a process to which I return in Chapter 3, to explore objects as places or 'events') as to Alfred Gell's proposition that we ought to apply ourselves to a theory of art that 'considers art objects as persons' (Gell, 1998: 9) – of course without such an application overrunning into some sort of animistic account. In these and further ways, black British artists' works have a status in a perceptual continuum, with an impact upon our tactile and optical registers. In short, this grants a clearer sense of how, in Merleau-Ponty's terms, we can 'reveal the mystery of the world and of reason' (Merleau-Ponty, 1962: xxi) from the starting point of the art object in black visual culture, by 'looking for what it is as a fact for us, before any thematization' (1962: xv). There should be little argument that a better understanding of black British art requires an account of visual perception itself, an explanation of how these artworks have set up perceptible spaces and critical sites that are the focal points in networks of phenomenal importance.

## Situatedness

The selection of artists in this book is largely consonant with the selections made through those historiographies and exhibitions which have promoted the discursive category of 'black Britain', investing in its historical recognition and cultural visibility. This apparent canonisation furthers the political initiative to bring such artists into the purview of critical and institutional attention. But unlike most other writers on black culture, I cannot profess to being socially positioned as a black subject, critic or artist. That does not mean that I claim to be operating from a (fallaciously) 'depoliticised' or even 'de-ethnicised' position or situation. Instead, in a sort of 'trans-situation' of engaged scholarship into philosophical thought, I suggest that a detailed study of the phenomenal and perceptual in black artists' works would contribute crucially to deepening a sense of their historical presence in newly found terms.

The issue arises nonetheless of whether the account given in this book is a warranted and desirable one in respect of the individuals it names. If the idea of focusing attention on the perceptual aspects of black artists' practices were mine alone, then there would be reason for concern, but there is a broader and shared politics to which I adhere. Calls have issued from various writers and artists identified intimately with black British art. Kobena Mercer, for instance, has urged the need for 'the dignity of objecthood ... [to be] bestowed on the diaspora's works of art';[2] Jean Fisher has set out a 'plea to attend to the work before us' (Fisher, 1997);[3] while Rasheed Araeen has called for an 'art theory' as opposed to a 'cultural theory' relevant to diaspora artists and their careers. Araeen has explained: 'As for the dominant discourse, it is so obsessed with cultural difference and identity, to the extent of suffering from an intellectual blockage, that it is unable to maintain its focus on the works of art themselves' (1994: 9). That complaint is shared in the United States, where 'It is an unfortunate fact that in this country, black artists' work seldom serves as the basis of rigorous, object-based debate' (English, 2007: 7). I am told repeatedly in discussions with artists that a fresh approach is long overdue for dealing with the intersectional complexities of politics and aesthetics; that we need to reverse decades of inattention to the particularities of individual artworks, rather than misremembering or forgetting the actual art that is the material basis of their artistic biographies.

Still, all such calls for a change of approach have come from those who no doubt imagine scholarly pathways that differ from my own. This difference has nothing to do with a dispute over the appropriate *disciplinary* location for theorising about black British art. Fisher blamed 'the strategies of anthropology, sociology and so forth' (1994: xi) and expressed a need to develop 'conventional art history and criticism' (2003: 13), while Mercer has advanced his 'sociography of diaspora' (2000) in tribute to Stuart Hall, before attacking Araeen during those

2   Kobena Mercer, quoted from his presentation 'Iconography after Identity', given at the conference 'Shades of Black, Assembling the 80s: Transatlantic Dialogues on AfroAsian Art', Duke University, North Carolina, April 2001. Mercer returned to this phrase, with the qualification that what he intended was not a call for an 'object-centred approach' but the need for scholarly attention to 'multicentric circuits through which works of art acquire universality as they travel across the imaginative realms of great time' (2016: 30–32) – a clear reference to the interest that has subsequently emerged on the spatialities and temporalities of modern and contemporary art in numerous diaspora settings around the Atlantic region, a topic I established elsewhere in another book-length study (Wainwright, 2011).

3   Fisher had earlier written that 'Useful though interdisciplinary studies have been to an understanding of identity politics and the socio-economic context of cultural productions, the strategies of anthropology, sociology and so forth nonetheless fail to account for the particularity of critical aesthetic practice, the complex role of historiography in the evaluation of art, the relations between art and its audience, and the nature of the art "object" as a material expression of both an individual vision and a collective experience that exceeds its status as a cultural sign' (1994: xi; see also Fisher, 1996).

times when he 'mis-recognises the epistemological revolution that was led by cultural studies' (Mercer, 2009: 76). All would seem to agree nonetheless that 'The emphasis on the artist's identity and on the institutional policies of the art world has, I think, significantly deflected our attention away from the relative autonomy of the art object itself'.[4] (Let us quickly pass over whether these very same writers helped to put the emphasis there in the first place). The most closely argued solution to the general problem is to take up 'questions of interpretation concerning iconography and iconology' (Mercer, 2005: 53). But this is precisely an approach that I problematise throughout this book, mindful that such models of iconographical and iconological interpretation in art history are as much underpinned by concerns with language and contextualism as is cultural studies (Panofsky, 1972; 1955; Bal and Bryson, 1991). Shifting from one discipline to the next makes little difference if a semiotic-like commentary on black British art persists, always falling short of the ontological interests proper to a philosophy of aesthetics.

What remains paramount throughout the discussion in this book is the need to avoid the suggestion of a discrete or unified aesthetics of black British art. There is no desire to overshadow the possibility of diverging perceptual experiences of those very same art objects. The discursive category of 'black British art' should not be misused as a founding analytical term for aesthetic philosophy. In the most basic sense, my descriptions of this art comprise prose passages that are textual constructions, formed after perceptual responses to this art.

Inevitably, this gives rise to a 'construction of a construction' nexus, when we consider that the artworks of the black diaspora themselves occupy the complex position of being constructed out of their artists' realities. Additionally, as Richard Wollheim has suggested, 'An artist must fill the role of agent, but he must also fill the role of spectator. Inside each artist is a spectator upon whom the artist, the artist as agent, is dependent' (1991: 101). That chain of constructions, to which one may add the 'spectator' who peoples the audience for art, is much like the range of positions explored in the ostensibly phenomenological texts of Clifford Geertz (1973). But Geertz was committed to wide-eyed acts of description that overlook their own interpretative procedures, since he gave in to the temptation to form 'projections' on to artworks. Doing differently, one has to be conscious that written accounts of perceptual experiences

---

4 Mercer, quoted from his conference presentation of 2001, 'Iconography after Identity' (published as: Mercer, 2005).

are already a form of translation and that the acts of construction and perception are ontologically distinct and dissimilar. Emphasising the fact that black British artists' works are bodily present before us in contingent ways can highlight the process of projection on the part of the scholar, and thereby avoid the pattern, demonstrated by Geertz and others, of striving to 'vanish' as an author from one's own text. The continual reference to my own situation in this book is an entirely necessary feature of knowledge production in a contemporary philosophical frame, in working on the textual edifice of a discourse of black British art.[5]

## A body of phenomena

I have argued for the need to dignify black British art by renewing interest in perceptual experience, an initiative prompted by the compelling nature of such art, in its visual and tactile peculiarities. That effort to recuperate perceptual richness and to try and understand its importance has entailed pointing to its general abnegation in the current critical field. The operations of black cultural theory seem to have submerged

5   My sense of caution towards the error of 'projecting' on to cultural phenomena, while 'vanishing' from the resulting textual record of that experience, is shared in Crapanzano's poignant conclusions on Geertz's attempt to write 'from the native's point of view': 'Despite his phenomenological-hermeneutic pretensions, there is in fact in *Deep Play* [Geertz's study of Balinese cockfighting] no understanding of the native from the native's point of view. There is only the constructed understanding of the constructed native's constructed point of view … [Geertz's] constructions of constructions of constructions appear to be little more than projections, or at least blurrings, of his point of view, his subjectivity, with that of the native, or, more accurately, of the constructed native' (1986: 74). There is a lively debate to be had here, which I will not elaborate, that could bring in Jacques Rancière's observations on the 'emancipated spectator' (2010) who engages with the artwork in order to extend an independent interpretation rather than assimilating the artist's message without discernment – in other words, the very opposite of trying to write or speak for or from the viewpoint of 'the native'. Crapanzano's assessment, drawn during anthropology's 'writing culture' debate of the 1980s, could be set against cultural studies itself, and with rather sobering consequences. The degree of detachment that cultural studies enjoyed from critiques of cultural contextualism that emerged during the same decade is notable – as is indicated in passing remarks by Mark Hobart (2000: 12). At the same time, Rancière's interest in the emancipation of spectatorship would be unthinkable had post-structuralist theory failed to establish that negotiated and oppositional readings of culture are always possible, since power never rests entirely in one place, and that such 'readings' may take the form of everyday practices that are examples of production as much as consumption.

the phenomenal beneath the critical weight of its attention to textual codifications and translations. Since disclosure of the phenomenal is forestalled by that more orthodox politics of criticism, it is worth entering into productive disagreement with any such singly led theory of black artists' material histories. A philosophical project attuned to understanding the explicitly perceptual value of black British art can then be taken up.

While the idea of phenomenal presence offers an orientation for a sustained analysis, it also has knock-on effects for our understanding of the historicity of diaspora art and artists in Britain, their social importance and meaning. Indeed, the concepts of presence and efficacy innovate upon a sense of the creative and material past of diaspora people by pointing to the complexities enabled and entailed in their artworks. This discloses a peculiar sphere in which the manipulation of physical materials under the rubric of art-making serves to bring black individuals into presence as persons and artists. A discussion of the contingencies of ethnicity and difference can be opened up by analysis of the general ground of embodied human experience. Questions about black British art from the starting point of curiosity about phenomenal efficacy may be theoretically distinct from no less crucial social questions that others have already asked, but this curiosity can extend the reach of those questions. The conclusions of this book deal with the task of showing how these several areas of concern converge. Simply put, the concrete, political objectives for understanding black British artists can be built upon valuably with a close treatment of their art as phenomena.

A specifically aesthetic interest would be worthless if it remained somehow sealed off from the very social world in which aesthetic experience takes place. We would also have failed to learn anything from traditions of writing about art in a way that is worth struggling over: in its political, gendered, sexualised and psychic importance. We simply need to look anew at the ideas of articulation and contingency which are so important for understanding material struggle and change. It is worth keeping in mind the complexities of practices of translation, and not oversimplifying textuality or misrecognising it as an artifice that is anything but existential. We should recall Bakhtin's argument that 'The text as such never appears as a dead thing ... We always arrive in the final analysis, at the human voice, which is to say, we come up against the human being' (1981: 152–153). Recognising black British art as a realm of vital materiality – objects and images with a phenomenal presence – does not mean having to do away with a sense of its modes of inscription as media of representation in the visually 'linguistic' fabric of culture. There is an intimacy felt with these artworks, and a plurality of ways in which they have the potential for affecting those who apprehend them.

This in itself presents an opening up of original ways of *being-with* artworks, an originality that is the material setting and prerequisite for struggle, agency and articulation. I anticipate some directly textual effects of such a discussion upon the critically oriented commentary in this field. The present philosophy may help to ground the facticity of diaspora peoples' art practices within a material and aesthetic realm, and thereby assist in the articulation of cultural struggles and the dynamics engaged in their diverse expressive projects.

## A pact with the world

Stuart Hall has written about 'reconstructing' the past of black Britain, saying that a 'sense of history' requires 'a delicate excavation, an archaeology, a tracing of the contradictory imprints which previous discourses have stamped' (1992b: 113). But for all its metaphors of reassembling and revision, the semiotically modelled and exegetical programme followed by black cultural studies has consigned to a sort of *souterrain* the prospect of a phenomenological apprehension of black British art. It is primarily a phenomenal analysis that can radically extend the archaeological-styled work that Hall has called for and do justice to the value of this art. Yet the necessary activity to ameliorate our philosophical awareness of the black British field has hardly begun. To unearth what lies beneath the feet of its commentators, not simply a special kind of intellectual attitude would be required, but a wholly bodily engagement, in a novel pact between our physical selves and a body of artworks. Making sense of this alternatively corporeal approach ushers in much more than a new 'regime' of vision, but rather what Marsha Meskimmon has called 'an affective state of wonder' (2013: 21; see also Bennett, 2001: 131) – an openness to the 'enchantment' of art as the basis for an ethics of perception, an object-focused project of description and disclosure through which to collect and embrace this art.

Black British art stands within a horizon of experience, as phenomena that come into being and have a presence that the philosophy of art can address by considering art's impact on the world. Such art is a source of orientation that should be saved from the objectification of cultural analysis and elucidated through existential thought. Not only has a surplus of meaning surrounded this art, but also a surplus of complexity in trying to answer the question of its value – cultural, political, existential. At phases in my subsequent evaluation of it, I elevate its simultaneously tactile and visual dimensions and thereby specify the phenomenal peculiarity of works, while never negating their social implication by discursive or semiotic means. This assists in seeing more profoundly *how* black British art has come to practise all of those processes that its authorities have claimed for it: imagining through imaging; hybridising in a politics of difference; building identity through identification with communities of displacement.

For a phenomenological procedure to hold sway we need to differentiate ontologically between the discursive patterns ascribed to black diaspora visual culture, and actual objects of art themselves. Analytical writing on culture and the philosophy of phenomenal aesthetics are different things. This difference *in kind* needs to be taken into view more fully, establishing not further epistemological certainty about diaspora and blackness, but rather unfolding aesthetic experience from the very designation of 'black British art'. That should transform the entire black British milieu by returning to visual works themselves as the very space of philosophical work; as a body of phenomena deposited before us, of things that can withstand extended contemplation for the profoundly visual, spatial and tactile experiences that they offer, for how they appear to us, how they exist. Mine is not a case for elaborating a 'diaspora aesthetic', but for showing how the locating of a given corpus of art in the field of cultural representation is a matter of grasping affective relations. Black British art appropriates cultural narratives, telling and retelling, articulating and signifying. But it does so by giving rise to perceptual, phenomenal experiences that give place and substance to all such processes, and make encounters with them possible.

**Chapter 3**

# Placing the past

It may seem a platitude or mere truism to observe that black British art has the status of being representative *and* phenomenally important. But holding that simultaneous status in view is crucial for apprehending how such art performs the work of memory, how it reflects the past (whether that be the historical or the personal past) and how it comes into being at all as a locus of remembrance. The topic of the past has proven to be a capacious one for black British artists. While such examples of their art demand a critical reading, they can also benefit from a more wide-reaching interest in the productive ambiguities of aesthetic experience in cases where artists have explored art's memorialising capacities. That sort of intellectual work requires the innovative philosophical approach that is the focus of the following discussion.

When set within a phenomenological frame, art's significations of the past become the starting point for a new sort of inquiry. First, it should be one that declines to sort out or divide the past into verifiable historical documentation versus a purposefully constructed narrative – the real or factual versus the imaginary, the recollected versus the fabricated. Conceptions of the past do not separate so easily, nor into collective versus personal histories, and least of all does black British art in its concerns with the past drive towards a conclusive or consensual view. Secondly, a deep suspicion towards the aim of historical truth, which is shared by critical thinking and phenomenology, concurs on the imperative need to be receptive to the role played by memory in suggesting *alternative* pasts. Much can be learned from the celebrated Foucauldian initiative to unmask the extent to which discursive practices often try to fix the past through the use of narrative. This is the case for black British art when it has confronted aspects of an ancestral past, such as in reimagining slavery or celebrating the continuity of Caribbean, Asian or African 'traditions' in a British setting. There has been a fundamental appeal to the visual as the means to oppose the meaning of dominant historical narratives by introducing lived realities and biographies, thereby complicating the record of the past as well as expanding notions of the past itself. Such is the visual language of struggle and discursive articulation through the imagination that black British art exemplifies in its cultural politics of the past.

While this style of exploration of black British art could be extended to a limitless range of works and artists, this chapter confines its discussion to a handful of examples. Sonia Boyce and Keith Piper have in differing ways engaged in thinking about the past and history, choosing themes that index wider efforts to flag up and construct diaspora identities. In a substantial literature, the critical dimension of their respective projects has been clearly identified (see, for example, Abraham, 2012; Bailey et al., 2005; Chambers, 2014; Chandler, 1997; Cubitt, 1999; Gibbons, 2007; Tawadros, 1997), while leaving aside any concern with the phenomenal dimension of black British art in its apprehension of the past. As we shall see, however, this art offers more than a medium or conduit for visualising or grasping the past, for signifying new standpoints on it. The historical themes in the art of Boyce and Piper that emerge through processes of recollecting the past are also intimately felt, affective relations. Historical themes are not simply augmented by perceptual qualities, so much as brought into being by them, as they go about revisiting and 'disturbing' the past (Wainwright, 2000a; 2017), with a pertinence for understanding the relationship between art and the difficulties and potential of memorialisation.

## Visual historiography and place

Revisiting and celebrating the past is a complex process and the routes, strategies and meanings that are taken and thrown up by that process are salutary for understanding black British art. An interventionist 'rewriting' of shared and emphatically collective histories is especially useful for reinscribing the historical presence of a community at the margins of Britain's narratives of nationhood. This, by and large, was the leading motivation for staging public events and exhibitions during the 1980s and 1990s which elevated cultural difference – a drive to 'visibility' in a new cultural politics of 'race', nation and art practice (see Chambers, 1998; Clarke and Tawadros, 1999; Keen and Ward, 1996).[1] This was a moment

---

1   Early examples of such exhibitions might include *From Two Worlds* (1985), Whitechapel Art Gallery, curated by Gavin Jantjes and Nicholas Serota; the GLC's *Reflections of the Black Experience* exhibition and programme (1986); *New Horizons*, which was

of particular malaise, with a sense of protest towards the existing 'cultural circuit' of representation (Hall, 1997), when the infrastructure of art display came to seem not only inadequate but actually in conflict with the desire that black British artists might 'enter' the dominant historical record.

Since those heated decades of struggle in the arts, exploration of the topic of history has continued to be instrumental for developing black British art as a discursive practice. Such art is a vehicle in the search for identification within a sense of the historical past, a counter to contemporary racism in its denial that black people have a knowable past at all (Gilroy, 1987: 11; Garrison, 1990). Indeed, the very removal of a black presence from the dominant historical imagination is a shared condition throughout the African diaspora or 'Black Atlantic' world (Gilroy, 1993a; 1993b). Identities that are fashioned from such an experience of being de-historicised have responded by voicing a fervent belief in the imperative need for people of African and Caribbean descent to reflect on their past, taking the collective process of such representation to be a source of recuperative power. Characterising black visual practices is 'not an identity grounded in the archaeology but in the retelling of the past', a past which 'is always constructed through memory, fantasy, narrative and myth' (Hall, 1990: 224–226). Particular energy has gone into tracing the historical past through art practice and a line of cultural criticism attuned to its political purpose.

I should explain what might be meant by ideas about the past in black British art. There are the named historical events and periods referenced by these artists' works which can be corroborated by formal scholarly history. Then there are those ideas expressed by way of reference to a personal history or past, namely autobiography. This is a type of historiography whose character derives from being an object of visual thinking, a *visual historiography* that treats evidence as a non-essential criterion for understanding the past. Instead what emerge are affective spaces which the viewer of artworks may enter, thereby moving into proximity with the artist.

Such an approach requires of philosophy that we elucidate exactly how signification and perceptual experience converge in a generalised

staged at the Royal Festival Hall in 1985; *Reflections of a Different World* (1984); the *Colours of Black* exhibition at the GLC Conference Hall (1986); *Black Skin/Bluecoat* at the Bluecoat Gallery in Liverpool (1985); *The Thin Black Line* at the Institute for Contemporary Art in London (1985); and *Plotting the Course* at Oldham Art Gallery, Wolverhampton Art Gallery and the Bluecoat (1988–89).

hermeneutics, where the dividing line between description and interpretation becomes less clear. Phenomenology's trump card is that it sits usefully at the threshold of a more properly interpretative method (Melville, 1998; Bontekoe, 1996; Gadamer, 1979; Ricoeur, 1981), since this makes it very useful indeed when encountering a critically engaged grouping of artworks and at the same time grasping their phenomenal importance. Black British art is a strategic, discursive cultural formation, for its ability to invert signs of otherness, to disrupt such cultural fixities as conventional signs of difference and 'race', and so on. At the same time such struggles go on with and through the actual materiality of visual representation. Identifying the structures of materiality is a matter of aiming for a pre-theoretical look – or, as Husserl termed it, an 'ante-predicative' look – at the 'thingly' nature (Heidegger in Krell, 1996) of these works, in a provisional step aside from cultural criticism preoccupied with the semiotic *langue*. Those same concerns may then be reframed by a mode of explanation that gives primacy to material objects and situates them within experiential *horizons*. This makes it easier to see a world of possibilities that is set up by the artwork's existence – in broad strokes, a philosophy of art that is mindful of Heidegger's analytic of *Dasein* ('Being-there' or 'Being-in-the-world'), a framework of thought dealing with the very issues of existence and its origins. On this more general ground of phenomenological description can be built a perceptual awareness of black British art *together* with a signifying one, in a more rounded and non-antithetical account that emerges from philosophy, which shows up the interplay among such approaches.

When speaking of the horizon of the work of art, we are already beginning to think about the notion of place. Considering the spatial metaphor of horizon brings to the fore a conception of artworks as places; not only as *expressive* places, or places of articulation (for the *placing* of ideas) but as materially present, 'place worthy' and ostensive, an instance of what David Summers has called 'place-making' (2003, especially chapter 2; Casey, 1997: 270). Artworks are visual places when they form a meeting point for artist, spectator/reader and idea(s); the work of art expands the possibilities of such elements coming to experience one another. When describing black British artworks, the poetics of the practice or 'event' of meeting needs to be kept in view, treated always as if 'on shared ground',[2]

---

2  A similar pronouncement has been made about meeting points in connection with film: 'cinematic vision in the film experience is articulated by *both* the film *and* the spectator simultaneously engaged in *two* quite distinctly located visual acts that meet

so that works of art may be apprehended as accessible places with which, and at which, experiences can be exchanged. These are the conclusions drawn from works by Sonia Boyce and Keith Piper, whose critical and phenomenal endeavours are characteristic of black British art's relations with the past, and succeed in giving place to the past through the orchestration of experiential encounters.

## Personal pasts and pictorial devices

Significantly bound up with an artist's memories are the places and spaces in which those memories were formed, and through which they are remembered and made. This can be seen in the domestic interiors and human bodies featured in drawings by Sonia Boyce which concern the artist's family and home, including *Big Women's Talk* (1984, fig. 5), *She Ain't Holding Them Up, She's Holding On (Some English Rose)* (1986, fig. 6), *Conversational Piece: Kitchen Table Talk, Strange Dreams* (1986) and *Bringing Up Babies* (1986). What gets included in these images has everything to do with the role of memory. As she perceives and recollects her personal history, the artist is subject to both forgetting and reinterpreting her past as it is transformed by time. Her drawings on the theme of childhood are at one level a careful retelling of her past, and on another a bearer or register of unchecked experiences. In this sense, to claim that Boyce's works amount to a kind of autobiographical project, a personal historical account, cannot sufficiently capture the degree to which unconsidered emotions emerge and register in her drawings, in addition to those she has deliberately sought.

Such ambivalence – the search for particular memories, alongside unsolicited appearances – is illustrated particularly well in the use of decorated surfaces in these drawings. In *She Ain't Holding Them Up*, Boyce pictures herself in a dress printed with black roses, standing against a highly patterned background, and staring out of the picture frame. Her face commands the most central part of this image, while above her sit four more figures – her parents and their two children. This area of the drawing also has its own fantastical elements, for in the space between the mother's head and shoulder a bright yellow bird appears,

on shared ground but never identically occupy it' (Sobchack, 1992: 23). The film's 'body' is a concretely embodied entity, whose visual and visible modes of perception and expression place it in a relationship of reciprocity and reversibility with its viewer (see Baker, 2011: 151; 2009).

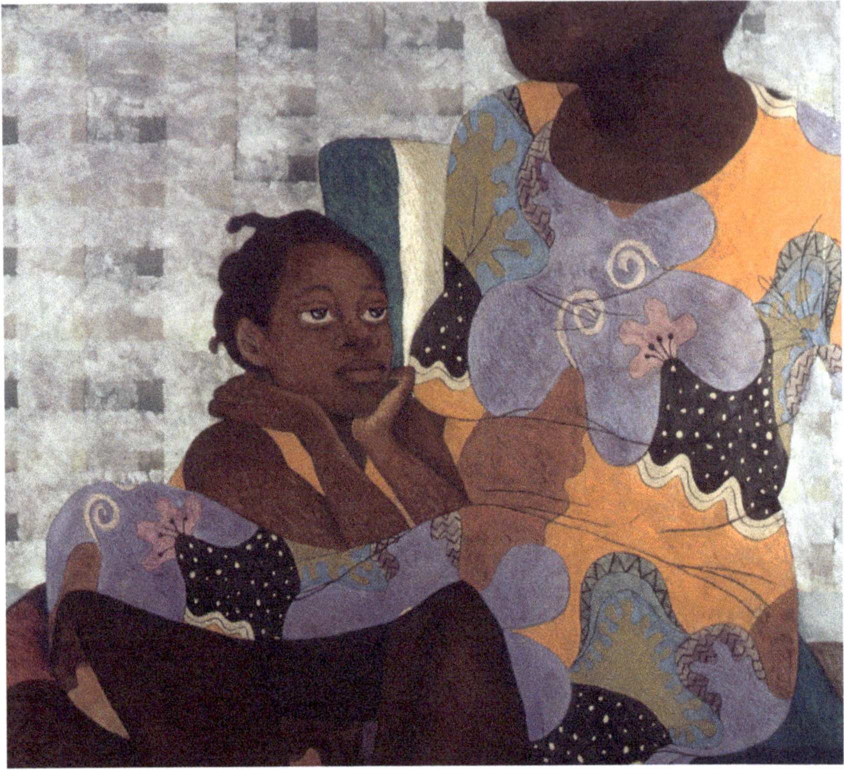

Figure 5: Sonia Boyce, *Big Women's Talk*, 1984, pastel and ink on paper,
148 x 155 cm. Private collection. © Sonia Boyce. All rights reserved, DACS 2016.

Figure 6: *opposite* Sonia Boyce, *She Ain't Holding Them Up, She's Holding On
(Some English Rose)*, 1986, crayon, chalk, pastel and ink on paper, 216 x 99 cm.
Middlesbrough Collection at Middlesbrough Institute of Modern Art. © Sonia
Boyce. All rights reserved, DACS 2016.

one of a pair that together carry in their beaks the patterned backdrop
by its ribbon-like upper edge, and behind the bird are several palm tree
branches, rendered against a blue sky.

The sense of the place of home is conveyed in the continuity of
patterned surfaces across many of Boyce's drawings in this group. The
prevalence of these decorated areas can lead us to know something
of the artist's connectedness to place by way of the mother, who in
turn becomes a site of emotional recollection. The patterns of her
drawings need not resemble the actual ones of her mother's house, and

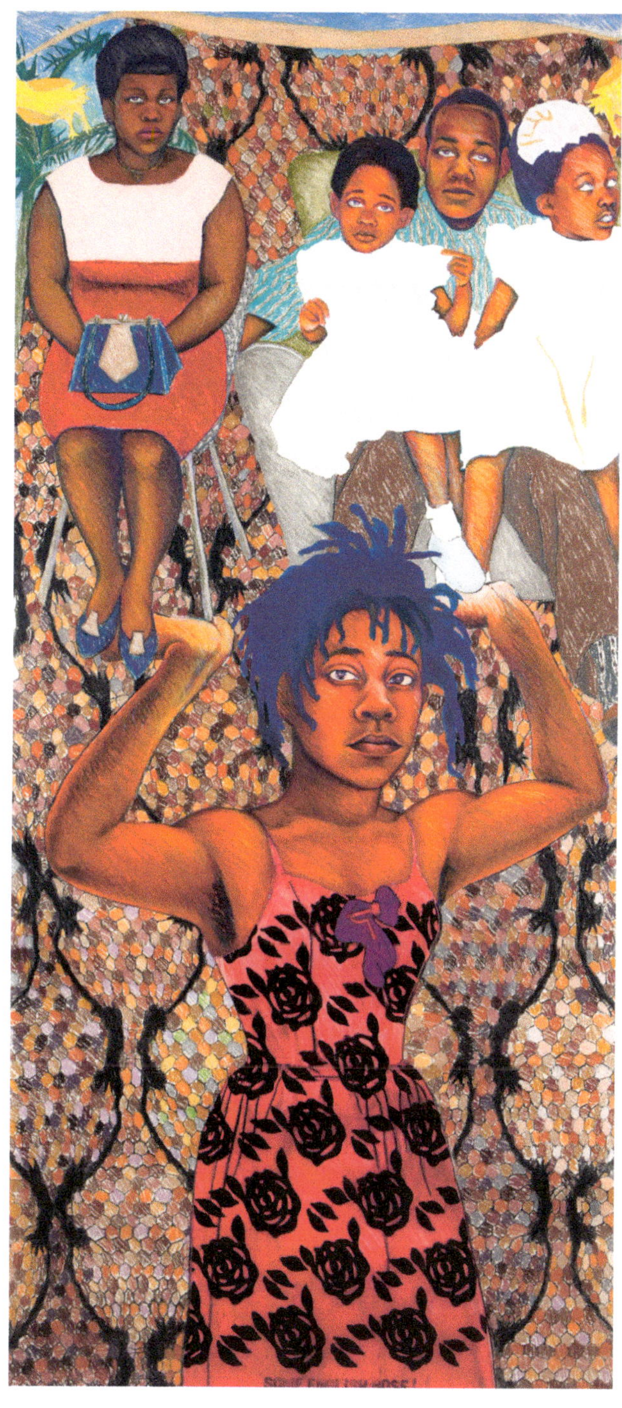

any discrepancy between them is significant of the ways memory and emotion have intervened to modify its decoration. This fascination with patterned surfaces is all of a piece with the artist's mother, with a use of colour and the repetition of decorated areas which become a traceable maternal presence. As Boyce has explained:

> My use of pattern owes a lot to my mother's house: your eyes can't stop blinking for all the patterns in the house. When you go in the living room there are patterns everywhere, on the carpet, on the curtains, on the wallpaper, on the ceiling. They have their own co-ordination. When I started doing drawings about my childhood … I realised I was including my mother's influence, or rather a West Indian sense of decoration. (Roberts, 1987: 62)

This comment that the patterns in Boyce's childhood home had 'a West Indian sense of decoration' serves to channel the meaning of these images. The text opens the way for a sense in which a visual language operates through pattern, both an index of an actual home and something more abstract and associative: 'West Indian'. As such, it forms part of an attempt to situate a social history among memories of mother and interiority, pointing to a family background of migration and diaspora. This may be separated into strands: the mother as a metonym for a West Indian cultural identification, and the mother as an intimately perceived maternal presence, outside ethnic categorisation.

The discursive and visual distinctions at play in Boyce's works of childhood memory are sharpened by the use of devices such as the cropping of figures within the picture frame. She gives us a child's sense of the home by ordering the frame and channelling the viewer's gaze to the subject of the child, bringing us closer and in line with the world through her eyes. In *Big Women's Talk*, the artist shows herself as a young girl sitting with her head propped on her hands at her mother's knee. The mother, wearing a highly patterned dress, holds a conversation with another woman, as we may suppose from the title, although no one else is in the picture. Her face is cropped by the picture frame above her half-open mouth, indicating it to be a point of interest for the listening girl who is seen to have the talking mother not in her gaze but in earshot. The division in her attention is a measure of the distance between mother and daughter. Yet, at the same moment, placing the viewer's attention on the intimate sheltering of the daughter in her mother's lap gains the effect of foregrounding the fact of their familial relationship. It makes for an elastic space between mother and daughter, widening and narrowing with the fluctuation of our sense of their proximity, heightened by the closeness of the child's face to her mother's breast and yet making the margin between face and breast seem variable.

The elasticity of space suggested by the arrangement of these elements is ideally conveyed through visual material, where the composition of an image invites viewers to move their gaze across the drawing in a non-linear fashion. The diverted glance of the daughter, the cropping of her mother's head and the alignment of our eye-level with that of the child would not have the same affective outcome in a verbal or written narrative form. This is true in general for how Boyce explores her personal history in several further images. The titles of drawings, *Conversational Piece: Kitchen Table Talk*, *Strange Dreams* and *Bringing Up Babies*, refer to the role of verbal exchanges within the home and between female family members. Each features a continuous background of patterned cloth, pressed upon by the spread fingers of two hands, and we can may suppose from the title and the projection itself that this is an aerial view of a kitchen table and tablecloth, that these are the limbs of two female family members meeting at the kitchen table. In *Bringing Up Babies* this is reduced to a single individual, with hands and forearms that smooth creases of fabric patterned with dark roses on a pale ground, perhaps a bedcover, tablecloth or curtains.

Within the setting of a domestic kitchen the relaxed posture of the hands and arms in *Conversational Piece* suggests, an understanding of the home environment as a scene for dialogue among children, and between children and parents, across generations. The work bears a notion of the domestic setting as the place to nurture openness, reflection and conjecture, an atmosphere for sharing one's ambitions, and as the subtitle would have it, 'strange dreams'. A sense of place is created through a careful composition that emphasises how the fluidity and pliability of dreams evade the fixity of visual narrative when such memories are painted and printed. This makes for histories of a particular kind, re-examined in a space that offers both the artist and ourselves the scope for imaginative travel, for travel to the 'memories of other places', which Gaston Bachelard named the 'land of Motionless Childhood, motionless the way all Immemorial things are' (1994: 6).[3]

---

3  He continues: 'We comfort ourselves by reliving memories of protection. Something closed must retain our memories, while leaving them their original value as images. Memories of the outside world will never have the same tonality as those of home and, by recalling these memories, we add to our store of dreams; we are never

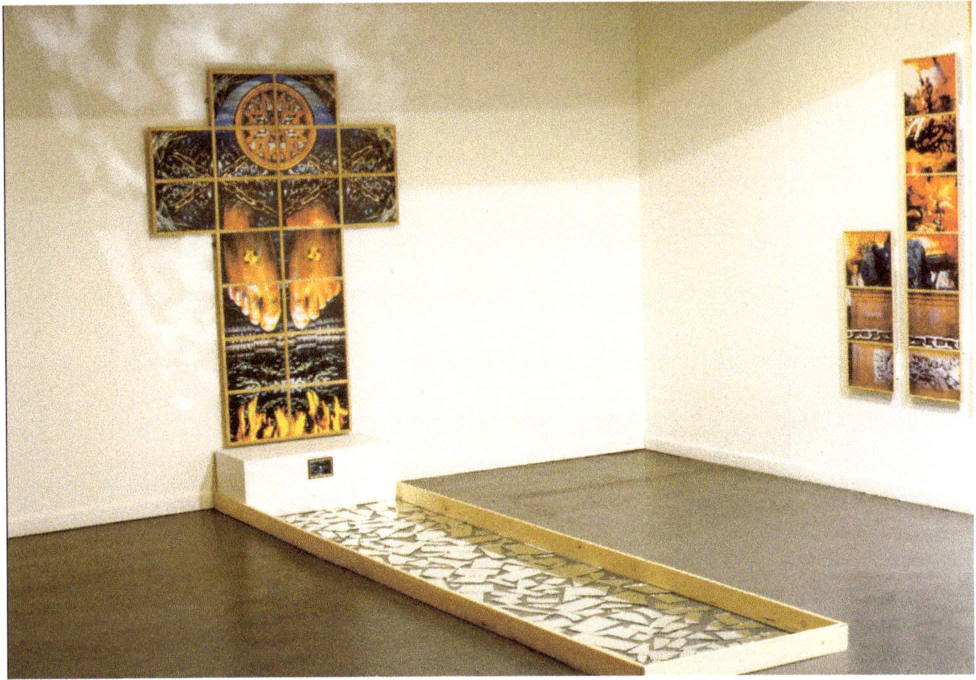

Figure 7: Keith Piper, *A Ship Called Jesus: The Ghosts of Christendom*, 1991, first part of the installation, mixed media with computer montage on timber. Installation: Ikon Gallery, Birmingham. Image used with permission.

## Assembling efficacy

Keith Piper's *A Ship Called Jesus*, an exhibition of installation and multimedia works compiled by the artist in 1991, addresses multiple historical themes in the role of Christianity, from the earliest period of English involvement in transatlantic slavery, to the rise and development of the black Church in the Americas and its movement to Britain in the mid-twentieth century. The first of three sections to the exhibition, entitled *The Ghosts of Christendom* (fig. 7), bears a strange mixture of elements with an intended resemblance to architectural and funerary features found in and around church buildings. On the right-hand wall is *Onward Christian Soldiers* (fig. 8), an arrangement of colour

real historians, but always near poets, and our emotion is perhaps nothing but an expression of a poetry that was lost' (Bachelard, 1994: 6).

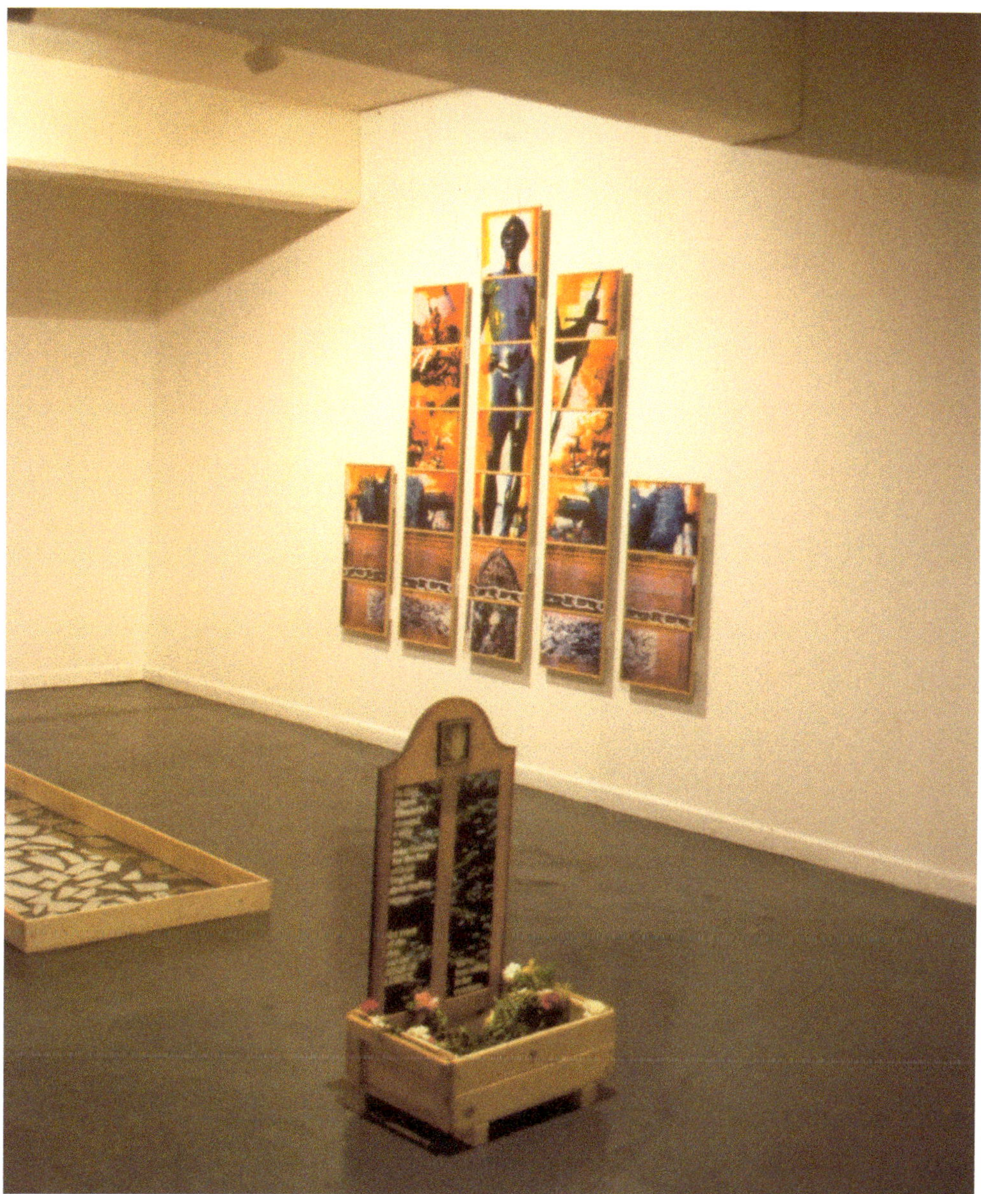

Figure 8: Keith Piper, *A Ship Called Jesus: Onward Christian Soldiers*, 1991, second part of the installation, mixed media with computer montage on timber. Installation: Ikon Gallery, Birmingham. Image used with permission.

transparencies mounted on electric lightboxes, with rectangular sections set out in columns forming an arched stained-glass window. On the left is a similarly composed arrangement of coloured panels, laid out vertically in a stout cruciform. At the foot of this illuminated cross is an enclosure the width and length of a grave, with an irregular mosaic of a hundred or so broken mirrors. In the foreground to both of these arrangements is a freestanding wooden panel shaped like a tombstone, a wooden box of flowers at its base, where Piper has inscribed the exhibition's first text:

> In 1564
> Queen Elizabeth I
> donated
> a ship
> to John Hawkins
> for the first
> official
> English
> slave trading
> voyage …
>
> the name
> of the
> ship
> was the
> JESUS OF LUBECK
>
> We've
> been sailing
> in her
> ever since.
> (Piper, 1991)

'From the point at which Columbus claimed the "New World" for the Catholic Spanish monarchy in 1492', he continues in an essay accompanying the exhibition, 'colonialism and Christendom became firmly locked in an unholy alliance of mutual self interest' (Piper, 1991). The artist's combination of emphatically Christian iconography with more recently reworked icons of slavery establishes a visual register of that 'unholy alliance'. The essay recounts the shifting relationship between the black diaspora community and Christianity from the period of plantation slavery to the present, arguing that Christianity was initially a means of spiritual bondage before its appropriation transformed that role to one of support and guidance during the later years of slavery and up to the present. He writes: 'Contained within [modern Christian] … modes of worship were both the expression of, and response to the various traumas of displacement and loss. These in turn echoed the earliest religious rituals forged by captive Africans transported to the hell of the New World' (Piper, 1991).

Body parts appear numerously across the framed areas of all of these assembled objects. Against a background of chains and architectural sculpture, filled in with areas of flickering open water and flame, are pierced feet that bear the sign of the cross. A similarly pierced hand is framed and mounted at the *titula* of the tomb, and in the arched columns on the right-hand wall a fragmented and reworked statue stands *contrapposto* bearing a sword. Arranging this imagery digitally has enabled the receding details, such as those of the feet, to overlap with boldly repetitive links of chain, an index of the Atlantic slave trade, and tight rows of illustrated slaves stowed aboard a ship. These bodies, minuscule beneath the feet, create a rhythmic effect, set against points of light in a stretch of lapping water which forms a broad band below, disrupted by tongues of flame. The composition acknowledges the complex role played by the Christian faith throughout the history of the African diaspora, especially its ambivalent attachment to religion. Here Piper has dispensed with the linear passage of history that runs through his written discussion in a range of indexical references to the institution of the Church – configurations of the cross, stigmata and traces of sacred architecture – and the artist's memorial to slavery, either inscribed on stone or sketched in shards of broken mirror.

Piper's accompanying written text is concise, only a few pages – and yet it succeeds in noting that Afro-syncretic religious practices in the Americas under conditions of slavery were part of more microcosmic elements of resistance that formed in the 'lifeways' of enslaved peoples (see Ferguson, 1992; McGuire and Paynter, 1991: 29; Vlach, 1990). His visual project retells such stories while presenting a distinctive form of aesthetic experience and a process of remembrance that differs from the sort of visual evidence that customarily provides a prop for historical narratives. While Piper's installations consider the ideological dimensions of Christian worship within colonial and slave systems, their phenomenological value is demonstrated by the different sort of truth that might obtain in a visual 'thing', compared to what can be gathered from the authorial construction of a written text. Such objects of remembrance – chains, flames and pierced bodies entangled in the form of the cross – do not issue from a flight of the imagination without limits, however, but from a sustained endeavour to recapture what an artist might regard to be a *credible* past, while turning away from a conventional historical textual practice. Piper's exhibition is a spell of guided imaginative travel that bears a crucial difference: it distinguishes an archival trawl across a received landscape of history from a properly material inquiry. Employing an approach to historical memory that centres more on personal post-memory of the Middle Passage and its horrors, these installations are a scene of actualisation for what the past holds for the artist himself in its phenomenal dimensions.

Art historical and curatorial research on 'visualising slavery' has surveyed art-making in several contexts within the African diaspora, mainly in the United States, to show how modern and contemporary artists might turn towards such histories while being bound by present circumstances (Bernier and Durkin, 2016; Copeland, 2013; Barson and Gorschlüter, 2010). In Piper's art the matter draws its character from a process of contending at once with the experiential depth of a multicomponent installation, and several temporally bound frames of visual perception; its affective relation to viewers pertains to work in the sculptural round as well as a continuing and open-ended project that unfolds over time. This art is spatially and periodically reviewed, strictly speaking, which has ensured that its core discursive issues remain live (for instance, Chandler, 1997; Wainwright, 2000a; 2003; Fisher, 2008). Indeed, in *emplacing* such issues within a physical arena, in the form of a work of art, our experiences may come to meet with the artist's. The horizons of the artist, those of the work of art and those of its viewers alter through a shifting relationship, merging and commingling to try to make sense of one another through the contingency of place.

Complicating such a process further is the 'relocating' of this installation to an entirely digital medium, as happened with Piper's larger multimedia project entitled *UnRecorded* (Chandler, 1997), which users enter via a virtual gateway comprising an altered reproduction of François-Auguste Biard's *The Slave Trade* of 1840. Interactive links at chosen points in the picture lead into scenes drawn from *A Ship Called Jesus*, along with many of the artist's even earlier works. We do not apprehend this art in visual terms alone, given the addition of sound, and viewers may form private narratives for themselves by threading their own paths, without linearity – phenomenal travel that in turn marks out a virtual place of memory for Piper's output until 1997.

## Personal and shared pasts

In their various visual and written works, black British artists have pointed unwaveringly to the interplay of historical evidence, textual and material, and the divergent phenomenal possibilities of memorialisation. They raise the question not so much of what supplies an artist's experience in order to make reference to history, but the outcomes of a search beyond referential relations per se. Viewers may bring to black British art concerns about the status of these artworks in relation to historical truth, and the nature of the truth about the experience they disclose. Attention to a perceptual experience of the past is simultaneously a process of place and place-making. Black British artists undertaking visual historiography have sustained Heidegger's sense of the work of art as something in which a world is 'set up' (*aufstellt*), and in which truth resides. They have asked: 'Where does the historical past belong in relation to the present lived experience of art, its makers and audiences?' and so moved closer to what phenomenology sets as its goal of enabling the 'unconcealment' of truth.

The limits of bringing narrative to bear on the visual are made patent by works such as those by Boyce and Piper, all the better to see how memory, emotion and belief can be assembled and disclose themselves. Keith Piper's installations point directly to history, set in the recent present and distant past, the Middle Passage of slavery, and to ideas about social control and religion. The phenomenal materiality of his practice is essential in allowing him to locate and *emplace* that history. Sonia Boyce's pastel drawings are figurative scenes of home and family that become sites of remembrance, places of physical and emotional attachment. They retell a childhood whose gesturing hands and bodies are grounded in pattern during a search for intimacy. The historical impulses felt around these figures are childhood 'dwelling-places' of protection, a material places and 'our store of dreams' (Bachelard, 1994: 6). Crucially, such images of the body and home are an artist's particular personal history which may be shared and generalised for viewers, in turn transforming the very terms of what comes to count as historical.

The existing scholarship on these artists has asserted the purpose of making art against a background of struggles over the representation of marginalised and excluded communities – the artistic drive for 'visibility' (Araeen, 1984) – which points to art as a useful social practice. In an important sense, this has the effect of presenting an art object as a phenomenon, as a 'thing' located within an economy and politics of meaning. This emphasises the notion of art practice as a matter of responsibility, implying that artists ought to approach their works with an awareness of the historical past and the need to engage with an aesthetics of struggle. In this scheme we can recognise a theoretical strategy to move beyond a distinctly modernist dichotomy of art's aesthetic value versus its use value, and into a situation of flux and play wherein art practices are caught up in the dynamics of discourse, signification and power.

Yet the split terms of this dichotomy have yet to be reconciled. We need to consider more effective ways of doing this, and to find a differently theorised approach to the problem. Going by way of phenomenology could be constructive here. Heidegger, for instance, chose to cast oscillating glances first at the notion of the 'ready-to-hand' (*zuhanden*) of the equipmental work, and the 'self-sufficient presence' (*Selbstgenugsamkeit*) of the artwork. That made for a certain sort of reflexivity and an arena of polemical thought that both sorts of 'work' bring into existence. This is what Heidegger described as the openness of the Open (*das Offene*), the emergence of truth from untruth, and in doing so he returned us to the spatial metaphor identified in black British art concerned with the past, which specifies places that are inhabited and set up by such visual works as they take the role of emplacing ideas at the threshold of experience. This more philosophical understanding of experience represents a renewal of descriptive focus arranged alongside a signifying analysis, raising a fresh consciousness of art, the past, memory and place.

While I began by outlining some paradigms in a cultural-political understanding of diaspora art practice, I have left trailing the more conventionally pondered questions of artistic motivation in order to describe how these artworks 'set up' a world, and create points of both reference and support for historical memory. This raises a major theoretical issue in understanding black British artists at large: the need to recognise that accomplishing a visual historiography of these artists' works can only be undertaken at a relatively 'late' stage of analysis, after having first described and delineated the boundaries of their art as material spaces of remembrance. The physical markers of the existence of these artworks as visual places are concomitant with a poetics of remembrance and imaginative travel. Each of these artists' practices are the result of a personal search for the very materials with which to establish those places travelled from and to, which produces a gathering of ideas and materials in a new physical context. The foregoing analysis of just a couple of artists' forays into visual historiography should show up the more foundational value of their art, without needing to draw further from the pool of black or diaspora cultural discourse. Indeed, the dominant procedure of semiotic analysis somewhat entrenchs the historical value of black British artworks within an account of their metaphorical and critical functions. With a new look at this art, however, there comes an appreciation of its artists' imaginative movements through time – in the intimate realm of art-making – as well as how this art carries indexes of historical revisionism addressed to experiences of diaspora, without any contradiction emerging from this more inclusive philosophical understanding.

Art can be a place for thinking about the past and it calls for a more flexible commitment to the available intellectual schemes for elucidating the historical imagination of black British artists. Such artworks hardly have an essential meaning, but rather become meaningful in the course of questions that are asked about them. Whether these relate to critical inquiry, or to inquiry of a more expansive, perceptual kind, in either case there is a fundamental ambiguity about them. At root, the historical presence of black British artworks, their memorialising roles and the cross-articulation of aesthetics with ideas about the past, all rely on their effectiveness as perceptual phenomena. How philosophy might treat this peculiarly material efficacy for artworks that, by contrast, have little such overt orientation to the past, and indeed how philosophy can specify many more of the ways that presence is manifest in black British art, is the matter I will turn to next.

# Chapter 4

# The body and perception

In the discussion thus far I have contended that appreciating more fully the historical value of black British art demands a closer aesthetic engagement with artworks. I have shown how this is the case when artists have sought new relationships to the past, producing a material presence through their art from which further and unexpected understandings of the past can emerge. Clearly, works of art that re-examine the histories of the Middle Passage, of Atlantic slavery and its horrors, colonial subjectivity and so on, are all relevant to the constructed meanings of black or diaspora community and identity. But there are also divergent and expansive dimensions of human experience at play here. They would be missed entirely should we settle for the view that such art is not much more than the fulcrum for raising historical issues or themes. Indeed, the various pastel works by Sonia Boyce, which untangle and recollect the memories of childhood, do so in a way that looks above the thematic, above signification and the dynamics of cultural discourse. The patterned interiors of Boyce's home and her parental attachments are also an emotional landscape, which puts concrete ground under a cultural politics of the artist's drive to self-identification. That process is similarly exemplified by Keith Piper in his turn to experiential relations in works around slavery and religion. Taken together, such art practices demonstrate that cultural identity, the imagination and memory deserve simultaneous consideration, and that analysis of the phenomenal dimension of artworks is needed before arriving at a cultural or social appreciation of them, and before trying to account for how they bear historical meaning.[1]

---

1 Indeed, the previous chapter has shown that it is conceivable that through such a phenomenological approach many such things are 'active' and present in and around these works of art at any one time – therefore refuting the suggestion that 'in its deep concern with the individual embodied experience, phenomenology conceals the potential meanings of an artwork; or rather it obscures the possibility that the artwork is meaningful in "other" ways' (Boetzkes, 2010: 54).

Evidently, what is needed in the setting of black British art is a philosophical attitude to inquiry that can ensure that this art is recognised for both its critical purpose *and* its ontological presence. Black British art offers a spectrum of perceptual experience that presents a distinctive basis for knowledge. This can be brought to attention in particular through philosophical analysis of the body, and what might be learned through it.

In order for that analysis to proceed, the cultural and perceptual dimensions of black British artistic experience need however to remain separated off from one another, and perception needs to be treated as having primacy. As Merleau-Ponty explains, while 'the perceived world is the always presupposed foundation of all rationality, all value and all existence', and 'there is a whole cultural world which constitutes a second level about perceptual experience', perception is nonetheless 'the fundamental basis which cannot be ignored' (1964a: 13, 33). The practice of separation or *reduction* (otherwise termed 'bracketing' or *epoché*) has been extensively scrutinised and espoused within phenomenology, with the aim of seeing the phenomenal body in a reduced condition, aside from its involvement in that 'whole cultural world' of which Merleau-Ponty speaks, and hence before the imposition of wider cultural meanings. The objective in this chapter is to establish the status of black British art within its perceptual horizons, and to reassert the importance of this aesthetic dimension even in a discursive context as palpable as the cultural politics of blackness and difference.

## Incarnate subjectivity

The complexities of art and perception are easier to grasp when we recognise that any analysis of perception is also an analysis of the human body. Phenomenological thinking focuses on the actual human situation as the starting point for any authentic philosophy and counters the assumption that genuine thinking must always be abstract. For Merleau-Ponty, the human body – what Husserl terms the 'zero-point' (*Nullpunkt*) of experience (described in his work 'Ding und Raum', discussed in Casey, 1997: 218), and what Lyotard names 'the locus of the event' (1993: 314) – provides the only means by which human being is possible at all, and the starting point and ground for all thought. Art historian Hans Belting in turn names the human being the natural '*locus of images,* a living organ for images ...' He writes: 'The body is a place in the world, a locus in which images are generated and identified (recognised)' (2002: 37). At the basis of any understanding of the visual presence of black British artists is the fundamental recognition that presence and body are one. 'The body is our general medium for having a world', writes Merleau-Ponty (1962: 146), pointing to the ability of the body to direct itself towards, forge links with, or behave and situate itself in relation to a world. Any reflection we make about the world is based primarily on the foundation of an 'incarnate subjectivity',[2] that is, an anonymous and pre-personal consciousness shaped by its perceptions as a body.

While enmeshed in anti-racist, diaspora and postcolonial cultural criticism, black British artists are committed simultaneously to exploring physical, perceptual connections with the material world. From this it may be said that if these artists are the subjects of cultural politics in a larger sense, then their visual projects emerge from the foundation of their existence in 'the perceived world'. This becomes more evident by temporarily leaving aside several issues – of the gendered, sexualised, racialised status of bodies, for instance – before returning to them in hermeneutic fashion, with the fresh outlooks gathered through a phenomenal analysis. This meets with the recommendation from Merleau-Ponty that vision must be accounted for as always bound to and produced within a corporeal and a social context (1968: 235). As we will see, this approach assimilates the primary texts of twentieth-century phenomenology with the benefit of historical distance, and is cognisant of the feminist critiques of Merleau-Pontian thought, along with the application of phenomenology to the field of art history and visual culture studies (see, for instance, Rycroft, 2013; Parry and Wrathall, 2011; Elkins, 2008; Jones, 2003a; 2003b; Schmidt, 1999; Butler, 1989).[3] Many

---

2   This idea has also motivated work on the sociology of the body, such as that by Shilling, who revisits a foundationalist view of the body: 'To begin to achieve an adequate analysis of the body we need to regard it as a material, physical and biological phenomenon which is irreducible to immediate social processes or classifications. Furthermore, our senses, knowledgeability and capability to act are integrally related to the fact that we are embodied beings. Social relations may profoundly affect the development of our bodies in almost every respect; in terms of their size and shape and in terms of how we see, hear, touch, smell and think, but bodies cannot simply be "explained away" by these relations' (1993: 10–11). See also Turner (1984).

3   In feminist philosophy, it is the politics of attention to difference that interests me most, and I am minded of Judith Butler's sceptical position – that feminist theory 'has something to gain and something to fear from Merleau-Ponty's theory of

of the works appearing here have a figurative basis in common on which to build remembrance and emotion. In such a central role, the body presents not the recurring trope for these things, but its ultimate ground. It is the corporeal 'anchorage' (Merleau-Ponty, 1962: 146)[4] that allows the emergence of perceptual relationships in which artistic projects permit us to characterise what it is to have a body and a world.

Keeping in view artworks that invest this same appreciation for the philosophical importance of the body, I am at pains to show how black British art itself drives forward phenomenological inquiry. There are several interlinked issues here about how our bodies take up multiple positions in the world; how they perceive and interact with it; how our interests are interwoven with it; and how the sense of an insuperable distance between ourselves and our world can be overcome. For an analysis of black British artworks, this illuminates a deeper visual poetics, inscribed through instances of figuration, portraiture and self-portraiture, installations of body parts, performance work and digitally based montage. These show sustained artistic fascination for the phenomenal world and our places in it: how we perceive our body (the issue of arriving at what might be called a *body image*), the way we move and occupy space, and the way we have temporality through being incarnate.

Accounting for the immediacy of art in the black British milieu, what follows is a description of how artworks maintain such a corporeal

sexuality' (1989: 86) – and yet take forward Silvia Stoller's suggestion that 'Merleau-Ponty's conception of difference could be used along with feminist approaches to further reflect on the extent to which difference could be analysed in its ambiguous versions, that is, to analyse the ambiguities and nuances of differences' (2000: 177). Reflecting on the discipline of art history and its encounter with Merleau-Ponty, I would obviously disagree with James Elkins's conclusion that 'Merleau-Ponty does not provide the vocabulary to describe individual artworks' (2008: 26); my entire discussion here proves otherwise. See also Clark (2001). Elkins may have a point, however, about the actually existing state of play for phenomenology within art historical scholarship specifically: 'Describing the materiality of artworks demands words that are more specific than the terms available in phenomenology, and yet phenomenology is the principal theoretical ground for accounts of the physicality and materiality of art. But what figures in art history as the materiality of, say, oil painting, is only intermittently related to the generative terms in phenomenological criticism. The result is that talk about materiality in art history and theory is effectively detached from the sources on which it depends' (2008: 30).

4  'To understand is to experience the harmony between what we aim at and what is given, between the intention and the performance – and the body is our anchorage in the world' (Merleau-Ponty, 1962: 144).

connectedness to the bodies of their artists and to our own bodies as their viewers. These appear in various dimensions: through attention to colour; the way the body touches and is touched; and in its relation with itself as a self-aware body. There are some striking examples here of how artists have treated diverse ephemera such as hair, body parts and food in a way that shows tactility, texture and sight to be deeply germane to what are at the same time critically engaged artistic interests. The results have important contributions to a philosophy of phenomenal themes: namely, of colour, texture, touch and movement, and the relationship between a visual ground and its figures. Finally, building on descriptions of how their works explore the 'overlapping' of the senses, this chapter looks at the inseparability of perceptual experiences from 'making sense' as such.

## Immediacy

I go into his studio and there's an unfinished painting. Figures, not painted from life but from books. Piles of books are mixed up with paint and palettes left on the floor; art history mostly, and an elephant volume that probably belongs on a coffee table. I notice Svetlana Alpers' book *The Making of Rubens*, and a reworked Jordaens. Artists raiding history hasn't been a new idea for quite some time. Still, the initiative has multiple outcomes that were impossible to predict, NB Phokela's own 'King Candaules Lets Gyges Spy on His Wife' has an incomplete painted nude with a Kung Fu tattoo. Probably not what Alpers had in mind for her readers.[5]

In 1992, long after he left South Africa, Johannes Phokela began painting at London's Camberwell School and then the Royal College of Art, becoming known for rectangular works, mostly paint on canvas, that are reminiscent of a line of northern European artists including Bruegel, Rubens, de Gheyn, Jordaens and Manet. I encountered these works in the company of the artist as he was completing two paintings, or at least a work comprising two parts, his *Mortal Diptych Surmounted by Cameo Emblems* (fig. 9). Composed like a 'Last Judgement', a cascade of human subjects transfixed by celestial light, here the light falls only on painted bodies themselves, failing to illuminate a ground, so that other than

5   Personal notes on the occasion of my interview with Johannes Phokela, London, 3 July 2003.

these figures – each exposed to the flesh – the scene is dark and bare and without a sense of place. No preliminary sketches were made of the overall composition; Phokela added each subject one by one until the canvas was filled. The result is an assemblage of details from other paintings: Rubens's *The Consequences of War* (1637–38, Florence, Palazzo Pitti) informs the top half, with Mars, Venus, Europa, Pegasus etc., arranged in a montage, each figure put into empty space. In the foreground is a reclining nude from Rubens's response to Titian's *Bacchanal of the Andrians* (1523–26, Madrid, Prado). Top centre, a clutch of horses and bodies compose a pyramid, reversed in its symmetry, from *The Rape of the Daughters of Leucippus* (c.1618, Munich, Alte Pinakothek), which is in turn a response to da Vinci's *Battle of Anghiari* (c.1504, Florence, Palazzo Vecchio). Helping these diverse strands to pull together are sets of white grids, 36 'cameo emblems'. Phokela told me: 'I worked on them part by part to produce a cocktail of floating figures, anchored or held together by this grid. They become a woven pattern of themselves'.[6] The second part of this duo of paintings emulates the first, a patterning of presence in which the image becomes a variant of itself. 'It was a bare surface, cut and stitched together – I felt like a surgeon making it. I laid the canvas horizontally and bled paint through the slashes from behind'.

Metaphor and metonymy are essential to the elaboration of visual meaning in the genre to which Phokela is drawn, but for present-day viewers these have become obscure. The passing of time since Bruegel's or Rubens's day has ensured the erosion or 'rupture' of the connections between the human personalities depicted in such portraits and the political events explored in works of morality and allegory – what the social anthropologist Alfred Gell might have termed their indexes and 'prototypes' (1998). As Anne D'Alleva has noted about *tamau*, lengths of plaited human hair from seventeenth-century Tahiti: 'We contemporary observers have lost the ability to be captivated by *tamau*, not just because they have become tangled and brittle with age, but because the metaphoric and metonymic connections between index and prototype were ruptured' (2001: 90). But for Phokela, the agency of these works stems from the mystery granted to them by their reappearance in an art practice of the present – the *curious* nature of their contemporary location: 'I'm not intent on the viewer recognising these parts from masterpieces'. Phokela suggests, then, not that we try to piece together

---

6 All quotations from Johannes Phokela are drawn from my interview notes, made during visits to his studio in London during July and September 2003.

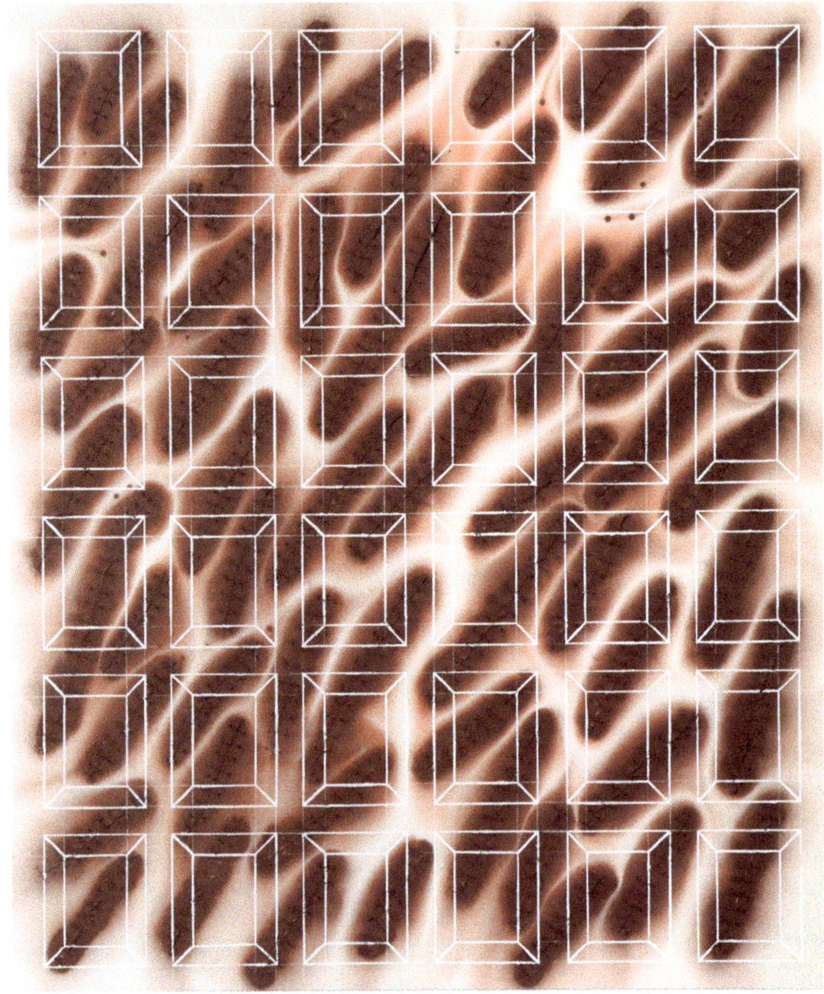

Figure 9: *both pages* Johannes Phokela, *Mortal Diptych Surmounted by Cameo Emblems*, 1997, oil and mixed media, each panel 198 x 168 cm. Courtesy of the artist.

the seventeenth-century significations of such works, the contextual ways that they might have captivated their Flemish observers, but that we look at their outcome and what they enable for Phokela as their primary agent.

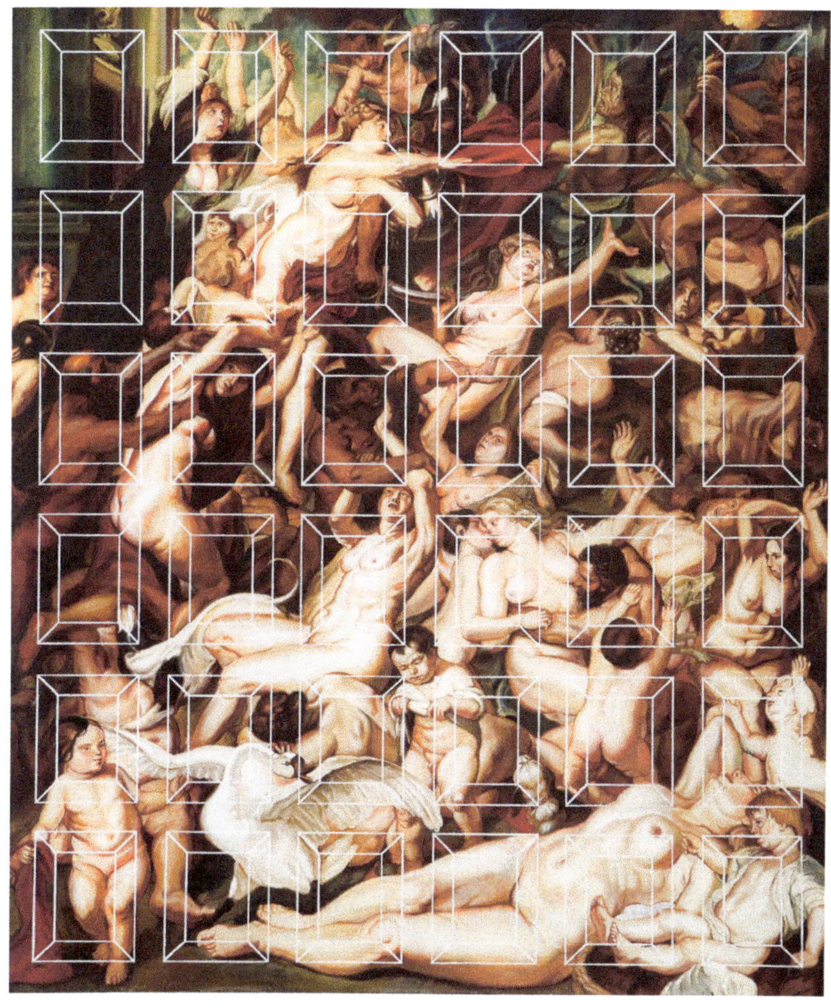

A similar interest in mining images of the past is shown by Aubrey Williams in his indigo-plumed serpent, his *Quetzlcoatl* of 1984, with its abstract coloured fields and Amerindian iconography. Here the artist allows himself the pleasures of play, irreverent towards an art practice circumscribed by 'signifying' themes. As Williams himself asserted, 'I haven't wasted a lot of energy on this roots business ... I've paid attention to a hundred different things ... why must I isolate one philosophy?' (Dempsey et al., 1998). Indeed, in his many canvases Williams radically overturned the sort of naturalism, the 'lifelikeness', that has so preoccupied European figuration, instead favouring – like Phokela – another modality of bodily 'captivation'.

Embodied looking is not a perspectival, ordered gaze cast in a rectangular frame – vision based on a monocular and fixed viewpoint. The eye is foveate, has definition, moves with the body, is binocular, expresses our height and enlarges with the approaching object.[7] As Norman Bryson suggests, we glance rather than gaze (1983: 94) and combine these fragmentary acts with sound, smell, touch and temperature.[8] What is more, the eye is selective (at least, it selects from among what Margaret Hagen [1986] in her study of the 'geometries of realism' terms 'invariants'), while vision unfolds in time.[9] Williams's abandonment of recession and monocularism is nowhere more obvious than in his *Olmec-Maya* series, with its traces of Aztec and Mayan iconography divorced from the rules of 'projective'[10] perspective. This is a trace of his larger search for a pre-colonial, Mesoamerican scheme of flattened surfaces and multiplying views (Walmsley, 1990). In his earlier *Symphonies* series (1969–81; see fig. 10 for an example from the series), by overlapping the aural and the painted, Williams apprehends music '*as painting*' (Armstrong et al., 2001), following the excitement and wonder

7   A summary of this position is given by Martin Jay, who quotes from Joel Snyder to summarise the differences between the photographic image and the human experience of sight: 'To begin with, our vision is not formed within a rectangular boundary; it is, per Aristotle, unbounded. Second, even if we were to close one eye and place a rectangular frame of the same dimensions as the original negative at a distance from the eye equal to the focal length of the lens (the so-called distance point of perspective construction) and then look at the field represented in the picture, we would still not see what is shown in the picture. The photograph shows everything in sharp delineation from edge to edge, while our vision, because our eyes are foveate, is sharp only at its "centre". The picture is monochromatic, while most of us see in "natural" colour (and there are some critics who maintain that the picture would be less realistic if it were in colour). Finally, the photograph shows objects in sharp focus in and across every plane, from the nearest to the farthest. We do not – because we cannot – see things this way' (Jay, 1995: 347–348). For an exploration of these and yet more limits of vision, and what came to dominate the rhetoric of aesthetic experience during artistic modernism, see Jones (2006).

8   For an analysis of this combination of acts, see Merleau-Ponty (1962: 305).

9   This is what Bryson in Chapter 5 of *Vision and Painting* describes as the deictic temporality of all seeing.

10   Again, see Hagen (1986) on the distinctions between projective, affine and metric perspective.

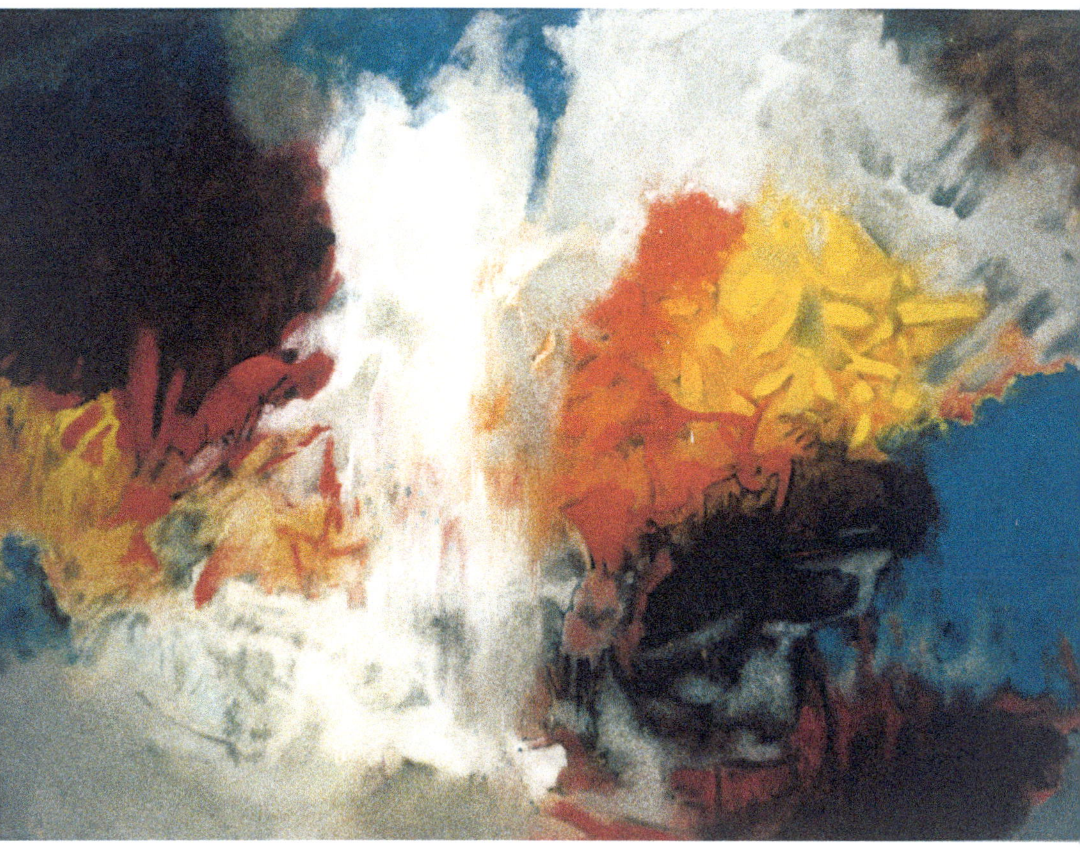

Figure 10: Aubrey Williams, *Quartet no. 5, Opus 92*, 1981, from his *Shostakovich* series (1969–81), oil on canvas, 132 x 208 cm, private collection.

he felt on first hearing one of the symphonies of Shostakovich in his teens: 'It hit me really hard, I was hearing a total sound … I could feel colour' (Dempsey et al., 1998; cf. Van Campen, 2011 on the synaesthesia of 'coloured hearing'; Williams, 2000). *Symphonies* connects to those musical works with its expanses of coloured space that darkly extend their drama, seen again in Williams's impasto starbursts and galaxies on canvases – his *Cosmos* series with its glissades of light, overlapping harmoniously with vacillating bubbles of celestial gas.

When Said Adrus and Bhajan Hunjan went *Trespassing* (the title of their collaborative painting and installation of 1993, fig. 11), among the transgressions they highlighted were illegal inroads into the same

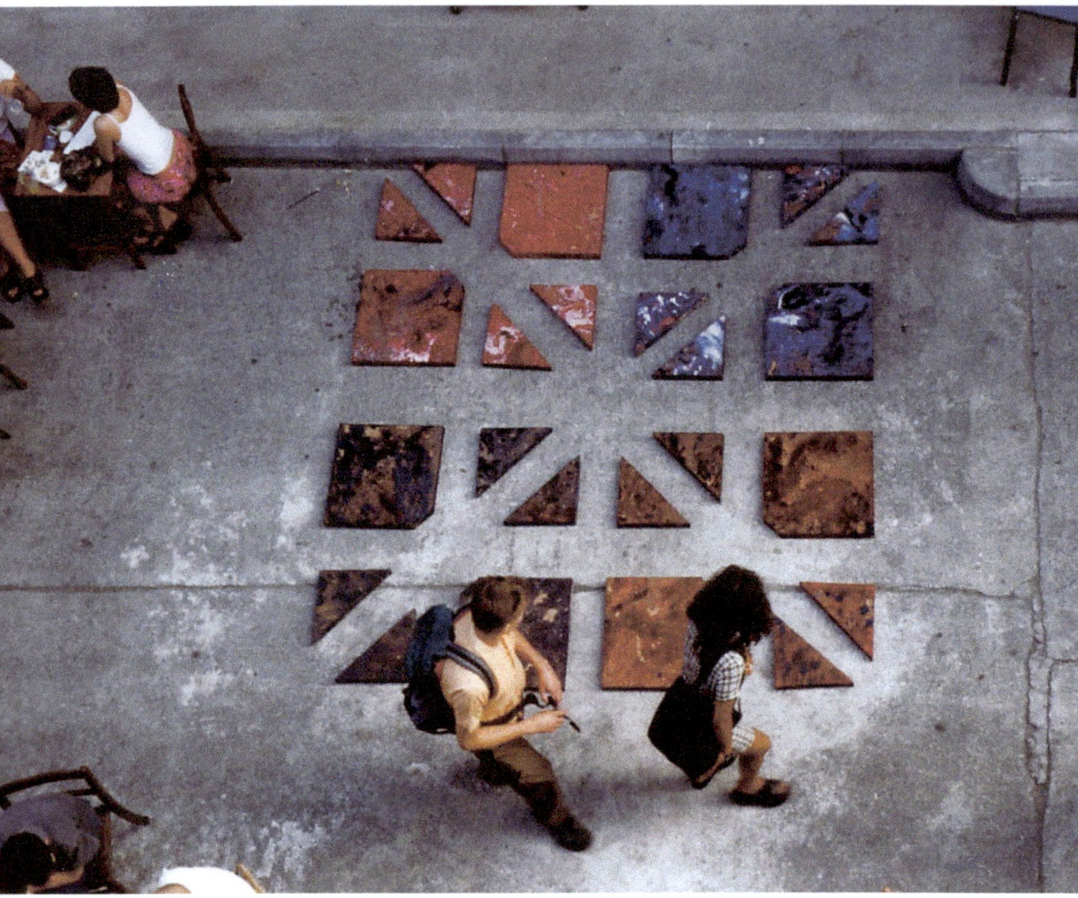

Figure 11: Said Adrus and Bhajan Hunjan, *Trespassing*, 1993, paint on wood, 31 x
31 x 1 cm. Photograph by Bhajan Hunjan.


'forbidden territory' of modernism.[11] Might not such a 'trespass' also be
a sojourn in a former colonial centre such as Britain, given loosely in the
work's arrangement resembling the Union Jack – even at a time when
'to perpetually counter a centre is to recognise it' (Oguibe, 1999: 322)


11   The first iteration of the work was included in the exhibition *Black People and the
     British Flag*, curated by Eddie Chambers (Cornerhouse Gallery, Manchester, 1993,
     sponsored by the Institute for International Visual Arts). A later version, illustrated
     here, was part of *It Ain't Ethnic*, a solo exhibition by Said Adrus at the One Gallery
     (Truman Brewery, Brick Lane, London, 1999).

– floating away from the margins, fancifully drifting to shore on panels of painted wood? As Williams offered a pre-Columbian cartography as a way of speaking to the postcolonial present, perhaps the oily film swirling on the grain of *Trespassing* also inscribes a practice of temporal mapping. This chaotic chart of geographical space, cut through with geometrical lines, serves as a window on to the difficulties of conventional cultural mappings after the advent of large-scale diasporas. It enunciates the contradictory idea of the shores of home as the place to which the migrant might sometime return; it materialises another instance of the 'myth' of homeland for those living in a diaspora, trying to cope with the 'impossibility' of making an ultimate return (Hall, 1990). If Hunjan and Adrus are indeed illustrating their arrival, homecoming or trespass in the territory of modernism's *sine qua non* – the medium of painting – then their wooden panels arranged horizontally on the gallery floor are both the flotsam and vehicle of that voyage. It is a journey sped on by an aggrandising, painterly act.

The difficulty of arriving as a painter in the territory of white (male) modernism, and of establishing oneself there, is compacted by the inaccessibility of that 'place' or 'position', since the European painter is the subject that they might never become (see Bhabha, 1994, arguing in a similar way about the literary author). How, indeed, does one take up such a coveted and colour-barred subjectivity, and moreover do so on one's own terms? This is the tension and dilemma that frames the issue of how to engage in representational painting, self-portraiture for instance, while avoiding the burdensome weight of its histories in a European setting.

In the striped mixing of colours, the gathering or reshaping through the painted medium offered by *Trespassing*, Hunjan and Adrus locate the uneven mixing of ethnicities and cultural identities in diaspora spaces, and an immersive ambivalence felt towards their hardships, shortcomings and freedoms. Broaching these topics of cultural politics, spatiality and selfhood through painting is about choosing a distinctly affective medium, and so it achieves much more than a topical, critical discussion. The phenomenal status of Hunjan and Adrus's painted panels indexes a reminder of how far 'colour in living perception is a way into the thing' (Merleau-Ponty, 1962: 305). *Trespassing* offers less an abstraction of the attempt to enter the histories of artistic subjectivity and an articulation of its problematic – a simple abstraction of the British flag – than the presentation of perceptual possibilities beyond those themes.

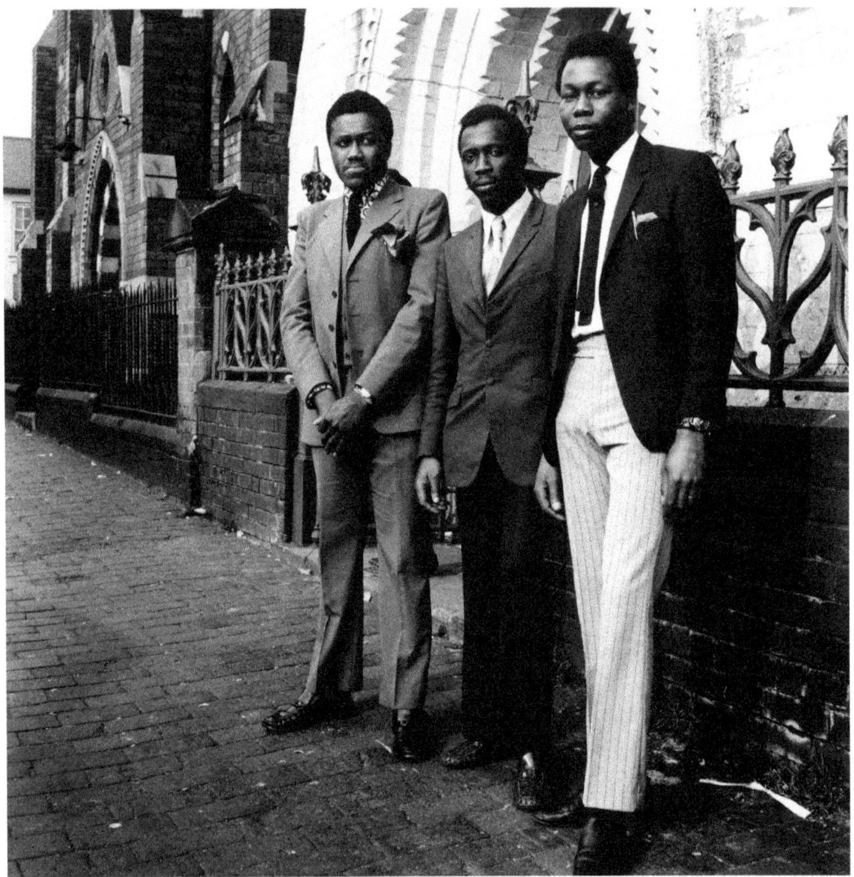

Figure 12: Vanley Burke, *Outside George Street Church*, 1972, monochrome photograph. Image used with permission.


Having seen these things in operation with painting, it repays attention to examine them at work in other media. Vanley Burke has described his photographic work as a sort of 'histograph', 'capturing the personal, social and economic life of black people as they arrived, settled and became established in British society' (Sealy, 1993: 12). Far from simply documenting 'black experience', however, Burke's crisply detailed portraits also prompt contemplation of the intimacy that he shares with his subjects. They distribute his familiarity with a humdrum, inner-city Britain – the drudgery of manual work, fraught relationships with the police and judiciary – and with sharing and celebration. Attending a

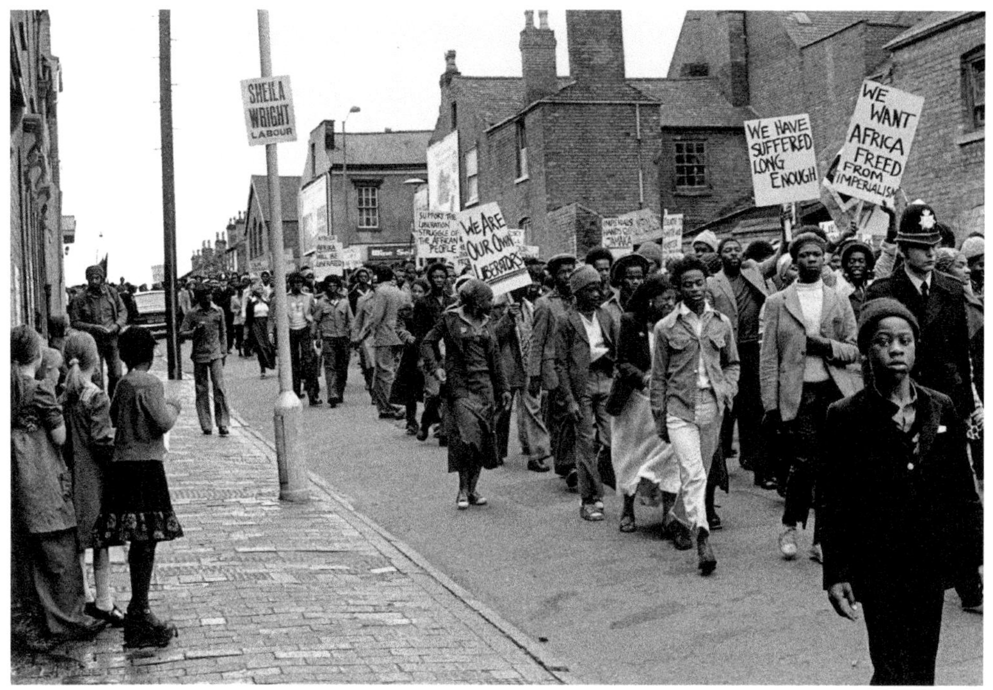


Figure 13: Vanley Burke, *The March*, 1977, monochrome photograph. Image used with permission.

wedding or going out for a night on the town, pristinely turned-out individuals make their way with springing step to a party or church (fig. 12). Excitement is imprinted on the photographic surface in discrete moments of Burke's empathy. While one image, a graduation portrait, marks out achievement, another venerates protest and resistance, as young people form a march on African ('Afrikan') Liberation Day in a district of the West Midlands in the 1970s (fig. 13). One placard reads 'Africa freed from Imperialism', others bring the message home with 'We have suffered long enough' and 'We are our own liberation'. These images disclose that no matter how distant these streets are from Africa, there is political thought and passion among young black Britons who project aspirations for change at home in Britain on to the African continent, visualising both as social spaces of racialised hegemony (cf. Herbert Art Gallery, 1983; Creation for Liberation, 1985).

What these photographs do for a phenomenal reality is configure distinctive moments of change, rites of passage, jubilation and frustration,

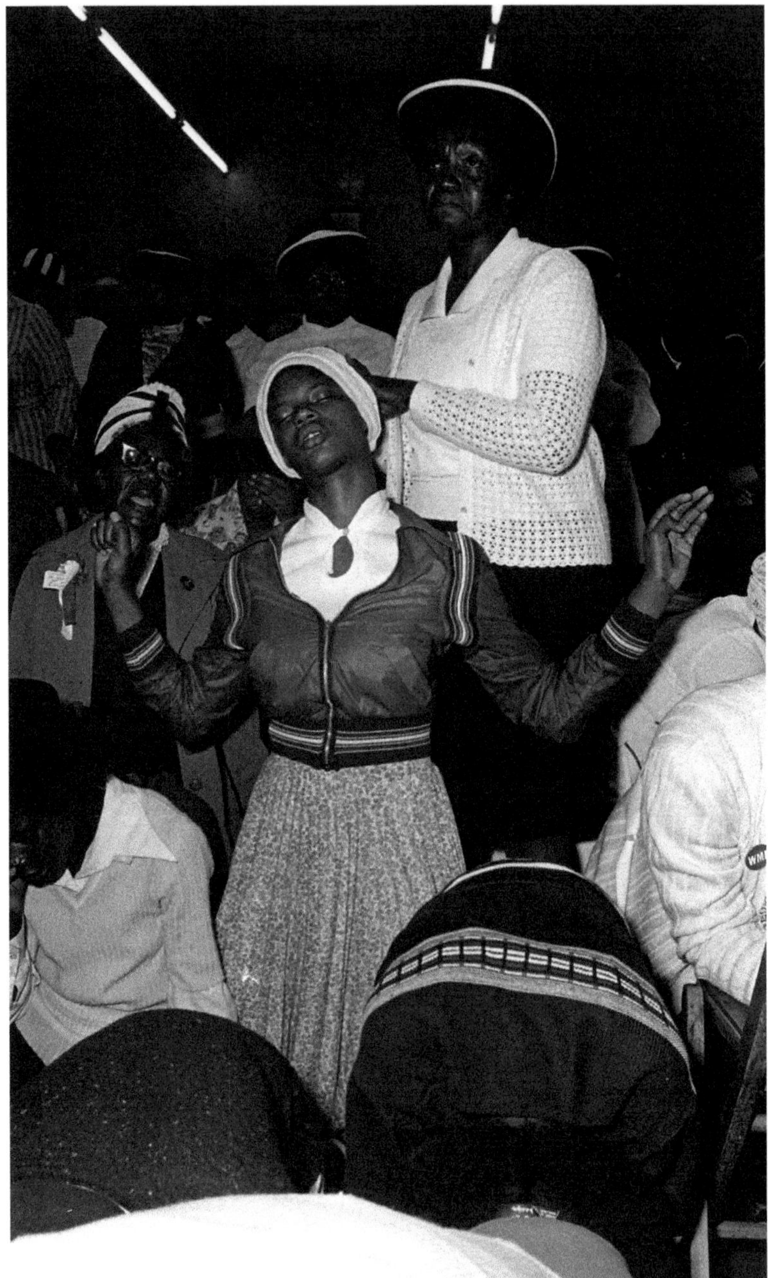

Figure 14: Vanley Burke, *Church Meeting*, c.1980, monochrome photograph. Image used with permission.

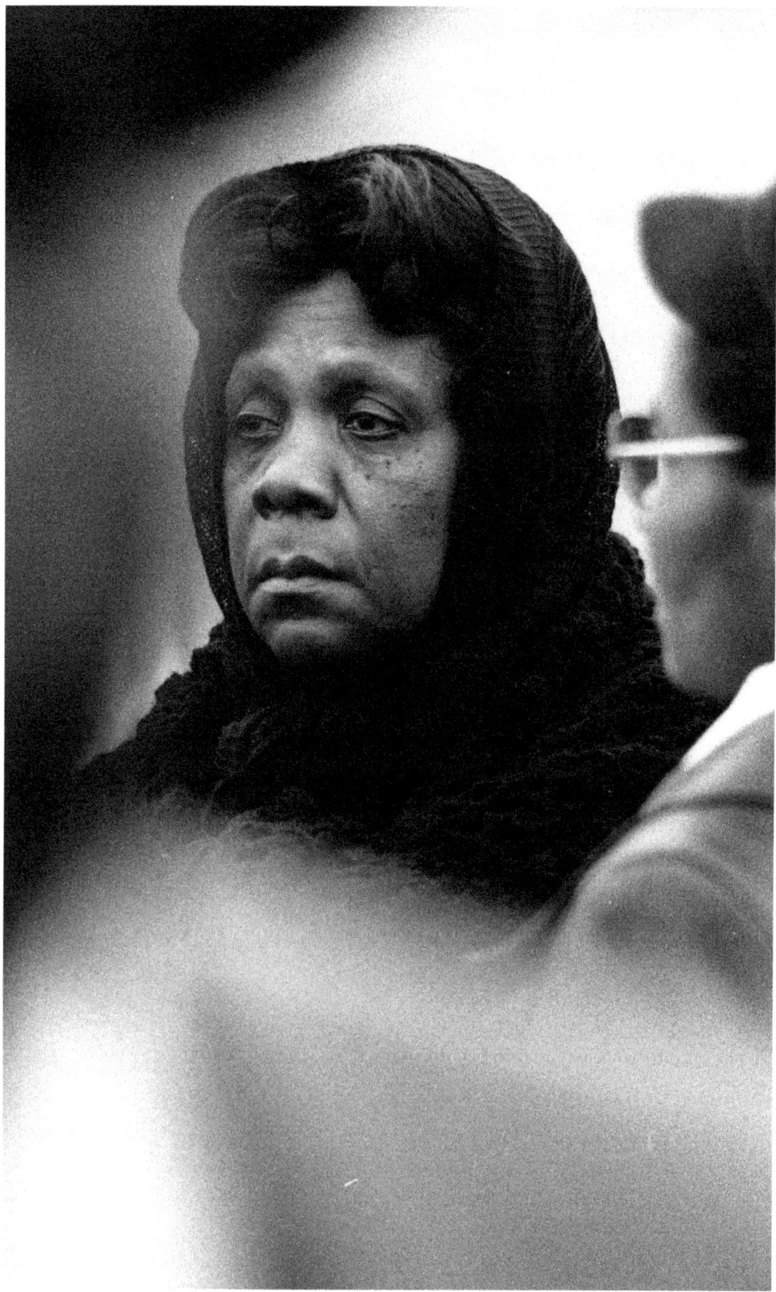

Figure 15: Vanley Burke, *Portrait of a Woman*, c.1980, monochrome photograph. Image used with permission.

and foreground their texture and attest to their energies. Such moments are often held within or in relation to institutions. Here is a baptism performed by black preachers, there a blessing given by a white vicar. Moments of prayer for women in linen headscarves open on to crowded gatherings and surges of exaltation for Christ and his Church. A young woman wearing an anorak and flowered skirt stands frozen, her head tilted limply in an ecstatic pose, an older woman gently resting a steadying hand on her crown (fig. 14). At a funeral, friends and relatives gather around to shovel earth into the grave. A long camera shot picks out the despairing face of a mourner lost in thought while others band in sympathy at a wake (fig. 15). This is indeed a sort of historicism through photography, suggesting that a portraiture of achievement and celebration, or loss and renewal, may be drawn along strands of private narrative and through metaphors of community.

The sharing of such histories is both the product and origin of black British artworks themselves – both a site of the representation of experience and its founding potential. With *The Traveller* (fig. 16),[12] Shanti Thomas provides a pastel inscription of her own past, at a moment of transition when a mother and child at a train station, wrapped together in blue cloth, are bearers of a childhood memory suggested by scant yet stark detail. Sooty traces of remembrance are the components of place. Light filters through the glazed panels of a great, arched roof, with its clock tower and waiting room, while further along the railway platform at the vanishing point is a passage into the open air. This is a conjunction of signs and tracings of the felt remains of a personal story: the smudged heads of Thomas's mother, perhaps, and herself as a child, as well as a more general trope of diaspora identities as constituted in flux, 'cultures on the move'. It is a corollary to other works based on the poetics of 'arriving' by Permindar Kaur and Manjeet Lamba (see Chapter 1), along with the attachment to the past exemplified in drawings by Boyce.

Juginder Lamba's wooden sculpture *The Cry* (fig. 17), takes up such a paradigm of the past by salvaging the materials of iron and wood. These found objects – wooden beams and planks – have biographies of their own, having once been part of the fabric of the Lancaster docks,

---

12  This work was shown alongside others by artists including Sutapa Biswas, Chila Kumari Burman, Jagjit Chuhan, Nina Edge and Gurminder Sikand at *The Circular Dance*, a touring exhibition organised by the Arnolfini gallery, Bristol during winter 1991–92.

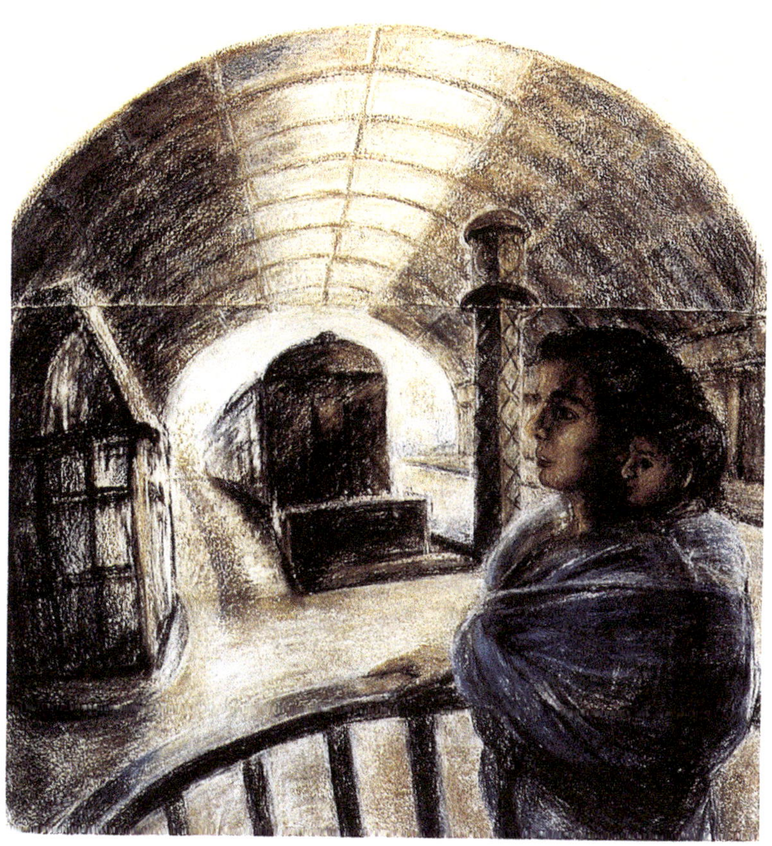

Figure 16: Shanti Thomas, *The Traveller*, 1988/89, pastel on paper, 141 x 132 cm. Image used with permission.

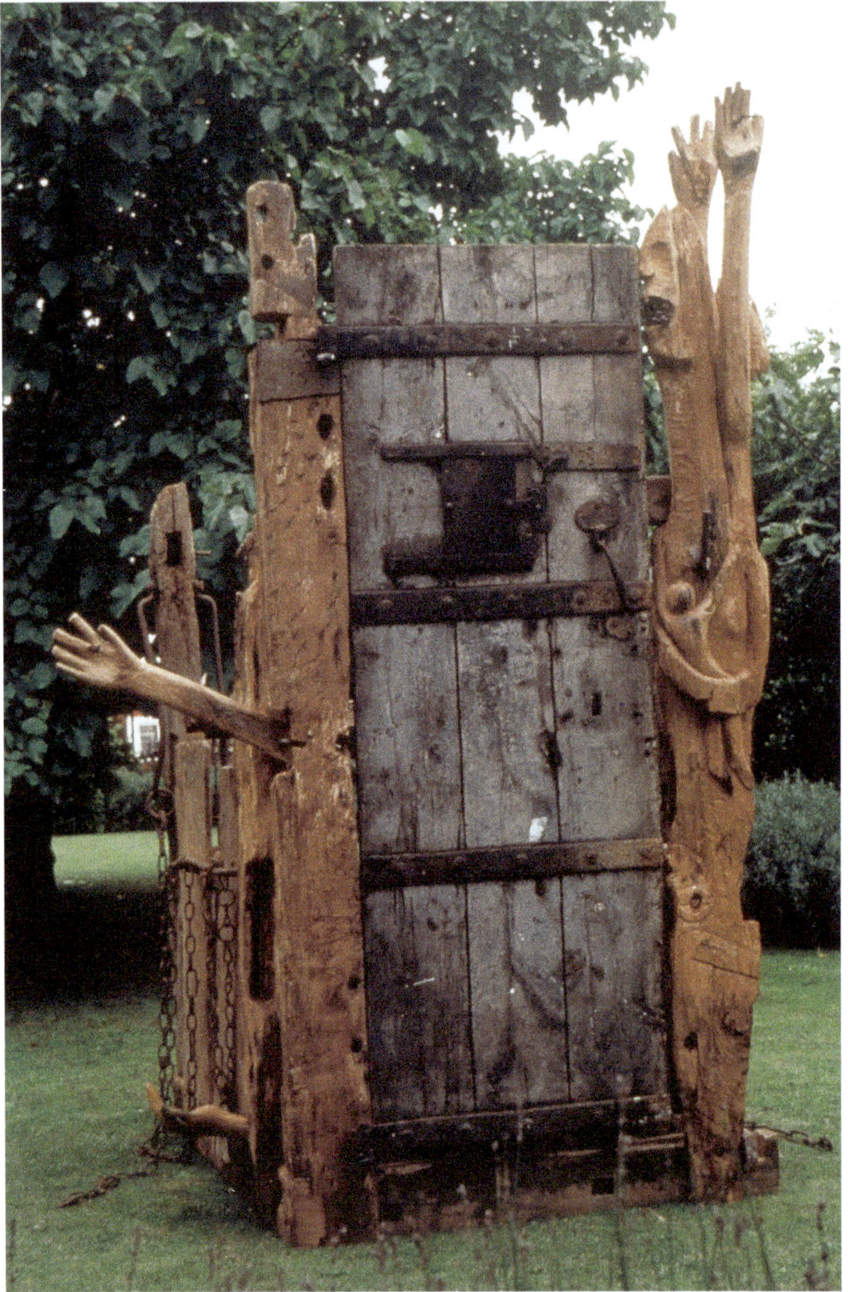

Figure 17: Juginder Lamba, *The Cry*, 1993, wood and metal, 213 x 152 x 107 cm. Wilberforce House, Hull.

used to build its warehouses, before which they were parts of ships (slave ships, Lamba assumes). This narrative of material reuse is brought to the artwork by Lamba's commentary,[13] the key to its immediate semiotic meaning: a metaphor of reclamation, the reapplication of construction beams as sculpture; invention of art from the abjection of a wretched past. In a gesture of rescue and retrieval, Lamba found a voice in the inhumane setting to which the beams may once have belonged, with the goal of finding and tracing the history of British trade and commerce back to the misery of slavery and indentured labour. The ship is the enduring figure of modern travel and colonisation and Lamba draws from this wood a cry of terror and lamentation, carving open-mouthed and gesticulating bodies. The doorway framed by these 'crying' posts is a further metonym of journeying and transition, a gesture to the long centuries of plantation slavery and the cruelty endured by people from Lamba's two continental homes, Africa and South Asia.

These reminders of the past – a project of returning it to visibility – come under a common theme in black British art, its artists' concern with injustice, oppression, 'race', and their interlinked, global histories. A sense of the ontological uniqueness of Lamba's contribution to that body of work has its beginnings in novel applications of labour to materials. In *The Cry* are weeping bodies that have a stiffness and angularity that betrays their wooden structure. Sand, a crucial component of this installation on which the sculpture stands, is a fragmentary patch of earth that has a theatrical role in creating a forum for a diorama of natural, raw materials. Producing a formally compact sculpture in the round, Lamba has pegged together materials whose level of finish and surface colour are slightly at odds; a clash of figures, textures and dimensions. These incongruities in the work (as well as its semiotic repetitions: so many bodies and limbs, where just one would have served adequately as a synecdoche) carry a feeling of the immediacy and presence of its creator.

With as much evidence of toil and manual dexterity, Lamba's *Pod* series of eight sculptures (see fig. 18 for an example from the series), begun in 1984 and continued into the early 2000s, is a set of monumental reminders of the artist's physical proximity and an elusive document of his technical procedures. Again the concern with retrieval is suffused with sculpture, even at the level of their preparation, since these are carved from logs discovered in a preserved state in

---

13   Conveyed during my conversations with the artist in autumn 1998, and his discussions
      with writers such as Nicodemus (1999).

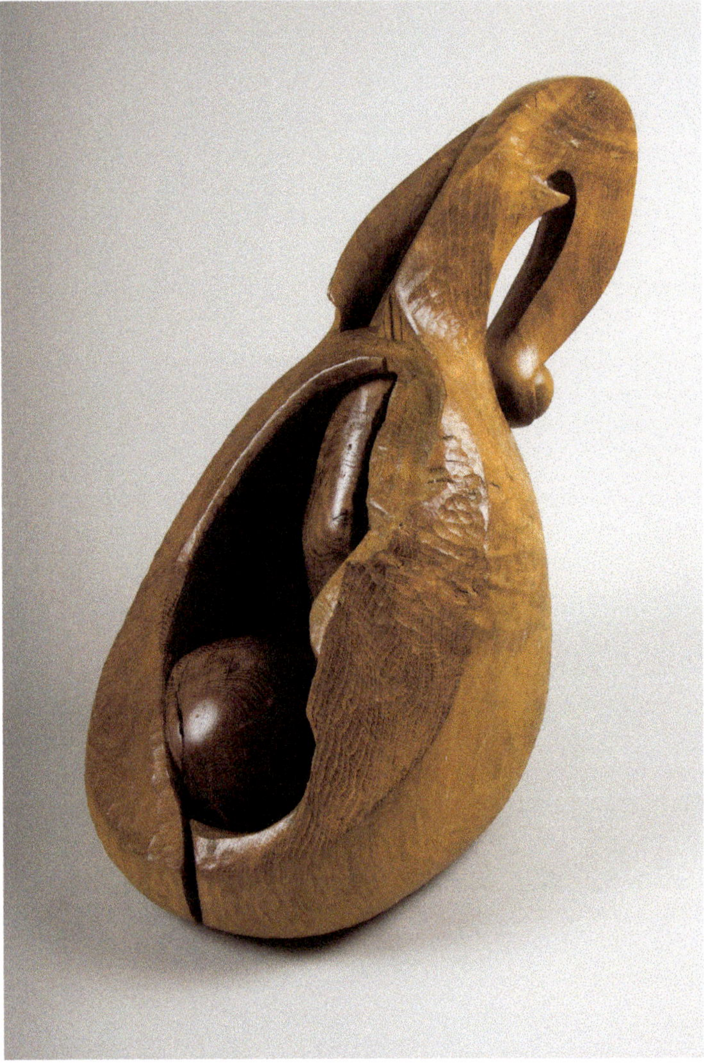

Figure 18: Juginder Lamba, *Pod Four, Phase II*, 1994, oak wood, 30 x 33 x 48 cm. Image used with permission.

bogs near the artist's Shropshire home. Reaching beyond their use as metaphors, each of the 'Pods' engenders an elaborate spatial experience. Their broad, scrupulously smoothed outer surfaces curve inwardly at crucial points, so that outside fields become interior ones, gently overlapping wooden 'flesh'. Lamba's *Local Marriage* of 1998 (fig. 19),

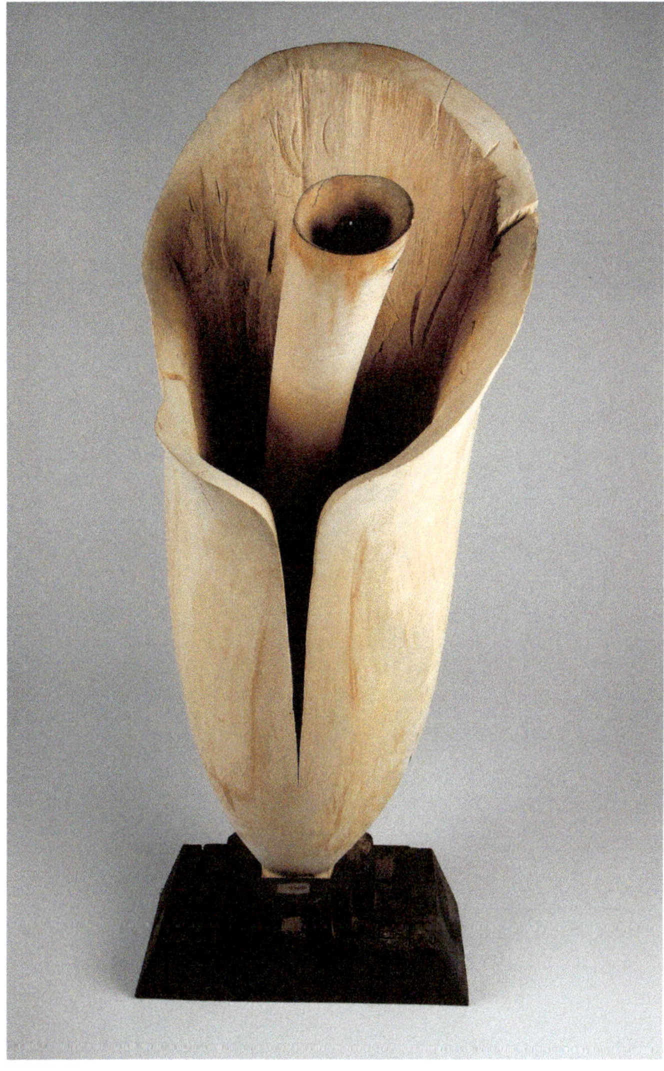

Figure 19: Juginder Lamba, *Local Marriage*, 1998, lime wood, 126 x 46 x 44 cm. Image used with permission.

in which the two sides of a huge conical flower-head split apart, offers a narrow gap to peep through to a chiselled interior. The space in turn cups a slender protuberance, tipped with a darkened filament. His earlier work, *Tree* (fig. 20), has great leafed sides that diverge in three layers beneath a flower. In effect, the careful movements of its

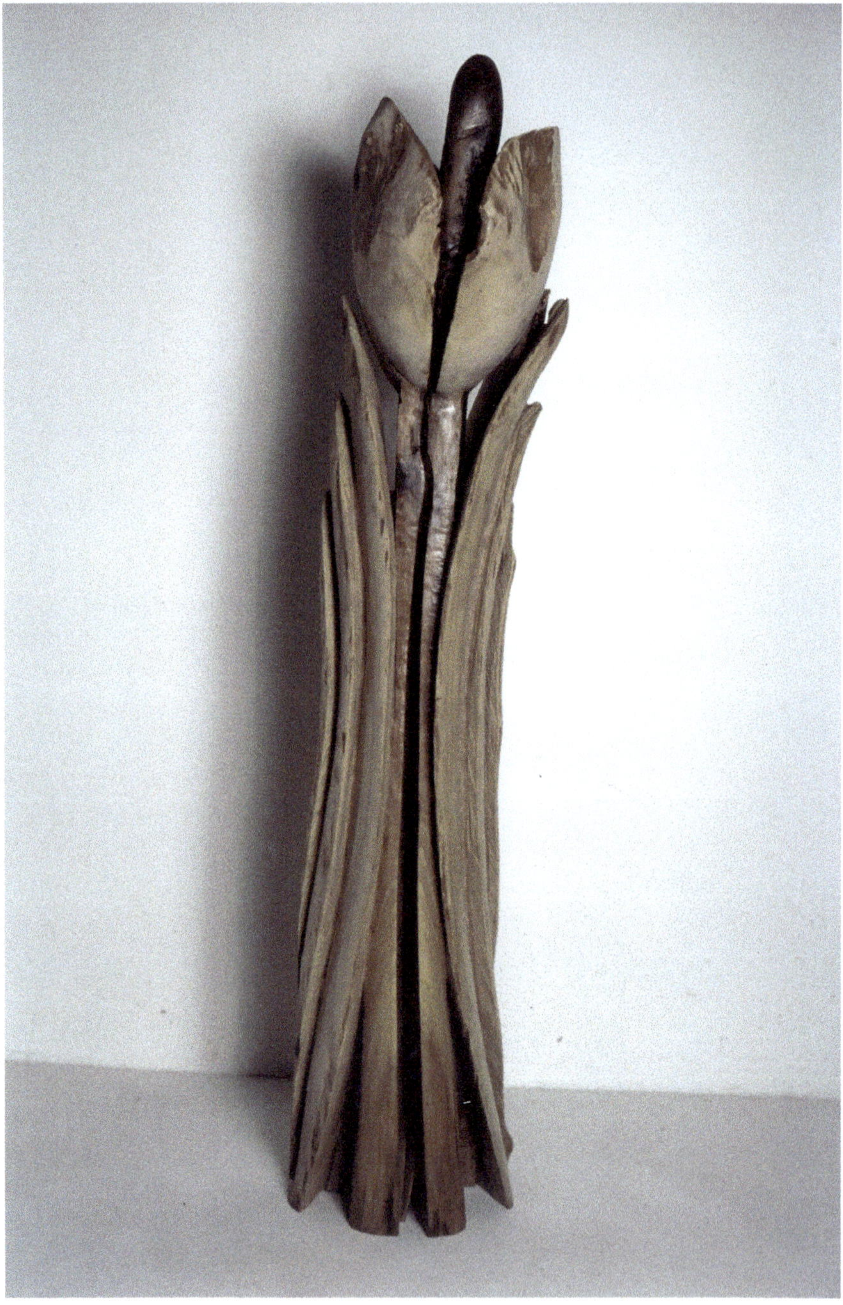

Figure 20: Juginder Lamba, *Tree*, 1995, walnut wood, 186 x 44 x 40 cm. Image used with permission.

artist are imprinted and made concrete at the place of all these edifices, as Lamba's hands endow the wood with mimesis – gigantic petals and stems – and at the same time a less indexical presence.

## Against objectivity

[S]cience manipulates things and gives up living in them …
(Merleau-Ponty, 1964a: 159)

[O]bjective thought is unaware of the subject of perception …
(Merleau-Ponty, 1962: 207)

The presence of the human body in work by black British artists finds a particular treatment by Keith Piper in his *The Fictions of Science* series (mentioned in my Introduction). Here it is the human face and head that concern Piper, undergoing craniological study for their irregularities as much as their uniformities. In inductive methods, such revelations follow a repeatable procedure. First, select a representative sample of cases; record and observe their features; formulate a suitably typical model of a single object's properties. From there, compare the single case to the general, thereby exposing variations and case-specific exceptions and deformities. *The Fictions of Science* image bears a critique of the search for deformation – or difference as deviancy – in human beings. Its 'object' is identified as a standard type, a classifiable morphology of head, ears, teeth and lips, within a diversity of types identified through induction. The image bears out a collecting of ideas on the standardisation of methods that order and produce knowledge of the human body.

Elsewhere in the same series, Piper points to ethnology, where a human hand controls a microscope lens, enlarging a profusion of technicolour sperm cells. The reference here is to the search for a natural basis that might explain cultural differences – a dangerously misguided proposition springing from a belief in an unequally weighted binary of nurture and nature. Piper's gloss may have confused biological anthropology with ethnology, generalising their relationship. Still it points at least to those disciplines' historical beginnings – alongside attitudes of imperialism, for instance – and their scientific predilection for an observable, provable, predictable catalogue of human nature across 'racial' groups founded on their morphologies. He also touches upon Foucauldian outlooks on the status of knowledge that scientific thinking, through its institutional discourses, might require in a visual form.

What in general differentiates an artist's launch of this same critique from one inspired by a formally argued reading of scientific knowledge is the body itself. The difference lies in asking how the body can be approached anew through visual representation, balanced against the extraordinary weight of its treatment in photographic recording and reportage pretending to science. What kind of understanding of the body might be offered by *artists* isolating it and its parts? What experiences of the body fail to be captured by 'the fictions of science', and in what form can they emerge?

Keith Piper's imagery is the starting point for a discussion of the visualised body by black British artists and maps out this very ground. His critique of scientific outlooks is a mouthpiece for other, un-vocalised beliefs in the sense of the body as a locus of experience, beliefs that slip beyond the analytical gaze. Piper's heightened critical tone is typical of how black British artists have rallied in favour of the value of the body. Their view of the centrality of the body within experience can be reached more fully through criticism of traditional, scientific ways of producing and supporting knowledge. The alternatives open to those engaged, by contrast, in largely visual work – the artists examined here – are alternatives that are posed by phenomenological attitudes to the body. Hoping to tackle the prejudices of science by recourse to a distinct tradition of philosophy, a more phenomenological manner of conceptualising the lived world has offered artists a basis for perspicuous thought as they explore alternatives to the objectivist enterprise of capturing and containing bodies as fragments of scientific knowledge. Articulating human experience by first recognising the primacy of the world of perception has helped to bring black British artists' thinking on the body into far sharper focus. The choice of photography and digital media to fulfil this task is crucial, for it means taking the same technologies of 'objective' recording and using them against themselves with contrary conclusions.

'Objective' thought has too often ignored the complex, ambiguous milieu in which human meaning comes to expression: as I quote above, 'objective thought is unaware of the subject of perception' (Merleau-Ponty, 1962: 207). Merleau-Ponty's suggested, and purportedly more edifying, response to this unawareness is to base our understanding of the body-subject on phenomenological description. In his discussion of science, he traces the 'intellectualist' assumption of a dichotomy of body and mind, and the objectivist, empiricist view of body as a simple sum of its parts. Here is a grave criticism of the refusal of scientific thinking in his day to scrutinise its own methods, and its inability to grasp an awareness of lived and bodily human experience and the very centrality of the body-subject (see Merleau-Ponty, 1962).[14]

The Merleau-Pontian view is that our insertion into the world is effected through the body with its motor and perceptual acts, by which we relate to the world in an unavoidably 'incarnate' manner. It is a conceptualisation of the body in opposition to racialised classifications – scientific ones not least among them – that disregard the subjective dimension. If we look closely at the procedures taken by black British artists in making their works, it becomes obvious that here too is a pre-reflective experience of the body. The imaged body can allow contemplation of the inseparability of self and world – the body-subject in its setting – and black British artists have attended to that project of visual understanding by investigating diverse aspects of the *body in perception*. As I will now show, there are many more examples of artworks that are made out of this background of experiences of the world from the starting point of the 'incarnate' subject.

## Body image

The outline of my body is a frontier which ordinary spatial relations do not cross. This is because its parts are inter-related in a peculiar way: they are not spread out side by side, but enveloped in each other [...]

I am in undivided possession of [my body] and I know where each of my limbs is through a body image in which all are included. But the notion of the body image is ambiguous, as are all notions which make their appearance at turning points in scientific advance. (Merleau-Ponty, 1962: 98)

When black British artists have undertaken a phenomenology of the body, using the technologies of scientific methods against themselves for alternative, unintended purposes, they have critiqued science – its 'foreswearing' – and rejected its traditional ways of objectifying and racialising the body. Such art thereby goes a step towards fulfilling the

---

14  Merleau-Ponty's perspective on the sciences has to be historicised in view of the changes that would take place in the later twentieth century, allowing the sciences to claim greater self-reflexivity about the methodologies they employ to explore feeling and affect. The link between science and the arts in the burgeoning fields of neuroscience and cognition is broached in Bacci and Melcher (2011).

ontological ambition of grasping an awareness of bodily experience in its *pre-objective* state. This second outcome, of course, bears a paradox, since the objectivising image-making tools of medical or ethnological investigation – the microscope, the camera – already shape views of the body and reinforce the selection of perspectives from which to observe the body and which bodies to observe. Those methods are also equipped with a pre-existing sense of the nature of the human 'object' that is under review. For example, before a human head is measured, its features have already been itemised through induction. Given that these forces are at work, it would then seem impossible to arrive at a pre-objective view of the body using the same technological apparatus used by science.

This very issue of how to maintain pre-objectivity has been skilfully broached by artist Mona Hatoum. In her work *Corps étranger* (1994) she made use of a unique tool, the endoscope, a minute camera for insertion into and around her own body (fig. 21). The resulting images were recorded. A presentation of the tool's journey was then projected on to a gallery floor within a cylindrical wooden structure. This porthole became filled with shots taken en route, filled with shining tissue. Bright yellows and pinks occupy knotted and dilated fields of colour, laden with short hairs, lengths and straps of organic support, striated tubes leading into darkness. Jagged edges border mucus-coated walls, asymmetrical, with no sense of up or down. In one circled view of herself, a bead-headed glottis in the throat waves at the lens, while elsewhere, dark hair on a forest-floor of whitened scalp or armpit or groin gathers densely about.

Wondering whether Hatoum knows what she is looking for is itself a loaded issue. On the one hand, we could assume that, before their encounter, she did not know the appearance of her magnified internal parts, having only some prior sense of the body's inside as so much mucus-covered, dilating lengths of tubing. Such expectations are little more than general. If she encountered irregularities – tumours, lesions, discolouring – would the artist be able to recognise them? Surely every visual aspect along the camera's journey might be viewed as irregular, since our everyday, unassisted sense of the bodily interior fails to take them in. Thus a high level of *un*-expectation characterised Hatoum's search. Certain bodily features are only marked off as irregular by an inductive vision, a model and abstraction, by the judgements they allow, and Hatoum is pre-objective without them.

It is just possible that the majority of viewers of these images will not recognise them either and in the face of this perhaps we are presented with a choice. We can connect her body to our own, imagining a range

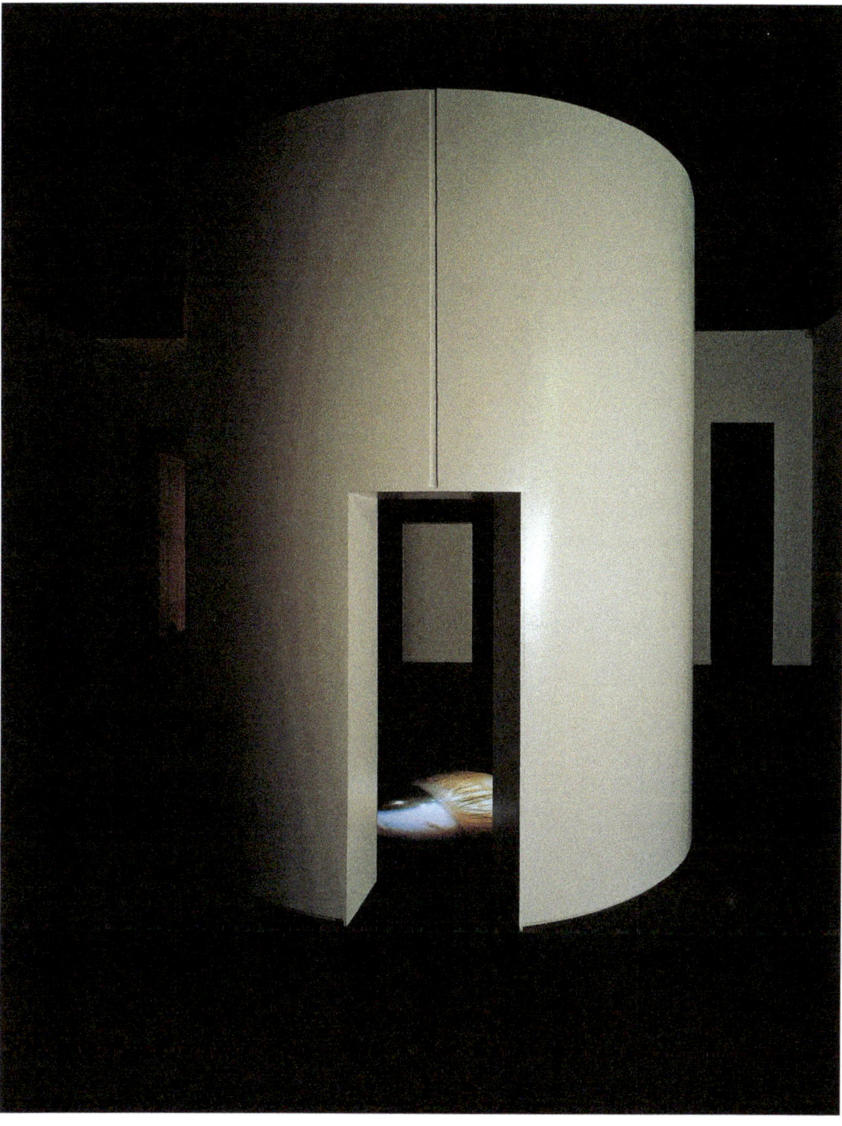

Figure 21: Mona Hatoum, *Corps étranger*, 1994, video installation with cylindrical wooden structure, video projector, video player, amplifier and four speakers, 350 x 300 x 300 cm. © Mona Hatoum. Photo © Philippe Migeat. Courtesy Centre Pompidou, Paris.

of similar functions for ourselves. But the hair colour? Those sphincters? Are some peculiar to Hatoum; some general to being female; some personal; some 'pre-personal'; all anonymous? It is not clear whether the artist has tried to decode these very features, or invited us to decode them. Would an attempt at pre-objectivity preclude that possibility? We are presented with the phenomenal presence of Hatoum's interior, unable to make sense of it. This pulsing circle, a frame of orifices, traces a consecutive order, in line with the endoscope's linear journey. Yet just as we are unsure where the body is entered and exited, it is not really certain if this is even Hatoum at all.

Such scientific technologies have greatly extended the possibilities for representing the body and its functions. But it is worth bearing in mind that there is a gap between the kind of knowledge those means can produce and the actual experience of both having and *being* a body. Objectivity makes the body anonymous. Internal exploration is assumed to be a way of making the interior known, yet it finds that interior to be a strange place indeed, with unidentifiable parts. Hatoum's images reaffirm how the experience of the body, on the one hand, and its material processes and workings, on the other, are each very different. She shows that a scientific gaze is a decoding gaze, an ordering and classifying gaze, capable of identifying the body's organs only by their function. That gaze observes, but it also imposes. At the same time, is there a 'body image' that remains intact?

### The body's colours

In Zarina Bhimji's *Vulnerable and Sticky* (1995),[15] animal brains, from pigs or sheep, are gently laid in a loose crescent on satin or rubber folds, positioned among the creases. The cylindrical cortex for each brain points

---

15  *Vulnerable and Sticky* was an incidental outcome of a commission for Charing Cross Hospital in London, in which a series of eight pieces entitled *Listen to the Room* were designed to lift the spirits of the patients. As images that emerged from a process of artistic research in a medical domain, they expounded on the qualities of fabric such as chiffon, of how it behaves for the camera, and materials such as rubber that may be layered and come to feel and look as light as talcum powder. In a subset of pieces relating to pathology, Bhimji sought to expose the unexpected results that may come from exploring with photography and showed the results in a medical lecture theatre, the series *We Are Cut with the Same Cloth*, which investigated the colour red. The artist has provided a selection of these images on her personal website: http://www. zarinabhimji.com/dspseries/6/3FW.htm (accessed 1 January 2017).

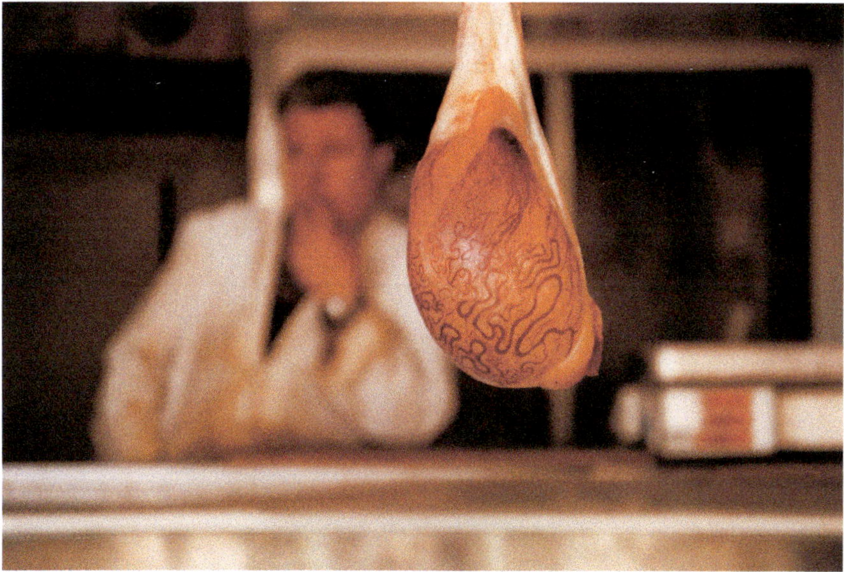

Figure 22: Mona Hatoum, *Baid Ghanam (Sheep's Testicle) (Jerusalem)*, 1996, C-type print, 18 x 26 cm. © Mona Hatoum. Courtesy White Cube.

away from the mass, with its tightly wound lobes and inner workings. Purples and blues caught across the cloth pleats are a royal setting for bright and shiny reds and pinks. The brains are not interchangeable, since they differ minutely in size, marking the metonymic absence of six living bodies, now with empty heads. Semi-circular, the crescent of this arrangement is an inverted question mark: why the need to extract these body parts? What really may be learned from corporeal investigation? It is indeed a sticky issue. A clear answer is that detaching and isolating these organic parts newly reveals their colours. Whether this is done through the use of a scalpel, through extraction or amputation, or by the cracking of the nut-skull to steal its contents, dispassionate operative strategies such as these make present to the photographic eye pigment for the camera's palette. The orange-pink of Bhimji's glistening brains, fruit or meat of the skull, is a wholesome colour. Here, seen free from their cranial shell, tight, elastic membranes allow colour to come through and make light bounce back.

An artist's search for colour can often take uncharted routes. Mona Hatoum pursues colour among the wiped-clean walls and scrubbed steel of the back room in a butcher's shop. Meaty entrails, displayed in

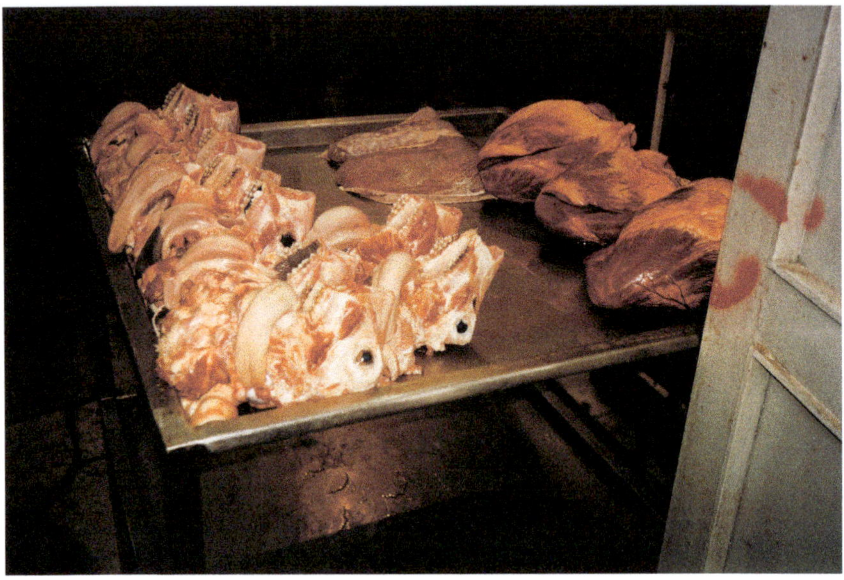

Figure 23: Mona Hatoum, *Rous Ghanam (Sheep Heads) (Jerusalem)*, 1996, C-print, 18 x 26 cm. © Mona Hatoum. Courtesy White Cube.

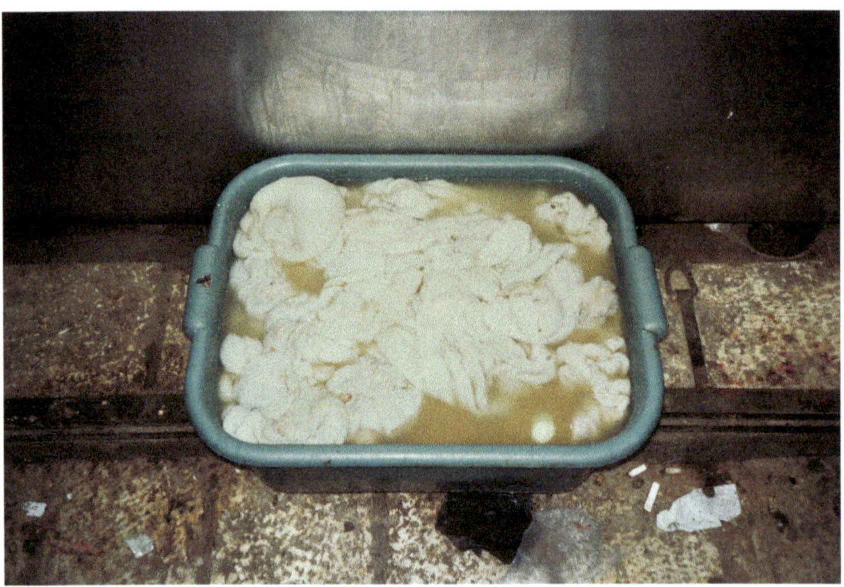

Figure 24: Mona Hatoum, *Kroush (Tripe) (Jerusalem)*, 1996, C-print, 20 x 29 cm. © Mona Hatoum. Courtesy White Cube.

their place of extraction, are found here freshly free from their corporeal context. Hatoum's hanging *Baid Ghanam* of 1996 (fig. 22) – a sheep's testicle – dangles before its liberator: a seated butcher, out of focus, chin propped on hand, no doubt curious about the artist at work. Tightly meandering blood vessels enclose its curved lobe. *Rous Ghanam* of the same year (fig. 23) – sheep's heads flayed bare of hide and wool – point, noses to the air, tongues lolling, silently bleating. Their tripe, seen in Hatoum's *Kroush* of 1996 (fig. 24) soaks meanwhile in a pale blue plastic bowl, like sluiced linen waiting for a scrub or a wring and an airing out. These flesh pieces are food, and so have a conspicuous object status in being made ready to be cooked and eaten. Then their original colours will be succeeded by others through being heated, before they are ground into a bolus of matter and swallowed. Fresh offal, glistening crimson, left to the warm and moving air, will fade into brown and green, as time quickly transforms the fragile body in pieces.

In their searches, these artists' photographed presentations are unmistakably both tactile and colourful. We cannot but notice colour and texture occurring together, the one never leaving the other behind, impossible to separate or bracket. Colours are always perceived in this kind of relationship with a sort of 'field'. 'The perceptual "something" is always in the middle of something else, it always forms part of a "field"', Merleau-Ponty explains, before continuing:

> This red patch which I see on the carpet is red only in virtue of a shadow which lies across it, its quality is apparent only in relation to the play of light upon it, and hence has an element in a spatial config-uration. Moreover the colour can be said to be there only if it occupies an area of a certain size, too small an area not being describable in these terms. Finally this red would literally not be the same if it were not the 'woolly red' of a carpet. (1962: 4–5)

Merleau-Ponty argued at length about the true relationship between colour and texture. Recognising how they are perceived leads us to do away with the idea that objects (brains, for instance) are not firstly substances – sticky and round – before being seen also to have secondary attributes or qualities, such as their pinkness. Indeed, we ought to resist the way our knowledge of the existence of objects, their ontology, has traditionally been based on this kind of substance/attribute relation (Merleau-Ponty, 1962: 3–14). Bhimji's brains present a range of reds within taut membranes and glazes. They are never pure colour, for these crimson head-centres also reach for our touch. Colour and tissue appear together, so that the white of bone, or the slowly rotting yellow of sheep's teeth, being white and smooth, yellow and hard, are always both colour *and* texture. This kind of rounded two-ness of experience shows that the body's colours are also textured, a reminder that we never perceive pure colour free from its material ground.

Such an insight from artistic practice, brought out through phenomenological analysis, has led to new ways of conceiving the grounds of ontological study in the case of black British art. It reframes our understanding of the critical and philosophical procedures and contributions that making art can entail. Just as the colour and texture of things are bound up together in the way I have described, so there are further such relations that pertain to perceptions of the body and its world, as I will now show in turning next to touch and its relation to vision.


## Hair and touch

Black British artists have often made art upon the recognition of the fragmentary nature of the body, the body as something that can be divided or separated, with detachable parts. Human hair is one such feature, appearing in several works, mostly of installation. Marina Warner (1995) has called hair one of the 'richest resources' of the self,[16] yet among its phenomenal peculiarities is the fact that it is a residue of human presence which can assume shapes and properties independently of the body or bodies on which it grows. And after being detached, it can also offer life to the world's inanimate features, such as in the built space of a room.

Mona Hatoum's *Recollection* of 1995 (fig. 25) is the result of years of retaining her own shed hair. This she rolls into neat balls, scattered randomly across the polished wooden floor of a long room, where they have settled in clusters. There are 14 balls in one constellation, 11 in another, nine in a further set. At a table beneath the window is a small, wooden frame loom, threaded with more red-brown hair (fig. 26). Work has already begun on the loom, rows and rows of a simple weave, kept in place with sticking tape, and a little way off is a bobbin wrapped with more of the same hair. Criss-crossing hair fabric created on the frame reflects the hair's deepest and lightest colours: almost blond, almost black, warp and weft dipping in and out, catching the daylight. From the

---

16  For an extended and vivid survey of the cultural history of hair, explored through
    contemporary art, see Hanna (2012).

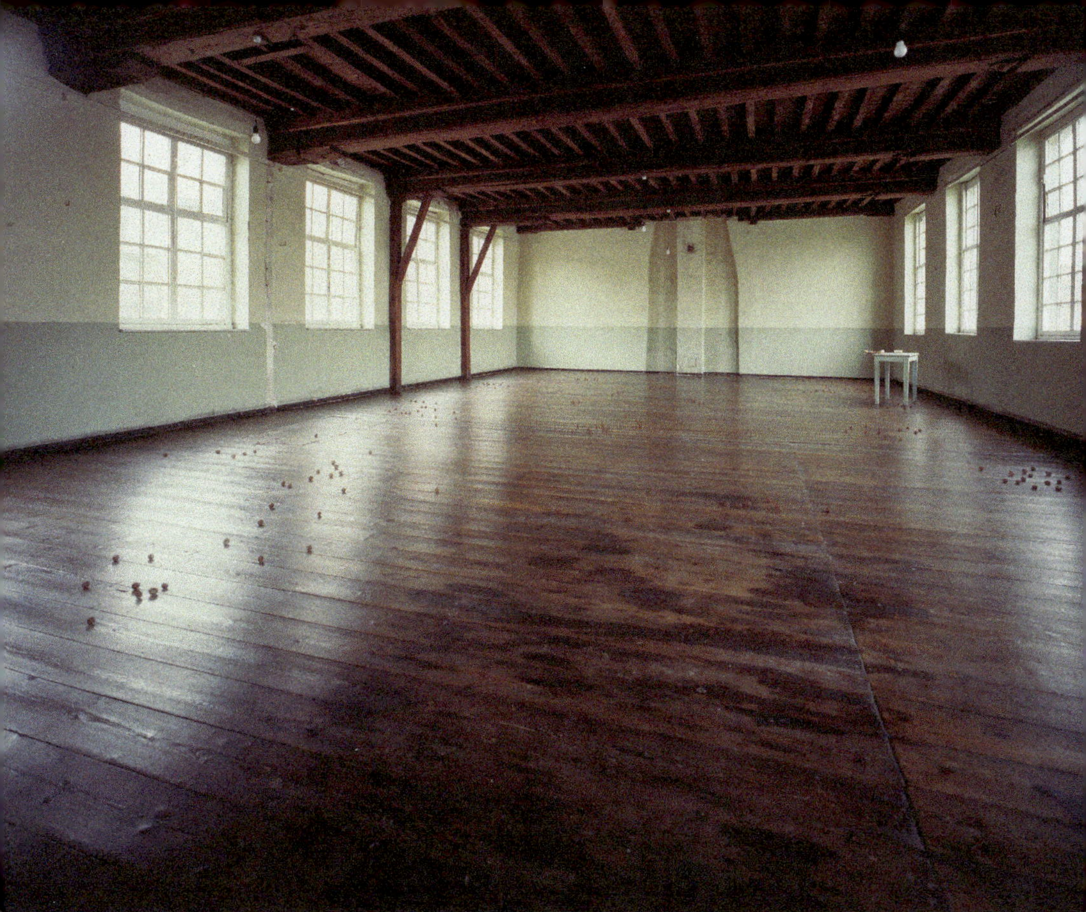

Figure 25: Mona Hatoum, *Recollection*, 1995, hair balls, strands of hair hung from the ceiling, wooden loom with woven hair, table, dimensions variable, installation. © Mona Hatoum. Photo © Fotostudio Eshof. Courtesy Beguinage St Elisabeth, Kortrijk, Belgium and White Cube.

ceiling, and barely perceptible, are more strands of hair hanging singly at shoulder height, touching the viewer's face when he or she traverses the room.

On a green table top the loom juts out, overhanging the floor. As with Hatoum's pubic triangle, we are presented with a geometric shape: a neat, patiently woven rectangle of the artist's hair whose geometry, forged from an organic material, is an ordering of the body's products, a way of patterning and introducing the body to a measured regularity. Hanging strands of hair are vertical lines, in parallel to the sides and walls of the room. That airy, box-like space seems to tighten the hair balls, reducing them to miniature. Yet this transformation of organic to geometric also moves in the opposite path. The room is inhabited by hair

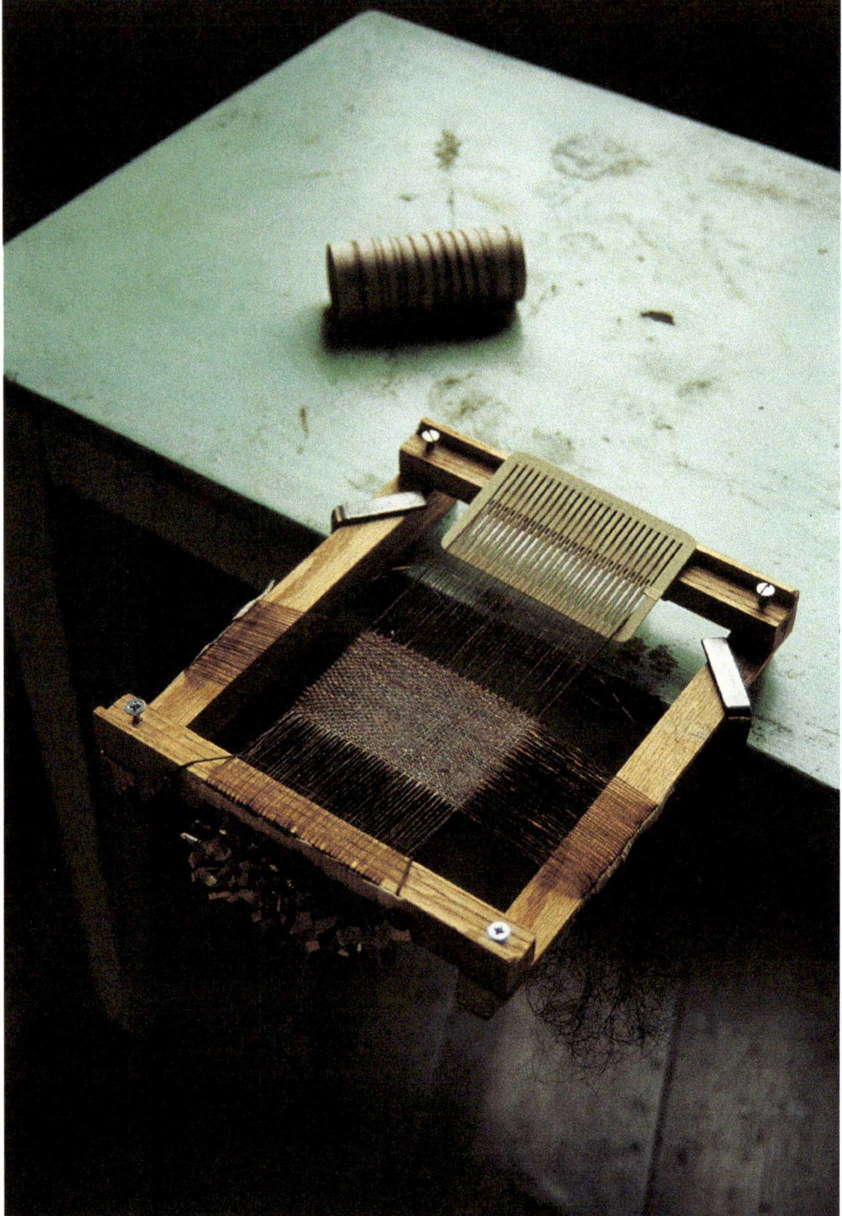

Figure 26: Mona Hatoum, *Recollection* (detail), 1995, hair balls, strands of hair hung from the ceiling, wooden loom with woven hair, table, dimensions variable, installation. © Mona Hatoum. Photo © Fotostudio Eshof. Courtesy Beguinage St Elisabeth, Kortrijk, Belgium and White Cube.

balls, hair strands and a weave, and is warmed by them, and as an empty plane the floor becomes a ground, the spheres of hair figures. There are live traces of their scattering. An opacity in the spheres emerges where they obscure their ground, and a transparency where they do not: the ground reflects daylight so strongly as to reveal their inner skeleton. The wooden floor, deep nut-brown from its oiling and polishing, then reveals its colours against red-brown hair. Such inhabitation of the room, itself a measured space, is thus made possible by hair in three geometric guises – spherical, rectangular and linear – and lends temperature and hue.

The interworking of strands of hair by Hatoum, together with their spatial positioning, is a minute deposit or tracery of movement – of the artist's touch. Indeed, hair seems to demand our touch, the very origin of Sonia Boyce's *Do You Want To Touch?*, a number of objects created entirely of synthetic and human hair. The largest of these is *Afro Blanket* (1994, fig. 27), a rug made up of 37 'afro' wigs pieced and sewn together.[17] Next to her blanket is a collection of 22 hair-pieces of all shapes and sizes, arranged on shelves around the gallery space, which confront the visitor with a semblance of the bodies of others. These body parts seem somehow closer to their growers and wearers than Hatoum's, since this is hair that is worked as if to be worn (although we are not told by whom, or when), while they are also removed and removable body parts, some synthetic, others not, and it is never clear which are what.

To touch another's hair is to connect in an exploratory way with something that is made distinct in the realm of social practice, not least the institutional conventions of public art installation and museum display. Boyce's presentation, although conscious of this very issue of untouch-ability, bears an invitation to pass beyond such everyday conventions. She has suspended a preoccupation with the social: bracketing norms or barriers of behaviour that order the spaces between human bodies, barriers whose narrowing is commonly construed as intrusion, threat, (sexual) adventure or a violation of taboo between perceived 'racial' groups (on the politics of touching black hair, see McClintock, 1986; Mercer, 1994; Caldwell, 1991).[18] This device of phenomenological bracketing furthers the artist's invitation for us to apprehend her pieces

---

17  This installation first appeared at the Central 181 Gallery (1993), and then as part of the touring exhibition *Fetishism at the South Bank Centre* (1995), before its inclusion in *The Unmapped Body: 3 Black British Artists*, Yale University Art Gallery (1998–99).

18  For opinion on the 'hair-touching burden' of street harassment, othering and 'impermissible grabbing', see http://www.theguardian.com/commentisfree/2013/jun/13/you-can-touch-hair-hottentot-venus (accessed 16 March 2017).

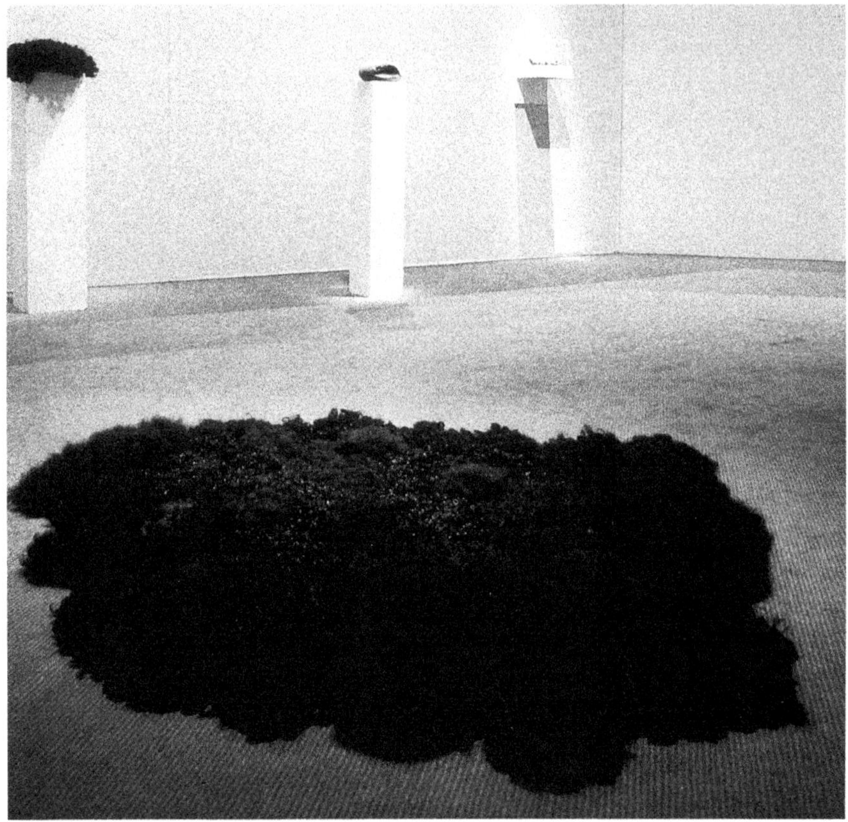

Figure 27: Sonia Boyce, *Afro Blanket*, 1994, 37 afro wigs, installation view at the South Bank Centre. © Sonia Boyce. All rights reserved, DACS 2016.

of hair as tactile objects. The invitation to touch has a distinctly personal mode of address. It urges the addressee to check upon the details of what we know of human hair, viz. that it is commonplace, that it is cared for by its wearer, an appropriate object of visual interest, and when worn, even of comment. There is at the same time movement and labour within these hair clumps. It is clear that they have passed through the hands of someone who has taken the trouble to press, plait, part, knot, comb, crimp and tie them. There is plenty of play here too, as the viewer observes the hair after the event of it being dressed. Invited to look, touch and perhaps even to sniff, we come nose to nose with a lighter exploration than Hatoum's, being left to wonder what the appropriate hairdressing might be for a carpet of wigs.

## Embracing the phenomenal

In the surrounding literature black British artists are regarded as individuals who are engaged in an array of art practices that promote processes of visual reading, and on which basis their works occupy a shared field of black or diaspora cultural politics. They are portrayed in the role of dismantling essentialist ideas about cultural identity and being generally iconoclastic towards fixed notions of 'race' and ethnicity, skilled cultural navigators moving across a dense landscape of cultural markers and resources in order to make art from the very experience of living in diaspora. They have assembled visual works both for the pleasure and provocation of their audiences, forging them from episodes of discrimination, from the contestations surrounding 'outsiderness', nationhood, belonging, and within the contingent conditions of migration and exile. On this view, such art elicits cultural meaning by being readable in the narrowly textual and signifying sense, and it enables a profound politics of difference in a visual context. The social environment of contemporary art may be its primary place of articulation, but it has a dynamics that is also comprehensible to viewers outside as much as inside the gallery walls, in the wider visual economy where cultural difference is constituted through quotidian acts of enunciation, negotiation and opposition in the contingent field of representation.

While retaining such a vivid awareness of black British art and artists, I have been suggesting that there is a decided political purpose in searching for a more roundly philosophical understanding, and what has emerged stands at a distance from black cultural criticism. That requires one to take issue with the existing field of discourse on black British art; indeed, it requires one to find further value for this art beyond a semiotic and textual interest in cultural difference.

Obviously black British artists have drawn from a wide pool of signifiers, a reservoir of modern imagery brought home by lived experiences of diaspora that are in turn reassembled within the contemporary conventions of public exhibiting. However, as a consequence, that sign-based epistemology of the visual has become a false end point for this art's audiences. More gravely, it seems to position black British artists as a mirror image of the very scholars who have given them critical attention. The impression is one of artists who speak only in the vocabulary of critical analysis. The situation bears parallels with the 'artist-envy' suggested by Hal Foster, especially in his comments on contemporary art and ethnography, where he highlights an attitude among scholars in which the artist is an ideal projection of the scholar herself. There the creative practitioner becomes 'a paragon of formal reflexivity, sensitive to difference and open to chance, a self-aware reader of culture understood as text' (Foster, 1994: 14). And although this approach has been productive in allowing commentators to elicit a complex dynamic within black British art, it has also narrowed the degree of divergence and intellectual difference needed for change and development. What may once have been a usefully illuminating approach to understanding this art has become an orthodoxy.

The habit among critics of portraying the black British artist in such a singular fashion as a 'self-aware reader' has delivered a mixed picture of the virtues of this art. It may have elevated artworks that show how the past – the history of colonialism and imperialism, racism and stereo-typing, exclusion and marginalisation – is an open record, to be robustly confronted with a view to effecting a lasting impact on the status quo. But too much is sublimated to a textual paradigm. When actual human bodies are brought into view, if at all, they go the same way of being codified as readable units, assimilated into a 'living archive' (Hall, 2001a), so that corporeality is relegated to being a prop for cultural mediation.

The result is that viewers of black British art may have found it hard to appreciate these works as phenomenal objects with more than one dimension. By addressing that limitation in approaches taken to the criticism of black British art, a new inquiry can emerge, set on a more phenomenological frame. This inquiry is a dedicated philosophy of this field that can find sutures, accommodations and syntheses between the extant theoretical options, and recognise that the invocation of art's representational capacities hardly exhausts the work of art's ability to disclose its phenomenal fullness. Through thick description, and accepting the centrality of the body and perception, an audience that remains open to a range of analytical opportunities can embrace the presence of black British art in a way that has hitherto evaded us.

# Chapter 5

# Equivalence

The examples of black British art considered towards the end of the previous chapter showed that looking at hair also prompts the need to touch it. This became obvious through encounters with art installations, where hair may carry a demand to be touched without permitting actual contact – the objects themselves being cordoned off by social and institutional convention. In general, such examples indicate how we are drawn into a closer bodily inspection when roused by a visual apprehension with art, how the textural appearance and the touch of objects accompany one another, the one anticipating and ushering in the next.

Indeed, black British art as a whole has provided an expansive locus of perceptual encounters and what may be called the phenomena of 'inhabitation'. Such objects precipitate detailed thought, and something of a lesson about perception emerges from them. Accounting for the affectivity of this art, I want now to explore further that same sense of curiosity – about how an artwork would *feel* if only it were possible to make physical contact with it. In particular, black British artworks allow the realisation that the senses of colour and of texture always appear together, the one never leaving the other behind, being impossible to separate or bracket off from one another. Just as things have colour *and* texture, there to be felt with the hands or body as much as to be regarded, that overlapping or 'equivalence' of experience is instructive for philosophical work. We can extend our attention to other physical relationships that may form between ourselves as viewers and the makers of art, emerging through diverse acts of perception. These are outlined in what follows, in a discussion designed to show how relations of 'equivalence' can be pressed into the service of a simultaneously linguistic and phenomenal analysis of black British art. The overall result should demonstrate that corporeal relations need to be taken far more seriously as the key to grasping black British art and, most importantly, that this should take a philosophical register.

## Indexing an 'Asian' presence

The various practices of black British art-making have often tracked a critical agenda to signify the ambivalence, contingency and construct-edness of 'race' and ethnicity, and yet in doing so they have also encountered notable material limits. This was made especially clear by the identification with 'Asian' differences performed by certain artists in Britain during the later decades of the twentieth century. Asianness became 'intersectional' in numerous ways. It emerged in the context of a wider declaration of the need to develop a black cultural politics in visual practice – most famously through 'black art' – and for artists of Asian backgrounds to use 'blackness' in common with other British artists of the African and Caribbean diasporas (Wainwright, 2011: 86–121). This complicated the 'black' in 'black British' by localising definitions of 'blackness'. It was a historic development that distin-guished the use of 'blackness' from other contexts of self-naming such as the United States, where 'black' persists as a specific cultural identi-fication within a larger grouping of 'artists of colour'. British artists of the Asian diaspora have shaped a politics of identity together with those of African and Caribbean diasporas, their participation becoming constitutive of the character of the British 'black arts movement' (Bailey et al., 2005; Leicester City Art Gallery, 1992). There has been a coalition of differences, in a jointly made black British art that appeared during that 'movement' to be indivisible along lines of ethnicity. And yet there were further, notable intersections with this articulation of blackness that were gendered, sexualised and generational, which have also been demonstrated through indexes to an 'Asian' presence, thereby encapsulating a wider spectrum of differences.

While analysis of these patterns of identification through and with difference and blackness would appear to be the domain of a critical theory of British art, a complementary role may be played by philosophy in allowing a more nuanced account of the interplay of difference and aesthetic experience. In particular, what repays interest is a look at the extent to which Asian British artworks prompt a meditation on the dividing lines between the linguistic and the affective. This applies to the linguistic per se – the communicative capacity of art – as well as the matter of language difference, and their interrelationship; indeed, a number of works by Asian British artists have tested the limits of a language-based engagement with the visual, since here there is frequent use of written languages other than English or any other European language. Such artists have drawn on a resource base of linguistic and iconological reference points from a broad cultural geography that includes India and Pakistan, and the lines or routes of multiple migrations and diasporas, such as from South Asia to East Africa, as well as identifications with the Middle East, South East Asia, Hong Kong and other East Asian contexts such as the Philippines and Japan. It is the matter of the relation of these works to their audiences – by and large viewers unable to read or comprehend such languages – that militates heavily for an intellectual engagement with art that is able to understand the limits of the discursive. Here, indeed, is a layering of linguistic registers and divergent modes of readership that are organised around a framework of concerns with difference addressed to matters of embodiment and the emotions.

Works such as Balraj Khanna's figurative canvases, narrative drawings by Manjeet Lamba (an example of which I explored in Chapter 1), and paintings and murals by Shanti Panchal (Greater London Council, 1985) instate their artists' ostensibly 'Asian' backgrounds by taking up figuration as a medium to articulate personal, collective, historical and *art* historical narratives, drawing upon a North Atlantic archive of such constructs centred around modernism. There is also an array of explicit references to visual schemes of ritual, performance and religion from South Asia. The play of Hindu signifiers in the sculpture of Dhruva Mistry, or the Hindu deity *Kali* as she appears in the painting and collage work of Sutapa Biswas, are characteristic of this ongoing conversation with visual languages distinct from those that were familiar to most British audiences in the 1980s and 1990s. These and other works, such as the cut-out collage and painted silhouettes by Salim Arif, and monumental wooden sculpture by Juginder Lamba (seen in the previous chapter), offer instances of intimacy with historically, spatially and culturally diverse visual systems hailing historically from outside Britain, which at the same time trouble the boundaries of signification and raise the matter of what sort of viewership these artists anticipate. More specifically, these are examples of written language and visual signification that are traceable to an Asian and diaspora cultural geography, variously interwoven or brought into conflict with the conventions and contexts of visual display typical of the history of British art. Through this contextualisation, such artworks in general have confronted the designation of their artists to a marginal or excluded community, and in particular have refused to be overwhelmed by terms of value that prejudice the appreciation of such art.

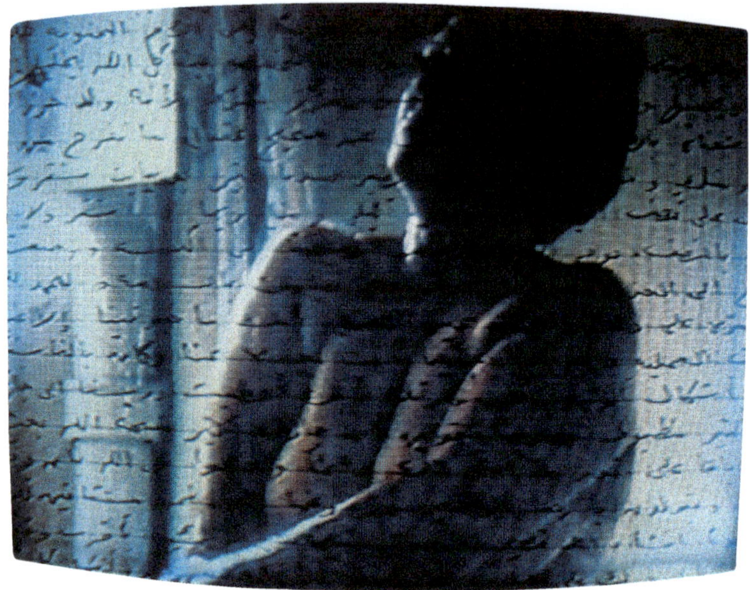

Figure 28: Mona Hatoum, *Measures of Distance*, 1988, colour video with sound, duration 15 minutes. A Western Front video production, Vancouver, 1988. © Mona Hatoum. Courtesy White Cube.

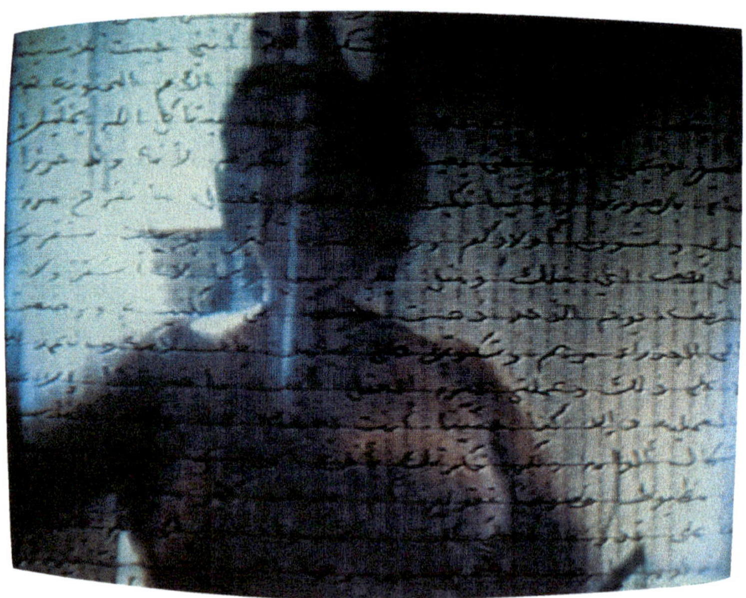

The story of how Asian British artists have tried to outstep the boundaries of such public reception is a fascinating one that emerges from a process of apprehending artworks themselves and problematising the view of them as textually signifying sites of 'Asianness'. Such artists have found paths through uncomfortable terrain in which the purportedly racial character of their art and its identification with 'Asian' differences operate alongside similar pressures and opportunities to those of their African diaspora contemporaries, who share an attitude of 'strategic essentialism' and a shared purpose to embed fine art practice in a wider cultural politics of difference.

At the level of what is required of viewers for the interpretative 'completion' of their works, it is safe to say that much awareness of Asian languages and cultures – within and without the diaspora – will have been unavailable to most non-Asian audiences of this art. This prompts a discussion of the extent to which the efficacy of these artworks may in fact have relied on them being inaccessible and closed to any sort of iconographic or iconological reading. Raising acute issues of translatability, John Roberts has noted of certain multimedia pieces by Rasheed Araeen, for instance, which include textual material in Urdu, that 'By including quotations from Pakistani newspapers on Benazir Bhutto's house arrest and Nixon's visit to Pakistan, the "final" level of interpretation is left with the Urdu speaker' (1990: 193; cf. Roberts, 1994).[1] Calligraphic formulations by Ali Omar Ames and Ahmed Mustafa (Naguib, 2015; Theophilus, 1994), and Mona Hatoum's celebrated video works that use Arabic, such as *Measures of Distance* (1988, fig. 28) also strongly establish this technique of multiple address to different cultural and linguistic communities.

---

1  Araeen's *Green Painting* displays this attitude, as Roberts has outlined (although the terms of his reference to Araeen's 'own culture' – as if he were somehow both representative and unproblematically at one with Pakistan as a coherent whole – is dubious): 'Conjoining modernism (minimalism) with the "primitive" (Muslim ritual) within the organisational spaces of modernity itself (the intertextual combination of various sign systems), he demonstrates his right to use elements of his own culture as components of an *international* art culture' (Roberts, 1990: 191).

## Feminism and language

Two of Zarina Bhimji's installation works are central to this discussion of how an artist may exploit similar linguistic differences and 'gaps', occasionally playing with, and at other times thwarting, a connotation of diaspora cultural specificity. Notable and initial works in this stream were *Live for Sharam, Die for Izzat*, a photo and text installation that foregrounds difference by the words in its title,[2] and a second installation by the artist, entitled *I Will Always Be Here*.[3] They are each examples of the interplay of visual signification and the exploration of the visual and material to emotionally affecting and more ambiguous ends. Nested within conventions of British art, Bhimji has an imperative to reassess the demand for a readable difference, for signs of minority ethnicity that may point back to the artist's biography. She rejects the idea that identity should be pertinent to her art, or indeed to any contemporary practice of visual creativity. This is complex territory, however, for the indexical surface of many of her works – their titles, appropriated elements, found images – do tempt the viewer to conjecture upon a migratory dimension, however hard that may be to pin down. Indeed, her biography escapes easy encapsulation, there being no simple label or quick distillation of identity for a woman who is not directly of South Asian descent, but is African-born of the Indian diaspora in Uganda, and who has been domiciled in Britain since childhood.

*Live for Sharam* comprises black-and-white photographs featuring arrangements of cut hair, lengths of white muslin, a nude male body, a brass cup and a reproduction of what appears to be a Mughal miniature, a postcard detailing a woman's portrait in profile. These offer a good range of semiotic references: the male figure, being motionless, is perhaps constructed as dead; nude and washed as if in preparation for his funeral, he becomes an object of ambiguous ownership – between the stakeholders of family, the state, organised religion. The installation also became an occasion for the artist to explore performance and how the idea of photographing the nude could entail judicious selections about

---

2   The piece was shown at the exhibition *Intimate Distance* at the Photographers' Gallery, London in 1989, and has since been made accessible as a set of plates published in Rutherford (1990). A single image from the installation is available online at https://www.art-tv.ch/files/zarina_bhimji1.jpg (accessed 1 January 2017).

3   Shown at the Ikon Gallery, Birmingham in 1992, a selection from this work can be viewed at https://artmap.com/zarinabhimji/chapter/images#_r2r7b (accessed 1 January 2017).

appropriate lenses for the camera and the texture of film, especially how it is printed and might suggest human skin. Some of these preoccupations are augmented in the objects and associations of the second installation: four large photographs, an array of objects that fill a series of glass boxes, made to order at a pet shop, based on size 5 shoeboxes and suggesting the materials of museum display. Above them is an arrangement of white cotton shirts, or rather off-white, in a shade of lilac cloth, hung close to the gallery ceiling. 'The white cotton shirts are for children', Bhimji explained, 'small ones that seem to fly out of the window like birds, as in Bachelard's writings – the cotton starched and folded to imply a bone structure'.[4] Patterned with great, singed holes, the shirts become partial screens, objects of utility spoiled by heat. This preparation of the cloth and its unusual display succeeds in shifting the clothes from functional items of vesture to scarred objects and the remains of measured procedures of harm.

In each case, the appearance of cloth has led certain viewers of these installations into insisting that the artist's Asian background is the ultimate key and arbiter of the value of this work. Obviously, the prospect of experiencing the work as a phenomenal presence in such cases is overtaken by the temptation to consider instead the matter of its authorship, with the danger of the artwork as much as the artist thereby being undermined by such a proclivity and caught in an ethnicising category. Indeed, what has commonly happened in the reception of these works is that Bhimji's aesthetic project has been bypassed or disallowed by critics who have preferred to dwell on the task of imputing biographical features to her art. Yet, as the artist described this process to me, 'Reading between the lines, other things go'.

A clear instance of that misdirected attention among audiences is the way that critics have placed importance on the damage done to the cloth by singeing and scoring, as if this action was a sublimation of some personal experience of violence – 'in order to make sense of a self that has "survived"', as was suggested in a review in *Women's Art Magazine* (Bradley, 1993: 24). Read in that way, the lengths of cloth surrounding the dead male may signal a widow's *sari*, with widowhood being colour-coded white. In turn, the hair clippings, brass vessel and painted image become offerings to the deceased: twists of burnt or cut cloth that wrap the man in an elegiac shroud. But little room is left outside such readings for the artist's primary involvement with the potentiality of

---

4  Conversation with the artist, February 2016.

hair as a sculptural object before it is codified as metaphor. Nor, for that matter, is there scope to appreciate Bhimji's response to professional art history's over-reliance on the female nude to provide a site of contestation, which by and large leaves the male body intact or discrete from the run of attention to the malleable meaning of nakedness. 'In order to bring that out I made a grainy image of the man, and used slow reacting film, drawing attention to the film itself', she has explained. On the related matter of ethnic difference and trauma, the artist is equally contrary: 'What is this European perspective that defaults to seeing the Other as damaged and sullied, and itself as pure? We seem to need re-examination of the implication of violence in my art. I didn't put it there'.[5]

The contemporaneous reception of such works as *Live For Sharam* and *I Will Always Be Here* was complicated by an obviously ethnocentric tone of readership. What is surprising is that this tended to be melded with perspectives that came from writers who themselves openly identified with the politics of marginalisation and exclusion associated with feminism. Here the sort of racialising gaze of critics met, or clashed, with a quite contrasting agenda of empowerment for women. That was an ironic turn, as it saw an otherwise progressive intervention (undergirded by the critical work of thinkers in the 1980s and 1990s who shaped feminist social-historical and psychoanalytic approaches to understanding art and its histories) which unfortunately appeared to skirt or entirely miss the point. A strictly categorical division of aesthetics from politics resulted in judgements that were ultimately about whether Bhimji had toed the line of white feminism (an unlikely prospect even from the beginning of her career, given the title of a work submitted for her degree show at Goldmiths College in 1987: *For the White Feminist*). More precisely, these were discriminations *not* about what aspects of an artwork may be considered political, but about what sort of politics was acceptable at all. For example, Jaki Irvine wrote for the journal *Third Text*, in quite categorical terms, about 'aesthetic pleasure' versus 'political concerns'. She betrayed an agenda that Bhimji plainly did not share:

> there would appear to be a contradiction between the concerns referenced by the work [*I Will Always Be Here*], on the one hand, and the means by which they have been articulated, on the other

5   Conversation with the artist, December 2016.

... Ultimately, it is the question of aesthetics, or, more specifically, aesthetic pleasure, which is particularly significant here as it strikes me as being precisely at the point that the work registers as 'beautiful', or decisions have been made on the basis of that criterion, that the political concerns referenced elsewhere seem to be undermined, allowing them to act more as a theme or a motif than as urgent issues to be thought through by the viewer. Obviously, this ambivalent relationship between aesthetics and politics is a difficult one to negotiate. (Irvine, 1993: 110)

Since the shirts in Bhimji's *I Will Always Be Here* are made to fit a child, they frustrate the easy application of a feminist social history of art that might seek to decode such garments for their significations of women in urban life – say, as statutory office wear – and sedentary employment, or else of gendered social mobility. Certainly, while the shirt at one time connoted masculinity, and that connection was unsettled through its appropriation by women in a new syntax of dress in the workplace, it would be a mistake to see Bhimji's installation as the occasion to plot the trajectory of that emancipation of women through 'Asian' social terrain. Feminist accounts of dress, design and material culture have insisted on cloth itself as a contested material, a medium of struggle against norms of gendered difference. It seems that such an analysis, once applied to Bhimji's works, fixed upon ethnicising the cloth that she photographed and took it to be material evidence of her biography. Critics were convinced that her art was a projection of her identity, even when such detail proved elusive, as if the artist was deliberately confounding the viewer who knew it to be there all the same. One has the constant impression that critics have suspected that Bhimji must simply be trying to hide from us some snippet of biographical information that would help us to decide about the artwork's final meaning, as if the bottom line can only ever be about ethnic difference. The title of Bradley's profile piece on Bhimji, 'An Audience Unto Herself', hinted at this suspicion as well as the author's sense of ambivalence. It generously suggested on the one hand that British audiences had a long way to go in coming to grips with Bhimji's contribution, while on the other it trumped up grounds to deny her art an audience among white feminists, blaming the artist.

## Shame and place

Whatever the case for Bhimji, the appetite for difference, whetted in the 1980s and early 1990s by the wide promotion of multiculturalist approaches to public art programming, has stood as an obstacle along the path that reaches away to the phenomenal complexity of her art. Only with the benefit of hindsight about that impediment and a more philosophical approach can the necessary analytical work be done to understand the chains of significations that feed into the materialising processes activated by this art. This analysis might begin by noting Bhimji's stated complaint against a general conservatism over dress styles within South Asian communities (whether in or out of the diaspora), which is evident in the text written to accompany her 1989 installation. She mentions Indian women in figure-hugging clothes, women for whom 'The Sari is given up for jeans, yet, the colour of one's skin, and eyes still/remains … it does not leave …' (Bhimji, 1990: 40). This assumes further meaning with the addition of clippings of hair. While primarily a metonym for the act of cutting or trimming hair, the clippings also suggest a rejection of the notion of the naturalness or norm of long hair and the recoding of femininity through alternative hair styling. Indeed, the dissemination of 'cuts' across Bhimji's visual and linguistic texts are also critical 'cuts' and interventions into the pervasiveness of various norms attached to the bodies of women. Cropped female hair may indicate a forbidden act or rebellious departure from a gendered norm; however, some far less celebratory meanings are also thrown up. The discarded hair at the same moment variously punctuates an act of despair (tearing of one's hair and clothes), prolonged self-damage or self-abuse, as well as a sign of punishment and humiliation. Equally, sliced shirts that imprint and recall the body's shape – its arms, its neck and torso – might as metaphors be slashed, stabbed bodies and wounded skins.

But rather than give this nexus of meaning further definition, perhaps by using the accompanying text as a gloss that would fix or narrow a visual reading, Bhimji chose not to supply translations for the foreign terms used in the 1989 work. This was ultimately a function of her discomfort about the type of public reception of her art that insisted on drawing associations with 'Asianness'. The word *sharam* translates from Hindi and Urdu as shame, and *izzat* as honour or respect, yet the keys to these interpretations are not given anywhere in the text. For those able to translate, the title offers a play on words by inversion, asking the reader of these languages the question: is the emphasis on the value of achieving a shameless life, submitting to an honourable death to avoid shame, or on death itself as a shameful end?

Even for those who appreciate how these words translate, however, there was still a lot of guessing to do, and audiences would join feminist critics in the dilemma about where to place the work's meaning in relation to the politics of gender. The work is shadowed by the suggestion of violence, which is cast across both its textual and visual vocabularies, among its twisted lengths of white cloth, burnt fabric and an apparently dead male body. Then there is the actual mention of self-sacrifice and personal compromise. The first stanza indicates an unwilling entry into marriage: 'TODAY MY HEART IS IN ANXIETY:/ Girlfriends paint her hands with henna and rub her body with jasmin oil,/ Preparing her for the …' The second is a rhetorical question and pronouncement issuing from a family member ('Aunt Nilofar's voice cracked in anger: "What kind of a man is he?"/ He … has NO IZZAT …'), perhaps in response to a confidence shared by the female persona who occupies the entire text. This communication prompts the aunt to call everyone to remember a *doxa* which is also a curse ('Once Aurat [woman] loses Izzat, She has no support, it's a high price to pay …'), which in turn frames the artwork's denotation of acts of desperation and self-harm.

Of equal fascination is how the inference of a particular social setting, which emerges via Bhimji's text, also inflects the specificity of geographical place. She writes, 'Anyway, what YOU do in Britain, does it really count?', to suggest being at a remove from a location of Indianness which is centred elsewhere. Indeed, this returns directly to the matter of language. By renaming woman 'Aurat', and disrupting her Anglophone narration with Hindi or Urdu terms, Bhimji invites her audiences to accept an art that is a figure of hybrid narration that requires a de-centring of Western feminism – sharing much with it, yet transposed uneasily to less trodden ground. As the artist explained to me: 'Consider an argument such as that of Dale Spender [the author of *Man Made Language*] and ask why is the concept of *izzat*, whether in and out of the court of law, only ever asked of a woman and not a man?'

Consequently, the works by Bhimji which I have highlighted place a full semiotic reading beyond the reach of most viewers in the British context. Bhimji has a continuing interest in the breaking up, or down, of linguistic units when they are translated into visual form and find material limits there. This challenges the tendency to categorise the artist under the pat categories of difference that have so dominated the black

British art milieu. This, ultimately, is the moral drama that black British art orchestrates, urging audiences to transcend the ordinary vocabularies for describing art as a cipher for the identity of its maker and confining art and artists to stereotypes.

When given its due, with favourable conditions of reception, art's material presence can serve as the counterbalance to such reductionism. Philosophy has a role to play in shaping the intellectual climate for this art. Without it, black British artists may seem for ever caught in a loop, repeating a mantra about their right to artistic sovereignty against the wind of a racialising discourse to which they also contribute. Regardless of whether an individual artist has achieved notable public prominence, there is a pattern of a host museum or gallery casting the artist's identity through promotional techniques aimed at piquing the interest of a certain public audience. Zarina Bhimji's experience on this score is a familiar refrain for black British art:

> In the press releases and advertising for an exhibition at the ——— Gallery, they wanted to say I am a native African. Which is Eurocentric, of course, because it simplifies 'for the sake of convenience', covering over my point of view, my self-perception. But I am not translating a personal experience for a Western audience. In the course of negotiating these pressures, in fact this art is not about the audience at all. I reserve the right to play with language, sound, metaphor, poetry, and to foreground the artistic process of working through these things, offering a space for doing so, for thought, for thinking about many different things simultaneously.[6]

### Food

Working with the operation of disparate cultural codes, and the aversion of the artwork to serving as a medium for the politics of looking, artists of Asian backgrounds in Britain have continued to pursue projects that raise a set of constructive philosophical problems. They complete a picture of the uses and limits of language in the turn towards materiality. Yeu-Lai Mo's work with food brings us face to face with the role of the senses in structuring a perceptual response to art that is not entirely and strictly speaking 'readable'. Using leftovers from her kitchen, Mo examines the visceral qualities of vegetables and sauces through a display of glass jars.

---

6  Conversation with the artist, December 2016.

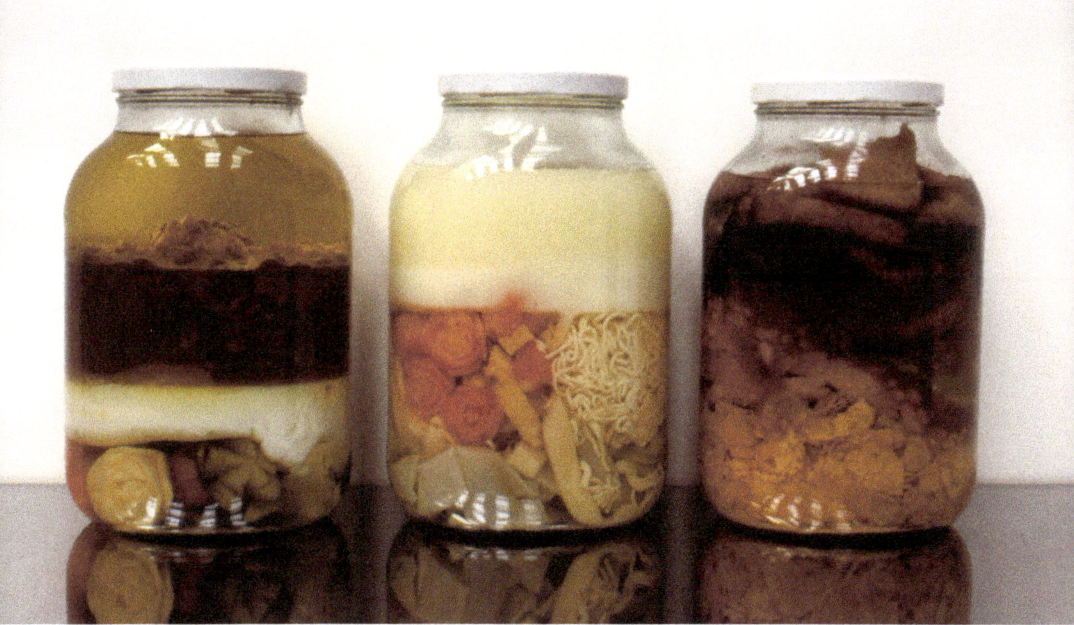

Figure 29: Yeu-Lai Mo, from the *Food Jars* series, 1998, curry sauce, lard, oil, water, carved carrots and radishes. Image used with permission.

Like Bhimji's *Charing Cross* photographs showing images of eyes and feet preserved in formaldehyde, the preservation of organic matter in Mo's jars mimics efforts to suspend decay. A consideration of process is also key here. Potatoes are carved to make ears and noses, and a 'castrated' carrot becomes a penis, which is rhymed with the qualities of an ephemera of black fungi, bean sprouts, radishes and raw eggs (fig. 29). Mo described this to me as 'borrowing from the kitchen' (as if such creations may one day be returned there, or even served as a dish), a borrowing that does not end but, in her words, '*begins* with an obsession'.[7]

An earlier work pursued this obsession through another selection of root vegetables. Radishes and swedes became roses and stars, while carrots and potatoes were petals and blossom, scattered upon water in a black photography bath, resulting in a spray of colours. These jars and later some rectangular glass fishtanks (fig. 30) also allow further meditation on the formal aspects of composition, directionality being the

7   Conversation with the artist, May 2002.

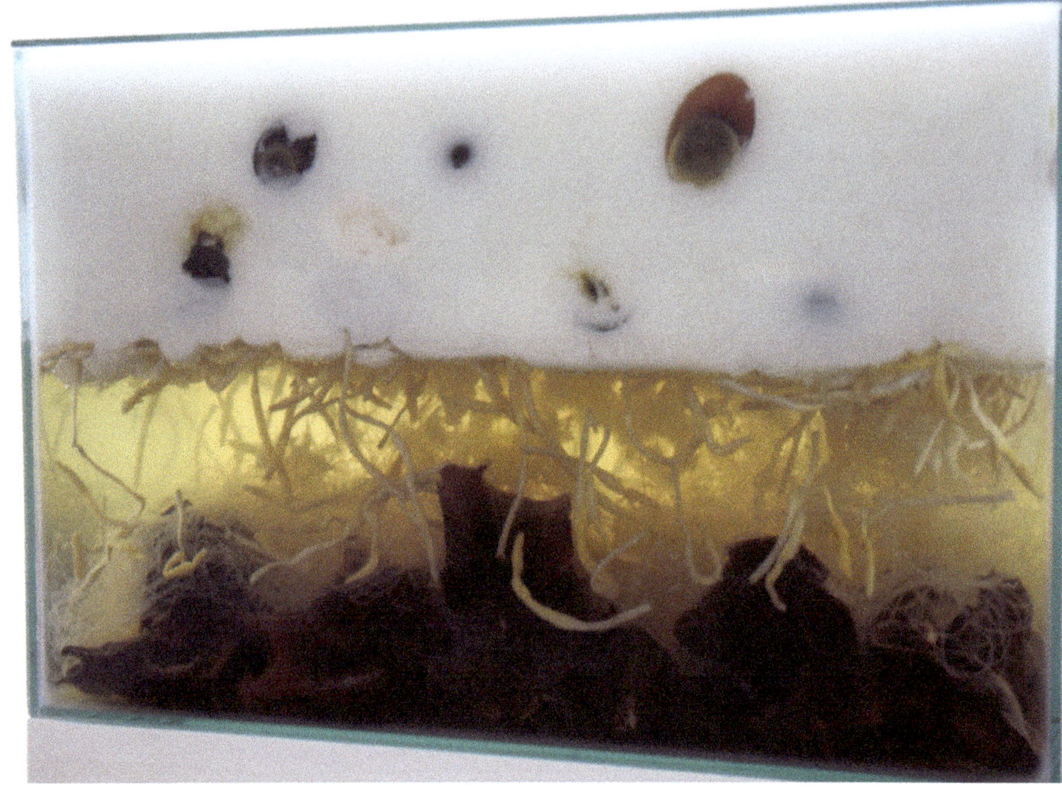

Figure 30: Yeu-Lai Mo, *Foodscape: Tank 3*, 2000, lard, hundred-year-old eggs
(preserved duck eggs), water, seaweed, lily bulbs, fine vermicelli noodles.
Image used with permission.

chief focus of their vertical stacks of long vegetable roots. By contrast,
later work saw a careful layering of sauces and viscous liquids to create
horizontal planes. This sedimentation, the result of a careful process of
cooking, preparation and pouring, has landscaped fields of colour and
texture in Mo's food tanks: a tangle of noodles forms undulating lines
and a copious amount of lard is a dense bench on which the artist has
poured a glowing bed of saffron gravy. If some of these ingredients are
recognisable from their everyday use in Chinese fast food, they all take
up obscure lives through being displayed in a gallery, while setting up
an affective relation with art as food – a sensitive treatment of racialised
looking that no semiotics of the kitchen seems able to capture.

## Black British art as a survey of Being

Given that the features of all these artworks point away from the centrality of visual language towards considerations of perception and the body, it is justifiable to conclude that black British art is at the very interstices of a set of philosophical problems. With artworks that usher in a concern with vision and touch, we saw an example of the overlapping – or what, following Merleau-Ponty, might be termed the 'equivalences' (1964a: 182; 1993b: 142) within perceptual experience – that has a place in the history of approaches to the ontology of perception. Merleau-Ponty's chapter 'Sensation' in his *Phenomenology of Perception* (1962), for instance, outlines just how far our phenomenological attitudes are out of keeping with traditional philosophical attention to sensation – such as in Locke or Descartes – where colour is taken to be a 'secondary quality' of an object and, as such, thoroughly distinct from what we understand of its texture or shape. For those earlier thinkers, colour does not belong properly to the object itself, but appears by affecting the subject who examines the object in a particular way. Yet colours are not purely subjective; regarding colours as such would render them indistinguishable, since differentiation requires an objectification on the part of the subject. In this philosophical scheme, pure sensation is a kind of experience that hits us with an undifferentiated 'impact', an instantaneous experience, which we later reflect upon and organise (Merleau-Ponty, 1962: 3–14).

This traditional strand of philosophical thinking is described and especially opposed in Merleau-Pontian thought, in an effort to show how previous attitudes to the experience of such things as colour and texture – that is, their attempts to explain sensation – lead us away from the meaningful and concrete setting in which colours and objects actually appear to us (Merleau-Ponty, 1962: 3–14; see also Hadreas, 1986: 43, 49). Sensations do exist, it is conceded, and are part of the sensory process, but they are not available directly to perception: we do not perceive sensations, nor are they a 'unit of experience' (Merleau-Ponty, 1962: 3–14). Merleau-Ponty argues that there are no such things as pure 'impressions', no colour and no figure free from a background, and this has profound implications for any analysis of perception. It means that perceptual experience is always seen to form upon a ground, and that (there being no pure sensations) when colour is perceived, it is never as a determinate quality of something external to the perceiver. That being the case, the suggestion runs that any belief in an external world itself must be duly abandoned: in order to understand why we perceive as we do – colour, shape, sound – we must return our attention to a pre-objective realm (Merleau-Ponty, 1962: 3–14).

Many of the offerings from black British artists – art based on and around the body – support this kind of ontological thinking about perception. They also underscore an agreement with Merleau-Ponty's objection on a crucial point of the philosophy of Husserl, at what was a key moment in the history of phenomenology.[8] Whereas Husserl's approach echoed much of Cartesian thought on sensation, Merleau-Ponty pronounced on the issue of the perception of colour and how it is inseparable from its coloured ground (the very issue that I took up in my previous chapter):

> We must first understand that this red under my eyes is not, as is always said, a *quale*, a pellicle of being without thickness, a message at the same time indecipherable and evident, which one has or has not received, but of which, if one has received it, one knows all there is to know, and of which in the end there is nothing to say. It requires a focusing, however brief; it emerges from a less precise, more general redness, in which my gaze was caught, into which it sank, before – as we put it so aptly – *fixing* it. And, now that I have fixed it, if my eyes penetrate into it, into its fixed structure, or if they start to wander round about again, the *quale* resumes its atmospheric existence. Its precise form is bound up with a certain woolly, metallic, or porous configuration or texture, and the *quale* itself counts for very little compared with these participations. (1968: 131–132)

He also argues a similar case for touch:

> distinctions between touch and sight are unknown in primordial perception. It is only the result of a science of the human body that we finally learn to distinguish between our senses. The lived object is not rediscovered or constructed on the basis of the contributions of the senses; rather, it presents itself to us from the start as the centre from which these contributions radiate. (1993a: 65)

The task of ensuring that sensation and perception are differentiated,

---

8 Even so, Merleau-Ponty does not discuss Husserl's account of perception in any great detail (a view endorsed by Moran, 2000: 420), only Husserl's interest in how perception grasps its object bodily, in the flesh (*leibhaftig*): 'As Husserl said, through the perception we have of them, things are given to us in the flesh – carnally, *leibhaftig*' (Merleau-Ponty, quoted from a radio broadcast in 1959 in Stewart, 1998: 495).

which involves rejecting all attempts to dissolve perceptions into sensations, is merely a beginning for perceptual analysis conducted on a phenomenological frame. Merleau-Ponty's expressed attitude towards colour, for instance, applies just as readily to other kinds of visual perception: form, depth, line, texture and so on. These dimensions are interlinked rather than separate in the traditional philosophical way that I have outlined, while any attempt to divide such dimensions into 'pure impressions' will come to nothing – their differences remain imperceptible (Merleau-Ponty, 1962: 4). Indeed, the interlinking of these different registers of visibility is a kind of system, it is a 'system of equivalences, a Logos of lines, of lighting, of colours, of reliefs, of masses' (Merleau-Ponty, 1964a: 182; 1993b: 142). And it exists since 'the world is a mass without gaps, a system of colours across which the receding perspectives, the outlines, angles, and curves are inscribed like lines of force; the spatial structure vibrates as it is formed' (Merleau-Ponty, 1993a: 65).

The basic claim I am making is that the sort of attention paid to perception among black British artists culminates similarly in this very 'logos of equivalences'. Their works show up a form of 'sensory universality' (Fóti, 1993: 305) to which each of the possible dimensions of visibility and tactility conform. The crucial identification of the 'logos' they offer distinguishes black British projects as part of a wider exploration of perception and offers a keen insight into the phenomenal. Such depth also affirms a vital dimension of the intellectual importance of their works.

As we have seen in artistic and critical attitudes to objectivity in works by Piper and Hatoum, a return to the body is in keeping with the phenomenological move away from scientific or 'common sense' thinking, after revealing their 'traditional prejudices' (Merleau-Ponty, 1962: 3–26). This particular attitude to perception signals a recognition of the fact that pure, undifferentiated 'impressions' are directly imperceptible: 'The structure of actual perception alone can teach us what perception is. The pure impression is, therefore, not only undiscoverable, but also imperceptible and so inconceivable as an instant of perception …' As Merleau-Ponty concludes in response, 'I shall therefore give up any attempt to define sensation as pure impression' (1962: 4).[9]

The search for colourful body parts in much black British art returns us to the very ground or situation in which colours appear: in the

---

9   Fóti describes this as Merleau-Ponty's 'notion of a sensory universality which is dimensionally organized and not amenable to conceptual grasp' (1993: 305).

butcher's shop, on the membranes of offal. Sonia Boyce has revealed that as we survey them, hair-pieces and fabrics reach out for our touch. For Mona Hatoum to launch into rolling neat spheres of her hair – to scatter them, playing with contrasting tones of hair and wood, and their random configuration within an architectural space – there has to exist a ground of perceptual wonder on which only those spaces and shapes can meet, however temporarily. The colour and texture of Bhimji's hair clippings, cotton and so on are enfolded with one another and endowed with the tactility of skin through photographing. As Yeu-Lai Mo demonstrates, food is also especially effective for its phenomenal presence, in which several aspects of perception interplay and cohere.

These artworks crucially bear out the recognition that the nature of perception impacts upon an ontology of the 'lived object' (which 'is not rediscovered or constructed on the basis of the contributions of the senses; rather, it presents itself to us from the start as the centre from which these contributions radiate'; Merleau-Ponty, 1993a: 65). They are a concrete artistic context in which claims about being and perception are grounded. Merleau-Ponty has claimed of the 'equivalence', or the universality present in perception, that it shows up 'a nonconceptual presentation of universal Being' (Merleau-Ponty, 1993b: 142). Examining perception and the body for black British artists on such a purely phenomenological frame represents, therefore, a thinking through of how as Beings we are rooted in the world – how we arrive at being-in-the-world (*l'être au monde*). As a form of ontological engagement with the body and its world, the breadth of these artists' works enables such a visual survey of Being.

Following through the implications of black British art, especially how it features the body and body parts – and how it finds distance from art history and cultural criticism in their continuing adherence to paradigms of semiotics, textuality and representation – returns us to the primacy of concerns with perception. Indeed, it leads to a renewed realisation of the importance of presence, counter therefore to its marginal place in the discourse of reception for these artworks. It is harmful to overlay evidence of any such perceptual experience with a language of critical explanation, since that would lose sight of the primacy of perception. All told, the type of crucial knowledge that is offered and unfolded by black British artworks suggests the need for a novel philosophy of this entire field.

## Criticality and form

Keith Piper's photographs of black subjects reworked with measuring tools and diagrams of body parts have references that are fairly transparent. Piper's digital works offer a key to understanding the use of both new and old technologies in racial classification, surveillance, control and the objectifying representation of black subjects; his works are a commentary on recent developments in what Piper views as a long history of 'othering' and oppression supported by visual means (see Mercer, 1997; Piper, 1991). Bhimji's *Charing Cross* series and other photographic presentations of fragmented body parts and entrails constitute a related project to illustrate the precise institutional settings in which knowledge regimes of 'others', and the paradoxical psychic melding of horror and fascination, are played out under the auspices of medical research. Similar themes are taken up by Hatoum in her explorations of the body using an endoscope, whose meaning critics have tried to short-circuit by referring to Hatoum's biography – namely her departure and exile from Palestine in 1975 and her art activism past – and the politics of gender and Islamophobia. The endoscope pieces are a response to the intrusion and violation of the female body through medical practices, and in other ritualised spaces and domestic situations, thereby raising questions about a woman's ownership of her own body, the stark realities of resistance and empowerment in the face of advanced technologies, and the prevalence and reproduction of gendered norms. The meat being prepared by a butcher according to custom urges her viewers to face up to a likely sense of disgust at seeing the finer grain of such practices, and to try to overcome a blanket rejection of diverse physical and sexual appetites.

Sonia Boyce's hair-pieces, essaying on similar themes, put on trial the institution of the museum and art gallery as an ideological space in which dangerous binaries of self and other are constructed. In these locations, prohibitions are made on intimate corporeal relations across perceived racial boundaries and a complex but ultimately contestable hierarchy of differences. Bhimji's arrangements of damaged shirts, a nude male body, lines of speech, Hindi idioms and so on are powerful for disallowing a white feminist and non-Asian 'reading' of an artwork that frustrates the dominant demand for black British art to signify ethnic difference. For Yeu-Lai Mo, a focus on food becomes an instrument for enunciating the ironic entry of Chinese people into that common, popular imagination, through a certain kind of 'contact zone' of the High Street takeaway, as

James Clifford (1997) once chose to call the ethnographic museum. Mo's series of works is part of a clutch of references to food in works among a network of artists of the Chinese diaspora such as Song Dong and Anthony Key (see Yeh, 2000: 69). There is a trope of personal experience in reference to her parents' restaurant, illuminating her father's 'materialistic attitude' and a stalwart position of 'self-subsistence, both culturally and economically'[10] in the face of over-the-counter abuse and daily toil in the kitchen, but the artist is defiant that her artwork will not be similarly regarded in the contact zone of the gallery.

Evidently, all of these artworks accord with a range of critically important political concerns and social dynamics. At the same time, as I have consistently argued, they operate with and through perceptual registers and prove the need to connect bodily with their grounded, aesthetic nature. While such a relationship to this art can be elucidated through detailed and patient philosophical attention, however, that is not the same as adopting an unreconstructed 'formalist' analysis (see, for example, Fried, 1998): the narrow sense of aesthetics that prevailed before the proper advent of criticality in the late 1960s and early 1970s, such as with the inception of feminist, Marxian and conceptualist approaches to art theory. Formalism is inappropriate, indeed, for capturing the historicality of much contemporary art in general. But it is especially unwelcome in the context of black British art, where the risk of ethnicising readings could be heightened by a formalist approach, whether unreconstructed or not.[11]

While the proper historicisation of black British works requires something better than mere formal description in order to handle their critical complexity, at the same time it is crucial not to force a false choice between aesthetic and critical discourse, as if there were a line of separation between them. This is where the turn to a notion of 'equivalence' is so crucial and may be put to best use. Remaining cognisant of the interrelationships between critical and aesthetic analysis, a philosophy of black British art can show how aesthetic concerns have

---

10   Personal communication with the artist, May 2002.

11   A similar situation has arisen with regard to black artists in the United States, as noted by art historian Darby English. Although he concedes to what he understands to be 'formalism', the dangers of this require him to qualify this approach by making it 'strategic'. He declares his choice of a 'strategic formalism, one interested in the peculiarity of works within their varied contexts of meaning, responsive to the specific artistic operations that often manifest relations and differences to which culturalist regimes of reception must remain blind' (2007: 32).

tended to be edged out by the primarily interpretative attitude shown towards black British art (they have been encountered as anything but equivalently), but also that they have never been subtracted entirely. Indeed, the status in the historical and intellectual record of black British art, and perhaps the future of this entire field, relies on making sure that a philosophical dimension becomes salient. We need to avoid misrecognition of the value of this art solely according to its capacity to demonstrate semiotic and textual theorisations of black or diaspora culture, as if it had no simultaneously phenomenal presence – or, more precisely, as if its phenomenal existence made no difference.

## The uses of equivalence

Theorising black British art through the idea of 'equivalence', or 'a logos of equivalences', to quote Merleau-Ponty, meets this objective. It brings out how artists evoke many of the vital aspects of human perception as such. The idea of equivalence establishes a sense of the common, equal relationship between texture and colour, shape, directionality and so on. As I have quoted above, here the perceptual 'world is a mass without gaps, a system of colours across which the receding perspectives, the outlines, angles, and curves are inscribed like lines of force' (Merleau-Ponty, 1993a: 65). Equivalence is the most forceful of the analytical schemes suggested by phenomenological thought, not least because it is not specific to a theory of art. As a manner of analysis it has advantages that extend well beyond its ability to disclose the phenomenal world, promoting descriptions that are a means to a further end, with considerable value in linking up the several theoretical shapes that surround black British art.

Equivalence is above all a template and a *vade mecum* for organising the perceptual responses and dimensions of visual readership that issue from black British artworks. Rather than seeming to apply only to perceptual categories, it has a usefulness beyond, which overspills the narrow domain of formal description and serves as a conceptual tool that is adaptable to wider contexts of thought and other conceptual issues. This expanded purpose for phenomenal analysis raises some pressing questions about the effects of allowing a 'system of equivalences' to adhere between otherwise discretely categorised areas of discourse on the visual arts. Much can be achieved by establishing the equivalence of pairs of terms such as 'content and form', 'aesthetics and politics', and so on; terms that are foremost among the 'natural' binaries of the commonly used language of art analysis, but fail to serve us in the black

British context. Subtending these issues is how a 'logos of equivalence' may enter that context to transform the notion of the relative autonomy of the art object by parsing the relationship between art's socially contingent meanings and those of a more concrete aesthetics.

## Art as a lived object

A sense of criticality is not merely retained while probing more plainly phenomenal themes, it is heightened or enhanced from the very starting point of a phenomenal analysis. Giving attention to the phenomenal can set firmer foundations under the interpretative work that has characterised much scholarly attention to black British art, making for a deeper complexity. Certainly, attention to the phenomenal can recast and rebalance within a relation of equivalence the two operative terms of the 'diaspora aesthetic'. But there are many more opportunities that need to be seized for transforming the critical models of art, blackness and diaspora visual culture.

A more philosophically trained focus on black British art can make possible a perceptual encounter with the very phenomenal world occupied by its artists. This new analytical attitude towards black British art, emerging after a more phenomenological excursus, can succeed in rebalancing around the point of equivalence the politics of representation and aesthetic experience. Perhaps the clearest merits of equivalence lie in its distinctive ability to bring out the idiosyncrasies of aesthetic experience before it is overlaid with categorical or 'conceptual' thinking. Merleau-Ponty claims of the equivalence or the universality present in perception that it shows up 'a nonconceptual presentation of universal Being' (Merleau-Ponty, 1993b: 142) and this warrants exploration of the phenomenological tradition in order to understand black British artworks that were produced mostly in a period when critical analysis had shunned aesthetic theory geared to ontological thought, even as artists themselves remained open and curious about its potential.

The really challenging work of historicising this art lies in a commitment to the idea that experience and signification are now, and have always been, in constant interplay. Seeing this art in a phenomenological frame means that nothing can cancel out the priority of experience; no amount of insisting on the mediation of it in or through language can rid experience of its foundational role. Experience is much more than a trace of meaning that can be decoded from black British artworks. For such works to be apprehended in view of their 'presentation of universal Being' (Merleau-Ponty, 1993b: 142), for all the philosophical generalisation that the phrase conjures up, is nonetheless a strategic break away from the habit of reducing art to the mere cultural media of social relations, where much theorisation of black British art stands. The alternative can afford a certain dignity to black British works of art so that their political and cultural value can be seen, felt, embraced and elaborated more properly – those many and diverse critical relations and 'contributions' to the world. Through such a detailed ontology of black British art as a 'lived object' – to use Merleau-Ponty's words – art may then 'present itself to us from the start as the centre from which these contributions radiate' (1993a: 65).

# Chapter 6

# Reversibility

The idea of equivalence as it pertains to perception, quite evident in the relationship between vision and touch, was taken up in the previous chapter as a way of establishing that there is a particular phenomenal complexity in the individual projects of creative practice identified with black British artists. Equivalence also pertains to matters of conceptual approach: it bears fruit for appreciating the simultaneously (or equivalently) critical *and* perceptual value of this art. In this second respect, the aim of delivering equivalence is about ensuring a greater balance of emphasis across the range of intellectual options that are present for understanding this art.

In both cases, of course, being able to capture the phenomenal presence of art has the consequence of empowering black British artists, by uncovering how they command efficacy through materialising practices. But what remains unspecified is the extent to which works of black British art and their creators can be said to stand in a relationship of equivalence with one another. As I will show in the following discussion, there is much at stake in being able to ascribe agency to artworks directly, rather than simply to assume that art is the medium by which artists seek or convey agency. A more precise way of thinking about this is to consider black British artworks themselves as 'persons', with the more specific suggestion that works of art are able to 'look back at us' in some way through the 'reversibility' of perceptual encounters. An extended exploration of reversibility is key to understanding the relation between perceiver and perceived, the body as sensing and the body as sensed, and between the phenomenal body and other worldly phenomena – relations that all in turn can have an important bearing upon black British artists as a significant creative force.

## Deviation

If, as we have seen, many black British artworks suggest the need to recognise 'a system of equivalences' in perception and its dimensions of visuality – reaffirming the ontology of perception's 'lived objects', and, in that respect, opening up a discussion of truly phenomenological problems – certain other works go beyond that stage by carrying a register of the '*deviation* in a system of equivalences' (Merleau-Ponty, 1964b: 54, 81). Chila Burman is one artist whose work offers this sort of deviation. Her art practice is a progressive culmination of over 30 years of experimental work in an expansive range of media, including photography and photomontage, graphic and plastic arts, video, sound, installation and performance (see Nead, 1995). Much of this emerges from a tradition of graphic political satire, generated from an adversarial position taken up within a political field in which gender, postcolonial identity and class are suffused within artworks that testify to a fascination with objecthood and materiality.

The terms of reception for such works, however, betray a tendency among commentators to select from among this enfolding of aesthetic and critical practices. Meena Alexander, for instance, takes Burman's art to be a 'theatre of sense' that is above all a touchstone for cultural politics: 'There is something in this species of image making ... that postcolonial thought at the birth of the twenty-first century must seek out, learn from' (2001: 12; cf. Burman and Hunjan, 1987). It is hard to disagree, except when such an aim diminishes the range of ways that this art complicates the habit of representing Asian British artists as a discretely categorised 'species', or encumbers the kinds of thought, let alone the perceptual experiences, that such artwork is permitted to generate. Stimulated by the need to enunciate her social background, the bulk of Burman's figurative work has dealt with portraiture and self-portraiture, exploring the production of her own sexuality and dynamism. While recent works concern the industries of 'glamour' and pornography, and make an obvious basis for phenomenological investigation, it is the earlier objects made during the 1990s that hold interest for the perceptual ambiguities they celebrate. Here the artist sharply apprehended the continuing 'othering' of the female body energised through the vogue for the Wonderbra,[1] interpolating the breast cloth/

---

1 Shown, for example, at the exhibition *Flirt*, Admit One Gallery of Contemporary South Asian Art, New York, 4 January–10 February 2001.

garment/device with the petals and heads of garden flowers. These take
the form of a series of billboards and installations of cibachrome prints
and 'durotran' lightbox works, and a set of drawings and etchings.

Burman's hypercoloured photographic prints have declared a disruptive
response to the status of visual representation in mediating binaries of
nature and culture. Precisely *how* this is undertaken becomes a matter of
investigation along ontological lines in view of the cibachrome print she
has made of objects found in and around her home, representing a close
study of the 'equivalence' of perception.

Her *For Tune* (fig. 31) is a panel of eight photographs crammed with
the petals and heads of garden flowers, interpolating variously patterned
bras. The reds of petals and satin are dotted with magnolia orange and
bright yellow, and a large white, many-petalled flower head beams out.
Burman's petals and underclothes are extracted from the home and
garden, from bedroom and flowerbed. These features are recorded by
being pressed close to glass above a moving, scanning lens, and light
thrown out by this device illuminates most those features proximate
to the glass, leaving the rest to fade into a sort of background gloom.
This method of photography emphasises colour and surface, enlarging
the objects it captures, displaying a panel of textures clarified by an
immediate, evenly spread light source. It entails a gathering of pieces
in an even-handed presentation, a balance and system of 'equivalent'
perceptions. These objects also have a provenance, an origin in the artist
herself, from around and about her body and dwelling. In other of her
works using a similar method of photography, the repertoire of her
gathering is extended to items of dress and accessories, such as lingerie,
bhindis, fabric, hair-pieces, jewellery and makeup.[2]

Accordingly, while these works offer the opportunity to explore
'equivalence', they also gesture clearly beyond that preoccupation. They
are a foray into the complexities of framing, layering and assemblage –
equivalence within the grounds of heterogeneity – but also cast a relational
look at the bodily presence of the artist herself. The materials drawn
from Burman's body within the prints are not simply the remainder of
her everyday habits of dressing, self-decoration, adornment, and planting
and potting in the garden, but the means for the artist to be in proximity
with the work through fragments of her dwelling-in-place. This subtle
yet significant sort of complexity is akin to the more general sort of
phenomenal relations that black British artworks allow, when they bring

2   For example, *On the Rocks*, 1999–2002, cibachrome print, ink jet, 42 x 55 cm.

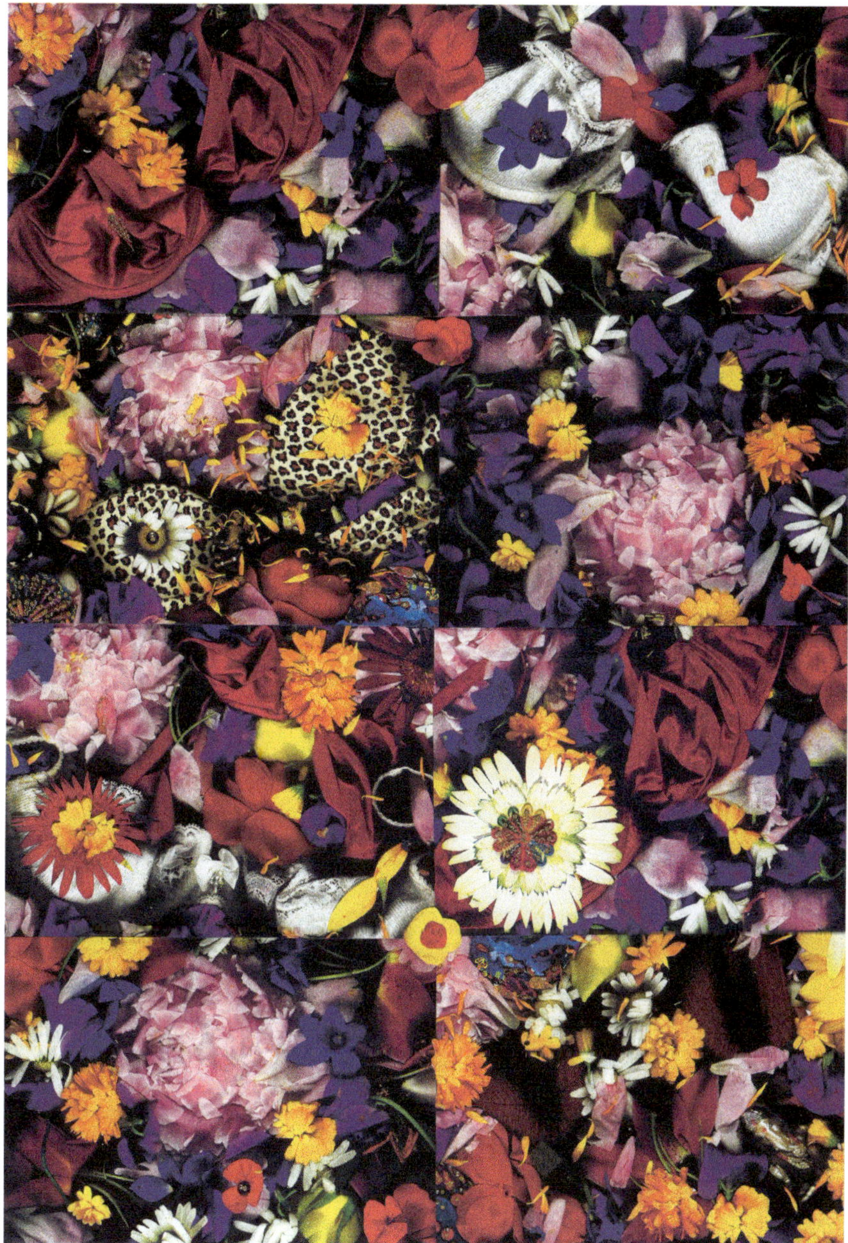

Figure 31: Chila Burman, *For Tune*, 2000, cibachrome and mixed media, 91 x 64 cm. © Chila Burman. All rights reserved, DACS 2016.

to the fore the body and its poetics in view of ontological concerns with perception and the world. With Burman's art, by contrast, there is the need for an ontology calibrated somewhat differently. The intimacy of looking that these works permit is an existential involvement with the artist, more precisely described as a phenomenal overlapping, and by engaging with this dynamics of looking, these works insert something like a rupture in the experience of equivalence. Of course, this problematises the centrality of a critical theory of art practice that signals black British art to be a 'product' of diaspora or postcolonial identity, since it suggests an alternative: that such works of art are, by comparison, themselves a source or origin for experience.

## Persons and the pre-personal

Chila Burman's art occupies attention and operates through a mode of visual perception that relies on its ability to set up perceptible spaces and a focal point of phenomenal importance that complicates a view of works of art in their capacity as media. In response, what is needed quite urgently is a more precise language to deal with how black British art in general enters our perceptual continuum and acts upon its tactile and optical registers. As an origin of effects, such objects take up places in the world, indeed occupy and dwell in those places, commanding and energising perception. That view broadly draws on Heidegger's notion of the way that a world is 'set up' (*aufstellt*) through the object, touched upon in Chapter 3 on objects as 'places' and 'events'. More so, it pays tribute to Alfred Gell's proposition that we ought to apply ourselves to a theory of art that 'considers art objects as persons' (1998: 9), without this being mistaken for a sort of 'animism', as it would be if its metaphorical value were overlooked. Gell explains:

> To suggest that art objects, to figure in an 'anthropological' theory of art, have to be considered as 'persons', seems a bizarre notion. But only if one fails to bear in mind that the entire historical tendency of anthropology has been towards a radical defamiliarization and relativization of the notion of 'persons'. Since the outset of the discipline, anthropology has been signally preoccupied with a series of problems to do with ostensibly peculiar relations between persons and 'things' which somehow 'appear as', or do duty as, persons. (1998: 9)[3]

3  In its refutation of 'animism', Gell's position should be set apart from the vaguely 'formalist' view typified in art historical writings, such as those of Arthur Danto,

It is worth drawing a parallel between this manner of 'defamiliarization' in anthropological theory and Merleau-Ponty's suggestion that we ought to recognise the 'anonymity' or 'pre-personal' nature of perception, an idea that offers distinct paths for exploring an understanding of the phenomenal and perceptual experiences made possible by black British art. Perhaps one of the distinctions Gell has in mind is the difference between 'individual' and 'person'. This has a tradition of relevance for anthropology in which the term 'individual', as 'the mortal human being, the object of observation' (La Fontaine, 1985: 125), is distinguished from 'person', a term referring to the social significance of that 'object'. I also recall, by etymological illustration, how the notion of 'personhood' retains something of the sense of the Latin *persona* as a character or mask worn on the theatrical stage, in order to consider social actors taking up roles or masking to enact a social drama.[4] Something like this same distinction is elaborated in Merleau-Ponty's separation of the 'ante-predicative' and 'pre-personal' aspects of perception from the social or cultural, which supports his claim for the anonymity of perception: 'Every perception takes place in an atmosphere of generality and is presented to us anonymously … So, if I wanted to render precisely the perceptual experience, I ought to say that *one* perceives in me, and not that I perceive' (1962: 215). And it also governs his understanding of the body and its social world, since he maintains this same distinction, as I have explained, to deal with the human body – the *'corps propre'* or 'one's own body' – as it is experienced: neither as a socialised body nor an object in the world.

where 'What makes the one an artwork is the fact that, just as a human action gives embodiment to thought, the artwork embodies something we could not conceptualise without *the material object which conveys its soul*' (1988: 31; my emphasis). A more sophisticated permutation of Gell's view suggests that 'film may be considered as more than a merely visible object. That is, in terms of its performance, it is as much a *viewing subject* as it is also a *visible* and *viewed object*. Thus, in its existential function, it shares a privileged equivalence with its human counterparts in the film experience. This is certainly *not* to say that the film is a *human* subject. Rather, it is to consider the film as a *viewing* subject – one that manifests a competence of perceptive and expressive performance *equivalent* in structure and function to that same competence performed by filmmaker and spectator' (Sobchack, 1992: 22; emphasis original).

4   Gell might also have in mind the exposition given by Radcliffe-Brown: 'Every human being living in society is two things: he is an individual and he is also a person. As an individual he is a biological organism … Human beings as individuals are objects of study for physiologists and psychologists. The human being as a person is a complex of social relationships … As a person the human being is the object of study for social anthropologists' (1940: 193–194, cited in La Fontaine, 1985: 125).

Granting the art object the role of person is also on a footing with Merleau-Ponty's ideas about reversibility in the relationship between bodies and the perceptual world, and yet here is an obvious point of divergence from Gell's notion of 'art objects as persons', given the margin left in Merleau-Ponty's early work for endorsing precisely the kind of 'animism' that Gell rejects. In Merleau-Ponty's posthumously published writing, however, this idea re-emerges with a new gravity as the notion that 'the seer and the visible reciprocate one another and we no longer know which sees and which is seen' (Merleau-Ponty, 1968: 139). It is this later understanding which should be taken more seriously, since it marks the crucial point of agreement between the more anthropologically applied notion of the *affectivity* of art objects as being in some way persons, and a philosophical assertion that black British artworks are phenomena of primarily perceptual importance.

The initiative from phenomenology to examine the notions of reversibility and the pre-personal raises some tough issues for the sort of philosophy of black British art that keeps perception at the centre of its analysis. The question arises of whether in dealing with perception we should hope to have engaged with the perceptual experiences of black artists, our own perceptual experiences as viewers formed by apprehending their works, or else a combination of the two (and if so, in what measure). If it were the former, then it would still have to be determined how to grasp black British artists' individual perceptions in their works, how to recognise or isolate those features by way of philosophical thought, and what importance to grant them. Since the task at hand is also to perform a similar study of one's own perceptual experiences of these objects, equivalent problems (of recognition and value) still need to be faced.

Consider too that a more advanced analysis can be achieved on top of these philosophical procedures. I refer to the larger task of relating the sum of all of this distinctively *perceptual* understanding to what has been established of black British artworks in the field of cultural criticism. How does perception relate to the framework of seeing such artworks as historical and social depositions, framed by the concept of visual creativity as a principally representational, culturally signifying practice? It is a question that I will broach in the remaining part of this chapter, beginning with a close look at works by a single artist.

## Overlapping and motility

[I]t is clearly in action that the spatiality of our body is brought into being, and an analysis of one's own movement should enable us to arrive at a better understanding of it. By considering the body in movement, we can see better how it inhabits space (and, moreover, time) because movement is not limited to submitting passively to space and time, it actively assumes them, it takes them up in their basic significance which is obscured in the commonplaceness of established situations. (Merleau-Ponty, 1962: 102)

The consistently challenging art of Sonia Khurana is comprised largely of video installations that are often the end result of performance work, a process she has encapsulated with the notation 'video/photo/sound/installation/object/performance' (Wainwright, 2000b). A highly skilled photographer, video and sound editor, Khurana shows great tenacity with the technical demands of a clutch of visual and audio tools. Bodies and faces emerge from the electronic texture of these media, demonstrating both her command of gesture, bodily expression and movement in her own body, and the ability to capture their essence in others. She sometimes pictures her own body, yet there is a sense in which Khurana's works aim away from direct self-portrait. Although recognisable as the artist herself, the manner in which her imaged faces and flesh appear points towards a concern with anonymity and the pre-personal perceiving body. In particular, a distinctive attribute of her works is her means of drawing us to the challenges of her technical apparatus and reformatting of time.

When mentioning Khurana's work in the black British context, it needs to be stated that this is not to attest somehow to her 'Britishness'. Khurana was born and grew up in India and has worked in New Delhi for much of her professional life, except for years of study in the late 1990s in London and the Netherlands. She has travelled extensively for residencies, art events and exhibitions throughout a global network, spending much of her time away from her notional base in India. It is the British context for her work or, more expressly, the works she produced in the United Kingdom, that interest me here, however, since they suggest an approach to art practice that was shared in the late 1990s with black British artists who were also seeking to challenge the centrality of categories of ethnic and racial difference that had so heavily featured in art discourse in the closing decades of the twentieth

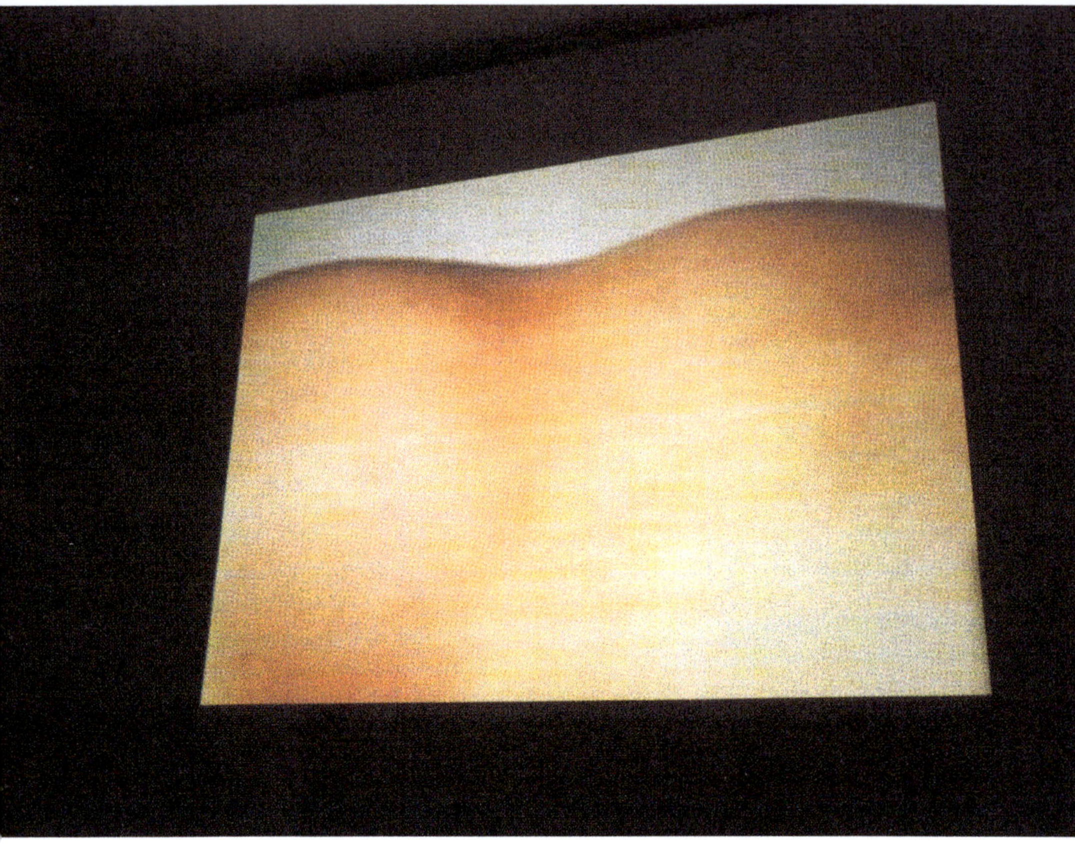

Figure 32: Sonia Khurana, *Breath 1*, 1998, single-channel video projection, colour, silent, 5 minutes, looped. © Sonia Khurana.

century. This is another way of saying that British art during the years of interest to identity politics and cultural diversity was also grounded in experimentation. Artistic creativity has often tried to sidestep or translate the lexicon of cultural identification through blackness, the institutional, market and curatorial pressures, and mixed opportunities that are associated with it. The complexity of the art that Khurana made in London should arrest any easily drawn art historical assumptions of periodisation and place, and assumptions about the strictures put upon art practice by identity politics. The same may be said of artworks by Johannes Phokela that I have already discussed, made during his sojourn in the United Kingdom before returning to South Africa.

Khurana feeds her fascination with phenomenal experience through an art practice that is in every sense an exploration of the uniqueness of ontological 'disclosure' in visual terms. These works are complex and ludic, endorsing an application to play in a grounded, embodied form. They also, in large part, form an appeal to bodily expression, and to the interweaving of spatial, perceptual and bodily presence. To understand these, it is crucial to think in depth about the notion of originality, and more particularly, origins. For Khurana takes a direct look at origins: the origins of movement or motility (what Merleau-Ponty called *motricité*); the study of the origins of spatiality or – in corporeal terms – of lived space.

There is a clear and notable effort in Khurana's practice to take an unmediated approach to the original nature of the body and its perceptions. A key experience of the lived body is the function of breathing. *Breath 1* (fig. 32), a colour video installation, presents the midriff of a torso in its continuous rising and falling breaths. Flattened on a digital screen, this is a shifting form, an expanse of pink flesh fringed above with a narrow finger of white space. The undulating line separating fields of colour, two smoothed ridges at the base of the ribcage, is our only register of movement. It is a steady movement, yet the isolation of the body section within the frame gives little indication of whether it is taking place in real time or at a slowed pace. Whether shallow breaths made deep, or deep breaths deepened, once imaged such breath allows the contemplation of gentle repetition in a silent form.

## To things themselves

Repetition and rhythm are measuring and orienting devices for another silent sequence, *I'm Tied to My Mother's Womb with a Very Long Chord* (fig. 33). This two-monitor video installation, one monitor fixed above the other, plays out two aspects of a hand-held camera carried along a shoreline. At the upper level, this appears as the shadow of a head and shoulders cast across shingle and muddy brown sand, interrupted by the utmost fringes of a lapping water's edge. Below, on the other screen, we see the lower body of a woman, stepping measuredly along a grey sand beach. Without stockings and wearing red-laced shoes, her feet pick their way across a landscape of flattened green seaweed, dotted with smoothed, egg-sized pebbles. Intermittently, the camera also catches glimpses of a flapping red skirt. The steps pause, edited into a freeze frame, letting several seconds pass before resuming their stride.

The figure's head, if these are indeed two aspects of the same body, remains at the margin of the upper frame. We look over her shoulder, effectively, at the field of sand and water trodden below, by feet that are out of sight. The discontinuity between upper and lower body, top and bottom sequences, itself becomes a focus of interest, the linear stacking of the monitors willing us to make them meet, to be aspects of the same figure, both on the same beach, at the same time, joined by a common rhythm of steps and sea and sand. But they do not conjoin, and so they come to trouble and play with any assumption of their equivalence: the very breaking of the body into separated frames of time and location excites the need to combine, to rejoin them, which is met by the gentle realisation that their differences cannot be reconciled. Stopping the wandering feet mid-stride, pausing to let head and shoulders walk on, brings a shrinking effect, halving and narrowing the area of movement across the split-imaged space.

These projects can be recognised as attempts 'to reveal the mystery of the world and of reason' from the starting point of our bodily encounter with the perceptual field. Indeed, Khurana's multifarious and rich descriptions of the body in its world – demonstrated, for instance, through the sketching of bodily movement in space – play out the famous declaration of Edmund Husserl to 'return to things themselves'. For Merleau-Ponty, after Husserl, this is taken to mean:

> to return to that world which precedes knowledge, of which knowledge always speaks, and in relation to which every scientific schematization is an abstract and derivative sign-language, as is geography in relation to the countryside in which we have learned beforehand what a forest, a prairie or a river is. (1962: ix)

It follows, then, in the open-endedness of visual sequences such as *Breath 1*, that Khurana has opted for an alternative to the 'derivative sign-language' which more commonly structures figurative artworks. It is as if by isolating the moving ribcage, or, as in her sand and sea locations, by fragmenting body parts, we escape the need to use visual devices that suggest body, and instead go directly to the body itself. Her walking feet have weight, and in their stride they measure out stretches of sand, weed and shingle. The dipping, swaying shadow of a figure's head touched at ground level by the washing waves presents an outline impenetrable by sunlight, the solidity and yet fluidity of a living form.

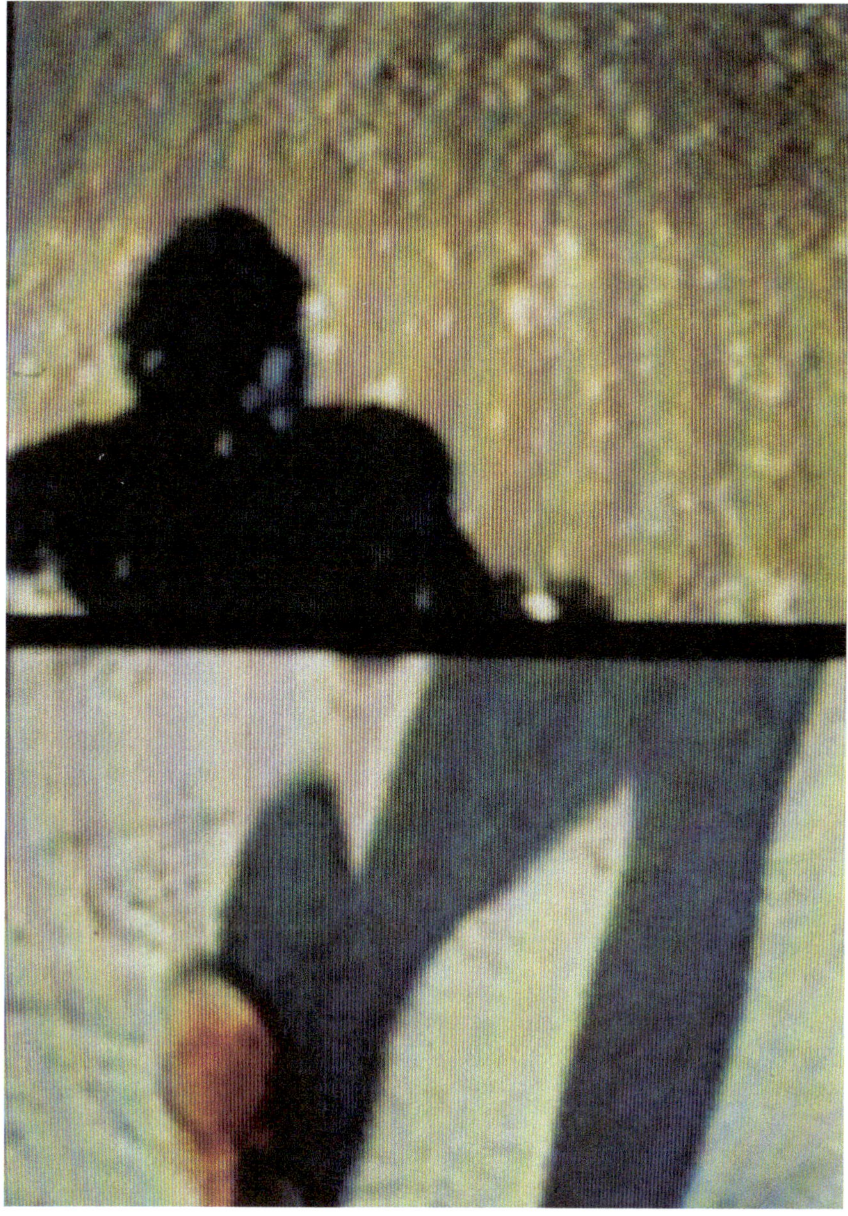

Figure 33: Sonia Khurana, *I'm Tied to My Mother's Womb with a Very Long Chord*, 1998, two-channel video diptych (stacked screens), colour and sound, 5 minutes, looped. © Sonia Khurana.

## Intra-action

To gesture towards these two poles of our experience of the body, as a natural, living object in the first sense, and in its abstracted, cultural guise in the second, is to investigate two related conceptions of the body in its world. Khurana's commitment to this further demonstrates the inadequacies of traditional objectifications of the body, urging us to abandon them. In their place, as her representations suggest, we are to regard the body as a dynamic synthesis of intentionalities, that is, as capable of responding to the solicitations of its world, of coming into being and having meaning in a plurality of settings. As the body responds to its world, it also makes sense of that world, bringing perceptual structures into intelligibility and exploiting their usefulness. The body then comes to have meanings in relation to the structures it sets up, in a ceaseless dialectic. Yet these encounters of body and environment are crossings that urge a close attention to the body that does not *dwell in* space, but that is *made of* it. Subject and space are entangled and co-constituted, rather than separate entities that meet simply to 'interact'. As the physicist and feminist theorist Karen Barad suggests, 'interaction' is better conceived as 'intra-action', where relata follow relations, rather than the other way around (2007). In such spaces of entanglement, the viewer enters in order to partake. We become complicit in the displacement of the boundary between the private and the public. Khurana's art exhibits the intimate as a venue for a shared, public intimacy, where the secluded is displayed, and the enclosed opens up to the viewer.

Having persuaded us to recognise this intra-action and intertwining of self and world, it is novel to find the artist involved in a contemplation of self, where the direct object of perception is oneself, which becomes the localised horizon of her attention. This is also novel in relation to the visual medium of video-recorded, time-based performance. In *Lone Women Don't Lie* (fig. 34), again using split levels with upper and lower monitors, dual appearances of the head and naked shoulders of the artist herself against a white backdrop perform a mutual adoration. Nibbling 'herself', the often childlike face of the artist engages in a nuzzling, sniffing, pecking apprehension of an original image or object that lies off screen. The focus of that apprehension, turned back on itself, now gently gnashes her teeth, now rapidly laps and flicks her tongue. The whole asymmetrical sequence ends with a sudden meeting of lips in a frozen, fleshy kiss.

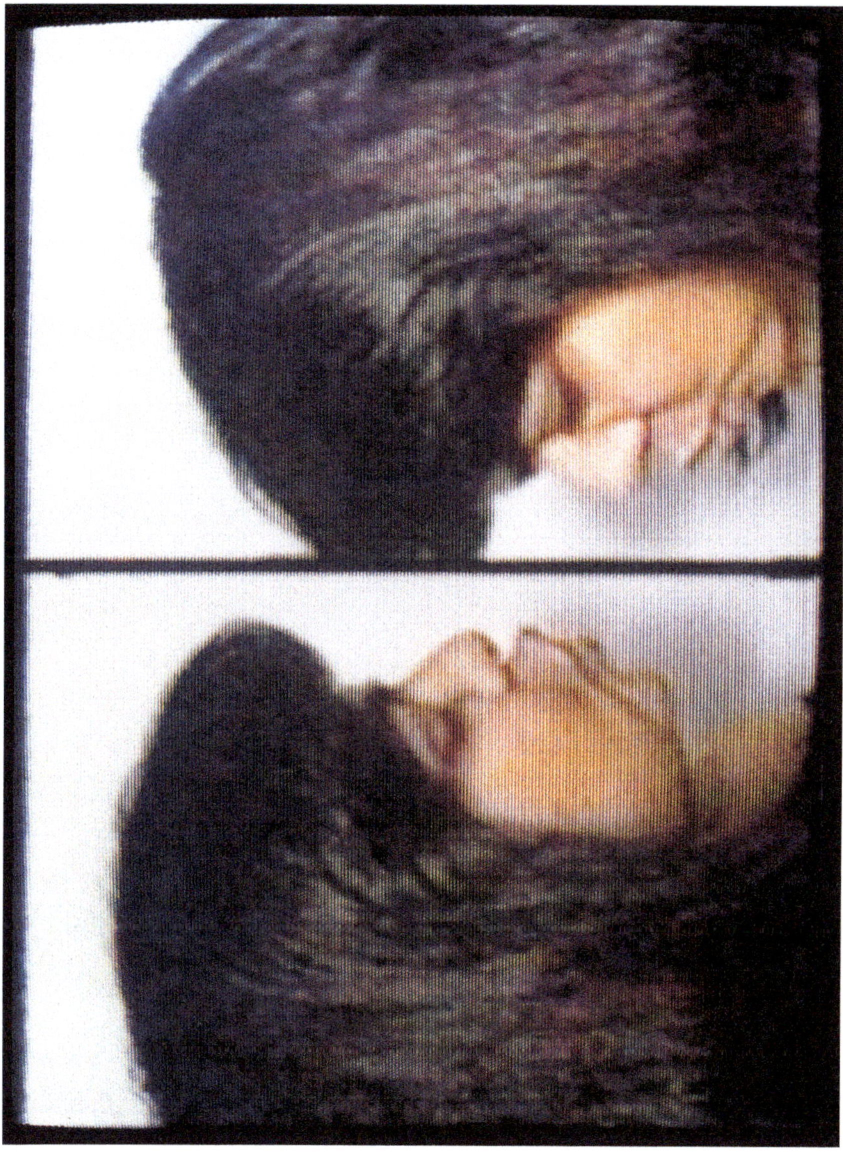

Figure 34: Sonia Khurana, *Lone Women Don't Lie*, 1999, single-channel video (vertical screen), black and white, 3 minutes 20 seconds, looped. © Sonia Khurana.

An amusing performance, no doubt, and a playful display of the exaggerated affections of the artist, ostensibly for her own image. Yet its philosophical significance lies in the fact that the sharing of a perceptual field and represented space across the monitors presents both a distinct simultaneity – two women playing in almost identical ways – and discontinuity, with performances happening at staggered times. Not only does it reflect by mechanical means the Merleau-Pontian idea of double sensation, but by elevating time in this way the artist puts forward a view of the body-subject as minutely differentiated by its changing situations in various temporal horizons. Even if Khurana's two performances were filmed on the same day, after the same meal, under the same artificial lights, her experience of them would still be subject to change. This in turn would alter and shape that performance. Which of the two images, upper or lower, we might wonder, precedes the other? The implication of the overlapping of the two performances, when the digital medium allows it, is to turn our attention to the novelty of adoration *and* of the visual medium.

## Playing with time

To have duration, we must entrust ourselves to rhythms, that is to say to systems of instants. Exceptional events must find resonance in us if they are to mark us deeply. (Bachelard, 2000: 21)

The open-endedness achieved in Sonia Khurana's installations depends largely upon her acute awareness of the technical effects of time manipulation. Across the range of her works, this is more obvious in some places than others. Taking various forms, the time element in many of Khurana's pieces ranges from a slowed or slower-than-real-time, through to real time, to accelerated time. Manipulating time in this way, their discreet differences help to orient the viewer's awareness of such things as sequence and repetition in her represented performances. Related to this, we might look more carefully at the role of time in enabling Khurana's foregrounding of bodily experience.

These three possible shades of temporal alteration in digital editing - slowed, real and accelerated time – betray the artist's interest in creating a sense of duration. As the quote above from Gaston Bachelard suggests, entrusting ourselves to rhythms, allowing ourselves to recognise in a digitally imaged sequence the measure and number of 'instants' or moments, raises duration to our awareness. For Khurana's *Anhad: The*

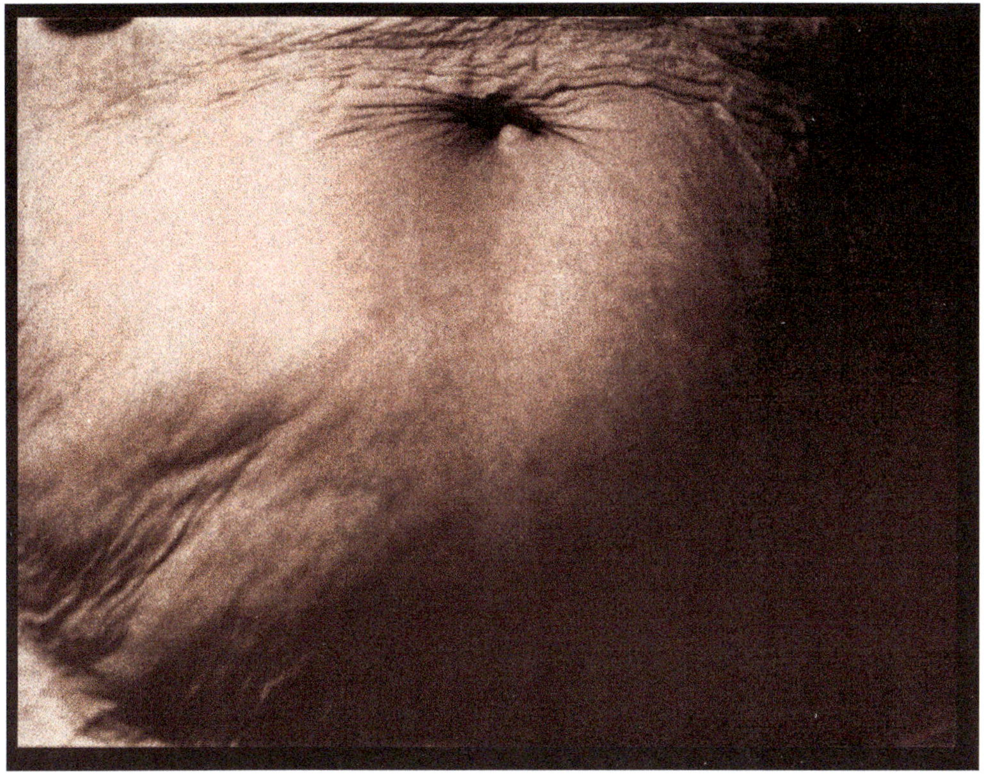

Figure 35: Sonia Khurana, *Anhad: The 'Original' Sound*, 1998, duratrans print photograph on lightbox and video projection, black and white, silent, 3 minutes, looped. © Sonia Khurana.

'Original' Sound (fig. 35), continuity is achieved in at least two ways. A still image, a black-and-white photographic print of an aged, hairless navel area, is placed to the left of a colourless surface of trickling sand and water from a back-projected video. There is no sound. Rifts and valleys left by water running across a sandy surface are shown enlarged, allowing the details of light and dark grains of sand to be picked out. The sequence is cut in places, overlaid with other aspects of the scene. From some aspects, the grains ascend, from others they descend, slipping across the channelled surface in a hypnotic cascade. Across from the sand, in a strong light source, the ridges of wrinkled skin remain unmoved.

In *The Waters, Forgotten of the Foot* (fig. 36), a two-part video and sound installation, continuity and duration are established in the form

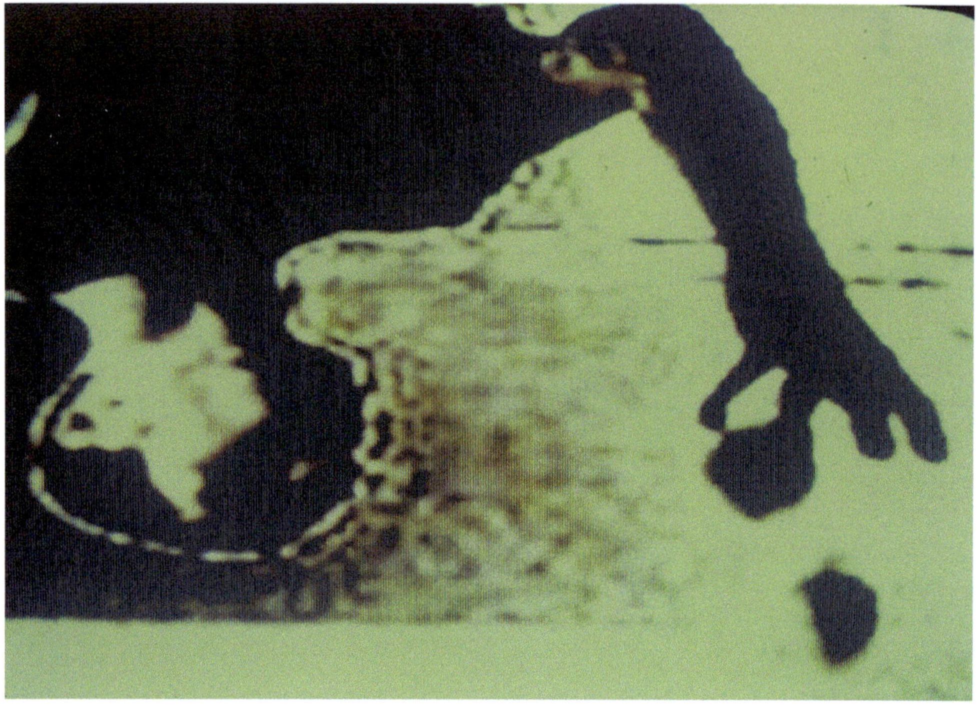

Figure 36: Sonia Khurana, *The Waters, Forgotten of the Foot: Part I, Juggler,* 1998, single-channel video, black and white, silent, 7 minutes, looped. © Sonia Khurana.

of falling objects. A man and his shadow, juggling balls or perhaps fruit, appear in slowed time. Yet these spheres seem to have buoyancy, not weight, for the image is turned upside down, so that falling objects rise, and what is thrown into the air first travels downward before coming up. The juggler seems not to throw but to push his tools, caught in a perpetual cycle of keeping them beyond and lower than his reach. In Part II of the installation, more spheres, the shape and size of apples, are dropped one by one from an extended arm (fig. 37). We cannot see where they land. A hollow striking noise persists, like the beat of a drum, sounded every few seconds. Below, on another screen, the artist herself is sleeping. Framed around her head and supporting arm, her sleep is interrupted, as she wakes intermittently, letting out a silent scream. She twists her head to face upward, over her shoulder and, as we view it, towards the screen above, her wide open mouth empty of sound.

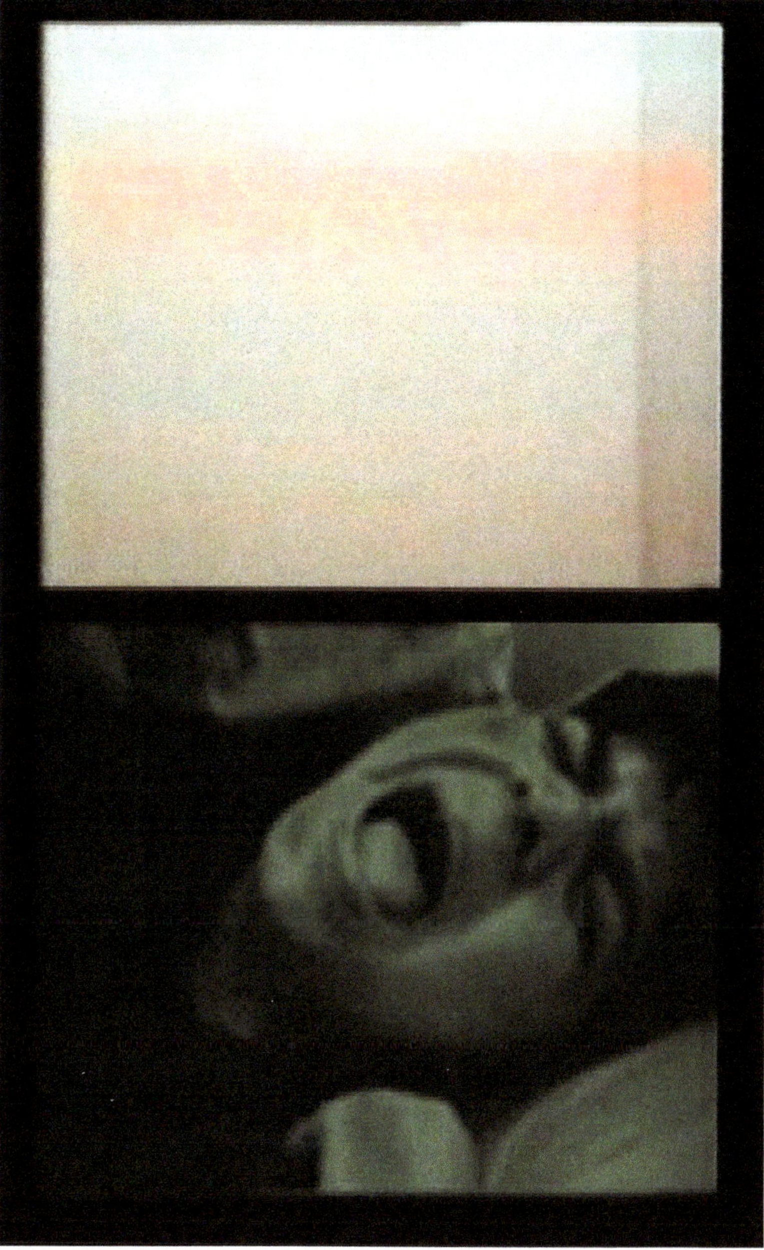

Figure 37: Sonia Khurana, *The Waters, Forgotten of the Foot: Part II, Big Sleep*, 1999, video diptych (stacked screens), black and white, with sound, 5 minutes, looped. © Sonia Khurana.

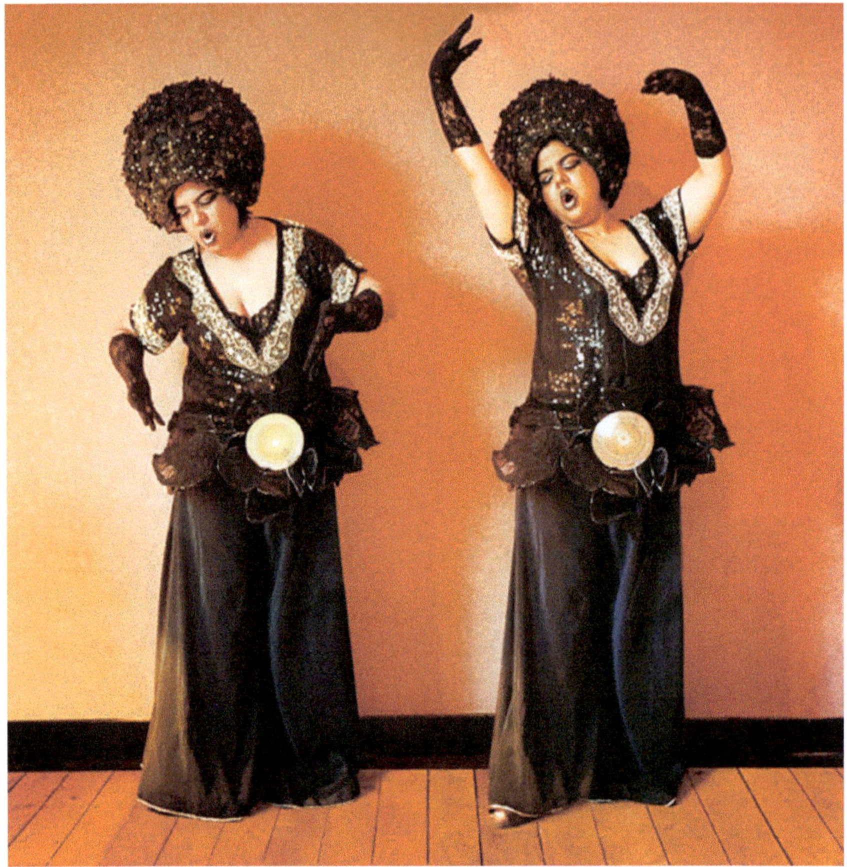

Figure 38: Sonia Khurana, *Zoetrope*, 1999, photographed simulated performance, on painted wood and metal kinetic object, 165 cm. Courtesy Kiran Nadar Museum of Art, New Delhi. © Sonia Khurana.

The repetition of these actions and the overlapping of their different cycles provide a continuous admixture. It is unclear when they begin or end. Duration, in that sense, is properly achieved within flashes of instants. This same application of cyclical movement is made possible in another of Khurana's works, *Zoetrope* (fig. 38). This interactive object demands of users that they themselves contribute to its path of repetition. Khurana's piece is much like the original zoetrope design, the drum-like object that once provided one of the few ways to bring movement to static images before the introduction of cinema. Spinning around, images arranged in series inside the drum can be spied through the narrow viewing slits within its circumference. The drum is to be turned quickly enough for the numerous images to merge into one, producing the illusion of movement. The subject of the display is Khurana herself, drawn into various poses, arms raised and open-mouthed, with head to one side, as if delivering a song. She is dressed all in black, with lace gloves and wig. At her waist is a reflective disc, tied in place with an elaborate bow.

*Zoetrope* represents a notable and striking departure from the other ways in which the artist orders the time element of her pieces. Here, the input of the object's users determines the duration of its sequences, and the point at which the movement of the drum and its contents might be returned to stillness. This extension of agency to the user or viewer of the drum is a development on the representation of duration in Khurana's digital and video installations. Duration is given its resonance for us since, as users, we establish it. And this means that *Zoetrope* enters the perceptual horizon of the viewer in alternative ways. Its tactility, its demand to be touched, its need for energy from those who apprehend it, means that its rhythmic effects are the rhythms we ourselves command it to produce, and its materiality is in this sense conjoined with ours. Interweaving our interests with the object and what it might show, in its potential to capture and deliver movement, closes the gap between the object and what we would make of it. Introducing movement to the 'zoetrope', we relate and inhabit it, in a spinning 'interworld' (*l'intermonde*, Merleau-Ponty, 1962: 357, 409) of experience.

## Hermeneutics, persons and things

Aesthetic experience, to be had before artworks, grants the opportunity to put aside the usual run of attention to critical modes of analysing black British art. The results recommend what such artworks offer, reflecting on the connection of artists to their works, and gauging their presence there. To view these works simply as a communicative channel between artists and their audiences would therefore overlook both the terms and textures – the motilities and temporalities – of such phenomenal involvements with and through works of art. Much rests here on being able to see such relations as social relations. To say that perception is pre-personal or anonymous, and that our apprehension of art is ultimately one of reversibility, raises considerations about the participation of all these agents – art makers, ourselves and art objects

– when caught up in mutually forming relations. This takes place only on the acknowledged basis that the human subjects involved are primarily corporeal, embodied subjects, capable certainly of 'decoding' and 'reading', but at the same time of hearing, sight, touch and so on. Recognising that larger affective presence for art suggests a more expansive notion of the 'ostensibly peculiar relations between persons and "things"' (Gell, 1998) in the setting of black British art, pressing our understanding far beyond the politics of representation.

Critics commonly misrepresent phenomenological interests as a method of inquiry that dismisses all others, as an either/or option (Melville, 1998). But phenomenology is more properly a set of initiatives than a method. Although what I have touched upon here points to a kind of hermeneutics established on phenomenological grounds, these outlooks have very little strictly *interpretative* content. These initiatives help us to understand the perceptual experiences of black artists in contemporary Britain along the narrow defile of their works, to offer us grounds for seeing *how* these artworks serve as affective fields of phenomena, and how their makers exist as artists who are as much embodied subjects as bearers of meaning. In turn, the sort of understanding based on the signifying processes by which black British artworks function is grounded upon a firmly phenomenal materiality.

## At the limits of interpretation

One of the main limitations of a phenomenological attitude, it must be said, is that it urgently demands to be qualified by precisely the sort of interpretative work that black British art has attracted. While a phenomenological approach has begun to emerge with the 'new materialism' of the humanities and social sciences (Fuglerud and Wainwright, 2015), such attempts to apprehend the phenomenal inevitably bring analytic work on to the threshold of more obviously interpretative exercises. While we should endeavour to set aside generally hermeneutic concerns in order to preserve the phenomenal as a category of the experience of black British art, still it must be conceded that certain hermeneutic concerns remain relevant. Taking up the phenomenal as an orienting category should never be allowed to obscure the gains for black British art from the application of critical theory. It remains a compelling problem that any discourse constructed out of a perceptual experience of black British artists' works is itself subject to the constructs of perceptual experience tacit in the schemes of critical theory. Our best response to this concatenation of interrelations can only ever be about recognising the merging of such horizons and seeing that one's own descriptive constructions are themselves a falsification of the innocent notion of phenomenological 'truth'.

Moving closer to hermeneutic methods than many earlier phenomenologists, Merleau-Ponty attempts to provide responses to these more interpretative issues. Although he has a lengthy discourse on expression as something that captures and conveys the act of perception, he does not deny that these 'expressions' are at the same moment accommodated and structured by figural or 'representational' languages.

In order to make the idea of the phenomenal a credible and workable one we would need, therefore, provisionally at least, to 'ride two horses' over the issue of expression. My treatment of black British art reflects this technique, by seeking out the tactile and optical perceptions experienced by black artists and evidenced in their works, and allowing their 'codified' aspects to remain accounted for in their existing signifying analysis. In some sense, one might say that the post-structuralist announcement of the fallacy of authorial intention as the ultimate site for understanding 'texts' – as begun in Barthes's famous 'Death' essay – is strongly at issue here. Barthes's idea, if applied to the current discussion, would serve to place emphasis entirely on the signifying importance of these objects, naming them as 'texts' and debasing the priority of their artists. This is done partly out of deference to the satisfaction sought by Barthes's contemporary critics for an 'explanation' of writing in terms of 'society, history, psyché, liberty'.[5] It more generally hails the 'birth' and 'rights' of 'the Reader'.

If we confine our attention to the pre-personal nature of perception – enabled by a recognition of corporeality in the Merleau-Pontian sense – then there is actually a large measure of agreement with Barthes's manner of 'defamiliarising' (as Gell might have put it) the 'intending' subject, whether 'Author' or 'Reader'. Indeed, we are permitted to ride the two horses together if, with Barthes, we look upon the 'Reader' and 'Author' as linguistically entangled, and thereby socially produced, while simultaneously envisioning these subjects as having a pre-personal

---

5   Barthes writes: 'Once the Author is removed, the claim to decipher a text becomes quite futile. To give a text an Author is to impose a limit on that text, to furnish it with a final signified, to close the writing. Such a conception suits criticism very well, the latter then allotting itself the important task of discovering the Author (or its hypostases: society, history, psyché, liberty) beneath the work: when the Author has been found, the text is "explained" – victory to the critic' (1977: 147).

relationship with perception and the body. Consequently, I prefer to believe that these more post-structuralist perspectives on black British art – and the work of Barthes, who inspired much of this writing – do nothing to hamper progress along a phenomenological path. Of course, this is the case only for as long as we admit to the importance of language in structuring experience, while maintaining the right to regard perception itself as a valid aspect of phenomenal experience, at the place of the corporeal. Just as Merleau-Ponty pursues the idea that 'perception takes place in an atmosphere of generality' or 'anonymity', perception is removed from 'personhood'. In this way the post-structuralist attitudes of black cultural critics, as in Barthes, can be productively drawn upon while bracketing the desire for explanation that is found in critical thought. At the level of a phenomenal analysis, it cannot be claimed that perception receives its meaningfulness entirely from social contexts and linguistic ordering – indeed from sites or practices of differencing, from cultural difference – but rather that it lies at their 'foundations', made present in the immediate, the tactile, the corporeal and the phenomenal.

## Phenomenal and social agency

Indeed, it is also true that Barthes and his post-structuralist followers in black cultural criticism inadvertently assist in what Gell declared to be the 'defamiliarization and relativization of the notion of "persons"' (quoted above). They do so through a treatment of the idea of personhood as either 'Author' or 'Reader'.[6] How, then, can something like the metaphor of art objects as 'persons' in Gell serve to be recuperative for a phenomenological project? The ability to answer such a question in the affirmative

6   We should be aware, however, of a potential confusion in the unorthodox use of the term 'personal' in Barthes. I believe Barthes uses it to indicate more individual than person, in the sense outlined above by Radcliffe-Brown, as a biological organism (1940: 193–194). It is debatable, however, whether this definition can be overlaid upon the distinction of pre-personal and social maintained by Merleau-Ponty. This is obvious from Barthes's comments in 'The Death of the Author': 'The reader is the space on which all the quotations that make up a writing are inscribed without any of them being lost; a text's unity lies not in its origin but in its destination. Yet this destination cannot any longer be personal: he is simply that *someone* who holds together in a single field all the traces by which the written text is constituted' (1977: 148). Barthes's use of the term personal is uncritical here and more akin to the kind of everyday speech that Radcliffe-Brown had sought to correct. But his *'someone'* is less likely to indicate 'somebody' in the sense of a pre-personal corporeality, than a subject expressed solely in language.

has until now been forestalled by a mistakenly assumed problem. Posed differently and plainly, it might seem quite impossible to support a view of art objects as persons while pursuing a Merleau-Pontian notion of the pre-personal nature of perception. Gell's idea of art objects as persons makes the case that what we ought to be seeking is the social importance of art objects, conforming to his sense of the goals of the 'anthropology of art' as the theoretical study of 'social relations in the vicinity of objects mediating social agency' (Gell, 1998: 7; Fuglerud and Wainwright, 2015). The matter presents itself succinctly thus: if phenomenological interest in black British art indeed lies in the pre-personal aspects of perception, surely we would be entitled to conclude (again, somewhat mistakenly) that social questions are no longer relevant?

The way out of such an impasse is to note that the objects made by black artists in Britain are as much a source and product of perception as they are a structure of expression. As expression, that artist's object is, of course, a signifying object, mediating or communicating (as so many critical commentators have shown). This means that we can submit to the notion of black artworks as 'objects mediating social agency' as much as to the idea of them as an origin of phenomenal *affect* and the very fabric of a phenomenal world. Certainly, no more does Gell believe in an animated person of the art object than does Merleau-Ponty believe that he is being looked at by the trees in a wood (Merleau-Ponty, 1993b: 129; and below). But they both arrive at a similar conclusion. It is the very presence of these objects that they agree upon, and the field of 'world alteration', to quote Scarry (1985), that they succeed in enacting – always, of course, with our help as their viewers.


## Being a body

It is in this manner of approaching bodies as relational phenomena that a philosophy of black British art resonates with a recently renewed interest in 'the somatic' in the humanities and social sciences. The interdisciplinary 'turn to the body' from the late 1980s has been indebted to a phenomenological tradition, by developing an engagement with the body in fields such as the philosophy of art, political theory, anthropology, the medical humanities, sociology and feminist theory (key examples from the respective disciplines might include Benjamin, 2012; Bennett, 2010; Csordas, 1994; Leder, 1990; Turner, 1984; Gallopp, 1988). With various concerns and agendas, these disciplines have focused on the centrality of embodiment and experience as exquisitely corporeal forms of 'being-in-the-world', juxtaposed to more abstract ways of theorising bodies. They have introduced a shift in the questions around experience, from the meaning of *having a body*, to the dynamics of *being a body*.

In the past three decades, this 'somatic turn' has also been shaped by a series of scholarly reorientations, which have grappled with concerns over 'being a *singular* body', problematising *what* a body can be, where its boundaries are, and what the potential for it may be beyond its physical boundaries. This has relevance for black British artists, as this chapter has shown, by way of art forms in which several bodies connect and expand their limits. While such questions are central to the current interest in 'affect' and its articulation through 'affective bodies' and 'affective practices', I have tried to ground this more closely in a notion of the phenomenal world as the space in which social relations emerge. This is similar to what the social psychologist Margaret Wetherell has described as attempts to put 'the visceral' in touch with 'the social' (2012: 11). Such an approach places an emphasis on bodies as always in process, with porous boundaries, defined by their capacity to affect and be affected. Hence the body becomes ontologically and quintessentially *relational*. The vocabulary and critical frameworks within this 'turn to affect' and interest in bodily experience come from various traditions within several fields, and Merleau-Ponty or Heidegger hardly provide all the starting points or definitive answers. For others in the field of philosophy or psychology, it has been just as constructive to orient their thinking to a range of contributions, from the seventeenth-century philosopher Baruch Spinoza and his adoption in Deleuzian philosophy, to telepathy and hypnosis in late nineteenth-century clinical practices (Ticineto Clough and Halley, 2007; Blackman and Walkerdine, 2001). While different, these vectors share an interest in the force of connections between bodies that reconfigure the idea of the singular and self-contained body while also examining its social and political impact.

Black British artworks lend themselves to similar concerns, through an exploration of the sensuous relationships that are mobilised between and among bodies. They show the need to engage with forms of perception that, while embodied, are not strictly located in or on the body. In this sense, 'the thing itself' that a phenomenological tradition aims to 'bracket out' in the pursuit of corporeal engagement before pre-existing knowledge becomes, in black British artworks, not only the 'material body' of sensual perception, but also the relational bodies that are produced and enacted in these bodily encounters. Like forms of proprioception and exteroception that qualify a bodily experience of the world, the body as a relational space is never static. It is composed of movements, twists, detours and deviations, as a space that moves with us. This motion is both an e-motion, a form of moving 'outside' (*ex-movo*) our bodies, and towards (*ad-movo*) other bodies. The space of movement is then one of kinaesthetic 'through-ness', at the limen between self and other, the material and the immaterial, the visible and the invisible.

The ontology of the body in movement, brought out so vividly by artists such as Sonia Khurana in her video and performance work, is thereby not one of self-boundedness and singularity. It has spillages and permeability. Its vocabulary pertains not to the realm of self-containment but to that of overflowing. It is a very useful basis to construct an ontology of relationality for black British art at large. The incarnated body of corporeal perception thus develops through reimagining incarnation without *carnis*, and here we should think of examples of embodied perception without physical flesh. Khurana's body, for instance, when mediated and fragmented through the video or projection screen, speaks through a language of excess and non-containment. Her body is often present through its absence. In expecting, looking for and mourning her body, the viewer gives it substance: this is 'reversibility' profoundly at work, with the viewer's role becoming primary. The consequence is that such a body is not *represented* by artworks, but *enacted* through them.

Black British art can be explored philosophically through these reorientations, projects that may benefit from a sustained focus on the forms that intercorporeal relationality may take. Such work interrogates the textures of embodied relationships that move beyond a traditional conception of body, before identifying spaces of encounter and trying to assimilate them. As viewers of this art confront the bodies of black British artists, they find that they are no longer contained in skin to be simply enumerated or identified according to markers of 'race' or ethnicity. Instead, through abandoning such categories and conceptions of the body, encounters with this art and these artists become e-motional – we escape (self-)containment, and move outside the body. Turning attention in this way to the body of the viewer through reversibility, this philosophy fundamentally rearranges the boundaries of black British art discourse, ultimately affecting, reorienting and reconfiguring its familiar landscape.

# Chapter 7

# Intertwining

If the notions of equivalence and reversibility have multiple implications for black British art, that is no more true of how this art can also demonstrate a surprising leap in the development of its ontological focus which this chapter explores in close detail. It is the sort of shift that is dealt with by Merleau-Ponty in the book that he was writing at the time of his death, *The Visible and the Invisible* (1964c: 222; 1968: 168). We have seen in various black British artists' attitudes to ontology a similar focus to that of Merleau-Ponty's early thinking, such as in *Phenomenology of Perception*, about how humans are placed in the world, and thus find ourselves being-in-the-world (*l'être au monde*), explicitly through perception and the body. Yet this thinking indicated the assumption of a consciousness–object relation, which was later thought to present certain impossibilities for ontological understanding: 'The problems posed in *Phenomenology of Perception* are insoluble because I start there from the "consciousness"–"object" distinction' (Merleau-Ponty, 1968: 200; 1964c: 253). The rigidity of that distinction takes the form of arguing for the presence of levels or norms within which our body operates in a 'field'; the way our body orients itself towards objects of perception; the way the body-subject operates in a 'pact' with the natural world.

This sense of being-in-the-world became familiar through black British artworks that show how the body acts upon the world through perception. Other works by these artists have more in common with how Merleau-Ponty radically revised this view, in an attempt to do justice to the way in which the body is more closely 'intertwined' with the world. The body is a thing among things, part of the world's fabric. Instead of seeing the body and the perceptual world and their interweaving as a system which comprises our world, therefore, it is vital to recognise the 'doubling up' (*dédoublement*, Merleau-Ponty, 1968: 139; 1964c: 280) of these several fields. Such fields take shape as 'brute or wild being' (*l'etre brut ou sauvage*), a sort of undifferentiated presence from which perception and consciousness emerge as a kind of 'rupture' (Moran, 2000: 428) – a 'deviation in a system of equivalences'. Merleau-Ponty's new overview, centred around this fact of 'intertwining', is a revision of his former sense of being-in-the-world. He described his later thinking as an 'indirect' ontology (Merleau-Ponty, 1968: 179, 233), with its claims that the various fields that humans establish indicate the ways we are possessed by or belong to Being (*l'être en est*) (Merleau-Ponty, 1964c: 136, 164, 314; 1968: 100, 123, 261). A focus on 'intertwining' suggests that we have a way of belonging to Being, yet without ever being able to differentiate fully between the overlapping fields of being in this 'wild' state, a 'never-finished differentiation' (Merleau-Ponty, 1968: 153; 1964c: 201). In short, we are 'enmeshed' in the 'flesh of the world':

> Where are we to put the limit between the body and the world, since the world is flesh? Where in the body are we to put the seer, since evidently there is in the body only 'shadows stuffed with organs,' that is, more of the visible? The world seen is not 'in' my body, and my body is not 'in' the visible world ultimately: as flesh applied to a flesh, the world neither surrounds it nor is surrounded by it … (Merleau-Ponty, 1968: 138)

Merleau-Ponty's aesthetics suggest that the ontological conditions of our being (as 'being-in-the-world') and the being of the world are in fact the same. The thing is a variant of myself, the latter being exemplary – and language, being the voice of no one, is, in a sense, 'the very voice of things, of the wave and the woods' (Merleau-Ponty, 1968: 155). To say that things have 'presence' is to say that they 'look at us', and that one self-same visibility is 'sometimes wandering and sometimes reassembled' (Merleau-Ponty, 1968: 137–138). Merleau-Ponty quotes the biographer André Marchand's comments, after those of Paul Klee, that:

> In a forest, I have felt many times over that it was not I who looked at the forest. Some days I felt that the trees were looking at me, were speaking to me … I was there, listening … I think that the painter must be penetrated by the universe and not want to penetrate it … I expect to be inwardly submerged, buried. Perhaps I paint to break out. (1993b: 129)

What appears perhaps to be more a feature of Merleau-Ponty's flamboyant style than a serious proposition is in fact central to his extensively argued thesis of reversibility (Dillon, 1988: 48). The idea re-emerges with a new gravity in his posthumously published work, as the notion that 'the seer and the visible reciprocate one another and we no longer know which sees and which is seen' (Merleau-Ponty, 1968: 139).

## Animated and talking presence

The relationship of reciprocity shows up with particular force through Mona Hatoum's play with the curiosity of human hair and furniture. She has presented to audiences a black metal chair, made from a sheet of wrought iron drilled with hundreds of holes, its seat section supporting a triangular field of curling mouse-brown hair. This is *Jardin Public* (1993, fig. 39), a patch of pubic hair offered on a flat metallic seat. The chair has design: a loose scrolling of wrought-iron bands and rings, in gentle curves; typical and familiar. As with any chair, perhaps, we acquire habitual familiarity with it as a functional object, come to know (and then take for granted) its main dimensions through use. The chair remains part of what Merleau-Ponty has called our 'familiar domain … as long as I have "in my hands" or "in my legs" the main distances and directions involved, and as long as from my body intentional threads run out towards it' (1968: 130). Hatoum's own hair is placed at the very point where the viewer might normally be inclined to sit. At this 'private' part of the seat – now on 'public' display – the viewer and chair undergo an 'intentional' drawing together. But the habitual action of being accommodated by furniture is here made unfamiliar, as its neatly threaded pubic tangle breaks with our habits of sitting. Moreover, this hair-out-of-place – Hatoum's *exuviae* – serves to animate its metallic support. The chair becomes hard and hairy, metallic yet organic; it stands as we sit, sits as we stand. We have not simply become a seer caught up in what is seen: in a relation of reversibility in which 'I feel myself looked at by the things' (Merleau-Ponty, 1968: 139), this is art that has moved over into *being another being*. It sets forward discontinuities in our expectations of its thingly-ness to become an animated presence.

Accordingly, what we should be searching for across all the works by black British artists is not bodies or body parts, but a perceptual relationship of reciprocation or intertwining instantiated through encounters with the work. This does not mean accepting the literal sense in which, as Hans Belting outlines its special history, 'The image … not only represented a person but also was treated like a person, being worshipped, despised or carried from place to place in ritual processions' (1994: xxi). Rather, it is to follow the more profound implications for understanding black British subjects who are engaged with the visible,

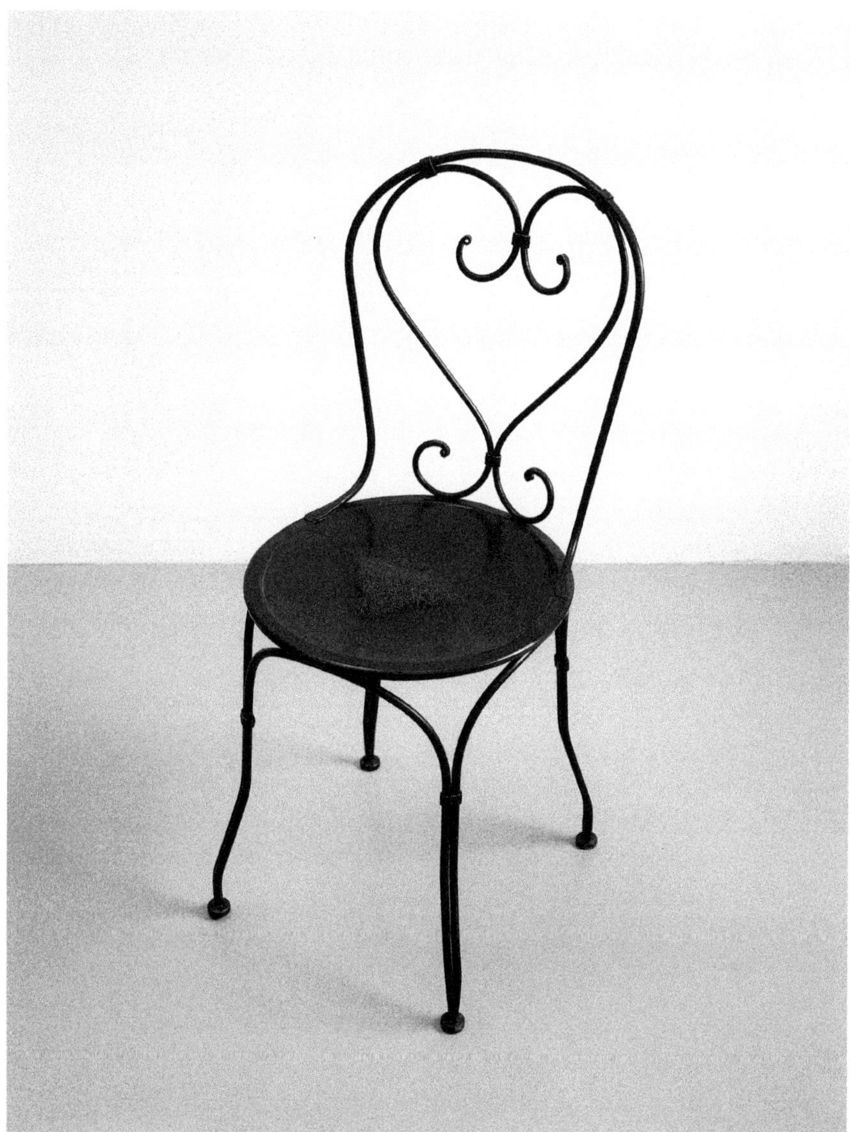

Figure 39: Mona Hatoum, *Jardin Public*, 1993, painted wrought iron, wax and pubic hair, 89 x 40 x 49 cm. © Mona Hatoum. Photo © Edward Woodman. Courtesy White Cube.

as suggested in Merleau-Ponty's exploration of seeing. It is an exploration that brings us closer to recognising the intertwining of black British artists with other subjects through their art-making. In their artworks, both being seen and feeling visible – through self-portraiture, through performance – must then be about a showing of oneself and a seeing of oneself within the world. But since that world is always at the same time a political world, its formations and differences have impacted directly on black British artists' attitudes to art-making and towards themselves. Conceiving that relation phenomenologically can disclose how the artist examining the world inescapably sets up her or his own presence there. While the critical aspects of subjectivity pertain to significations of presence and subjectivity in the field of cultural representation, the phenomenal basis of presence is no less situated.

The point is illustrated succinctly in Sonia Boyce's *Talking Presence* (fig. 40). Here is a certain grounding of two figures, one female and the other male, within an architectural pastiche of an urban landscape, recognisable as London. The woman's gaze scans the built space, while the male gaze rests upon her. There is a surveying of a world in those gazes, which look out from flesh – their corporeal frames – on to a 'flesh' of the city form. The city is in reassembled pieces, and the night sky sketched across with winking stars. We are shown through this London in its piecemeal condition that what is perceptible of any city is always partial, always the result of a 'rupture', and yet never actually felt as anything but whole. The reciprocation of gazes, cast back from this fleshly city, is conspicuous to the figures. That reciprocity is inescapably felt: for both the female and male seer, 'the vision he exercises, he also undergoes from the things, such that, as many painters have said, I feel myself looked at by the things' (Merleau-Ponty, 1968: 139). The drawn figures thereby exercise a vision that they also undergo from the things they see. What is more, 'since the seer is caught up in what he sees, it is still himself he sees' (Merleau-Ponty, 1968: 139).

There is an established way of 'reading' works by black British artists as a critical assertion of presence, through the repeated interest in self-picturing and identification through the black body. In Boyce's drawing, that black presence is given a place within Britain's capital city. The work suggests the need for a resetting of expectations in the style of an intervention; it frames or houses black figures in an urban setting where their social and cultural importance and belonging are often contested by the spatial imagination of contemporary racism which makes black subjects seem strange and unwanted. The work offers a

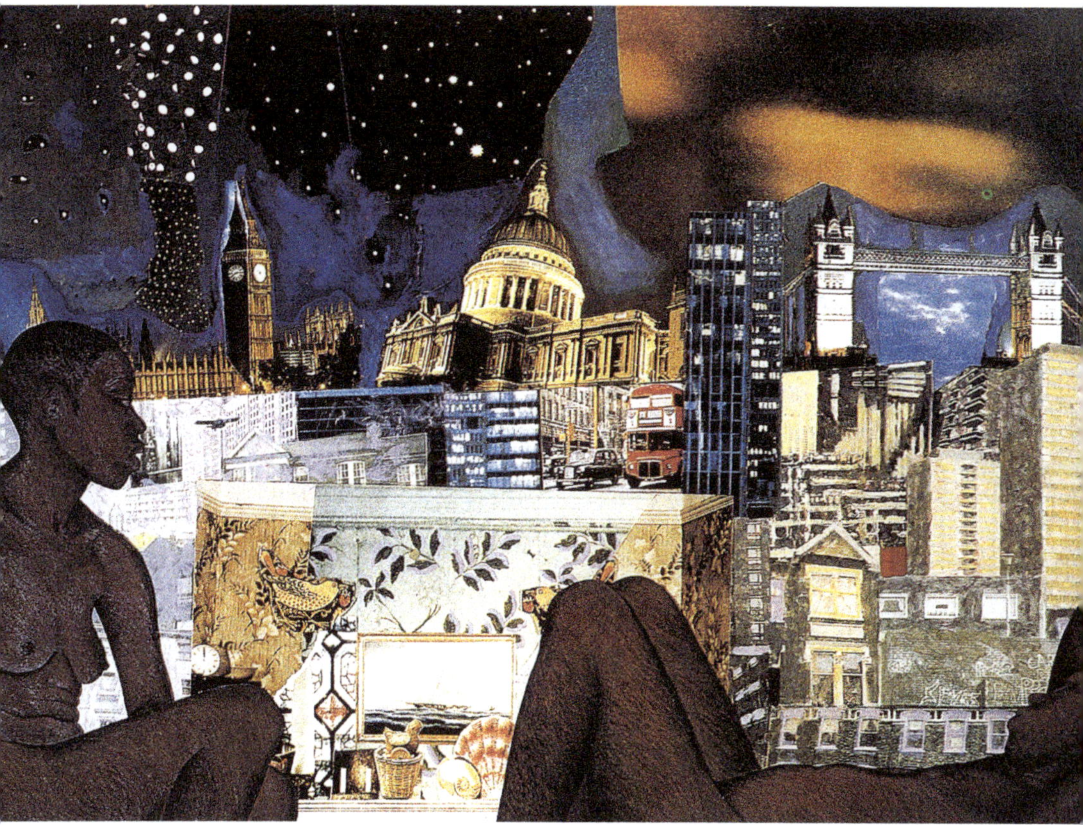

Figure 40: Sonia Boyce, *Talking Presence*, 1988, mixed media on photographic paper, 165 x 122 cm. © Sonia Boyce. All Rights Reserved, DACS 2016.

sign of resistance, housing those subjects as an enunciating, 'talking' presence, speaking for themselves rather than being spoken for or about.

The point of returning to this issue via phenomenology should now have become clear, since enlarging on the perceptual dimension of anti-racist politics has a transformative effect. The reversibility of glances and the intertwining of the art object with its viewers are phenomenal aspects of experience which reassign value to the practices of constructing and asserting cultural difference. The 'talking presence' of Boyce's figures in their social world is a form of witnessing and a scene of phenomenal difference: the artwork sets up a world of difference in which to resist the ethnicising of figures, the projection of expectations on to black and gendered bodies.

By insisting on the primacy of perceptual presence when encountering black British artworks, their important existential locus becomes more obvious. They can best be seen as both discursive and phenomenal at the same time through examples of figurality, and by treading a path between attention to art's status within textual fields of representation and a broader aesthetic domain that exceeds the practice of visual reading. This recalls Jean-François Lyotard's sophisticated work on the figural in his celebrated essay 'Discours, figure' (1993). As David Rodowick summarises it neatly: 'The figural … is not primarily a montage or chiasmus between the said and the seen … It is a third dimension, neither sayable nor showable' (2001: 12). Ultimately this suggests that a phenomenology of black British art is above all a critique of the concept of the cultural itself, by identifying an alternative basis for the cultural through an intertwined figurality.

## Intertwining critical and phenomenal relations

Black British art is distinctive for offering a special case in which artists have engaged carefully with some compelling perspectives on the cultural politics of difference, finding within them their own individual responses to the recommended critical means to make sense of the place of creativity in contemporary Britain. Above all, compelling accounts of black visual culture have specified the social value of artworks by unpacking their role within processes of codification that map uneasily on to the classic accounts of ideology, emphasising how cultural meanings are always contingent upon fields of representation. This is crucial for seeing how black British artists have negotiated and resisted dominant meanings through strategies of visual production, engaging models of semiotics that show how artists come to appropriate systems of signification in an effort to bring about change and take on agency.

Evidence of struggle through visual practices is abundant in such a setting. This is a fought-over field of sign-based meaning, where artists have sought an impact on the very visual language of contemporary 'Britishness', 'blackness' and difference. When artists examine ethnicity and 'race' through material signs, sites such as the black body, gender and sexuality provide the means to disrupt the visual conventions that give them meaning. This impulse to affect and alter the social contexts of these codes is an inherently political act, even if it emerges in ways that do not always conform to an everyday sense of the political. Indeed, black British artists have repeatedly undermined the dominant terms for evaluating culture as an aesthetic realm outside the political. Central to their politics of representation is the idea of visual-making as a site of self-construction: creative acts that make possible the formation of identities, feelings of belonging, notions of community and cultural specificity. More importantly, perhaps, black British artists have also striven to overcome social practices of 'othering', the particular ways in which the visual is implicated in the complex constructing of self and other according to indexes of difference which may seem fixed but can nonetheless always be resisted. This extends to showing how gender difference and sexuality can usefully complicate expectations about cultural difference by adding a vital tension and critical depth to art that foregrounds a thoroughgoing contestation over cultural practices of looking and expression.

More specifically, black British art urges consideration of our subjective, corporeal relationship with vision by virtue of artists' frequent focus on the body and their insistence that it provides a key site for cultural signification. In doing so, they link art practices to the cultural field at large; bridging art discourse and more everyday and habitual settings. I have touched upon how theoretical ideas about diaspora culture have been reassigned to actual artworks. A 'diaspora aesthetic' has been claimed for black British art that combines cultural codes from several cultural 'locations' and indeed geographical areas (such as Africa, Asia and the Caribbean), articulating them in a notably hybrid way.

Such cultural practices are acts of 'encoding' (Hall, 1980b) and of 'identification' (Mercer, 1994) in a particular sense: they are a dynamic and hybrid gathering and 'syncretising' of disparate elements. Generating cultural values through this kind of art practice has involved visual references to artists' individual and group identities; the production of narratives about personal and historical pasts, explored in Chapter 3; and 'narratives of displacement' that emerge through attachment to the past – as pointed out by Hall (1990), in his thoughts on how diaspora subjects face the impossibility of a 'return to the beginning', of origins. Such diaspora identities cannot be reduced to their 'Africanness' or 'Asianness', for example, and the art practices that assist in imagining community and identity are exemplary of how visual representations can be instrumental for constituting a sense of belonging and commonality.

Questioning the consequences of this characteristically post-structuralist formulation of art in black Britain needs to be done with extreme care. While I have directed attention away from the models of signification and textuality that cohere in the salient accounts of black visual culture and representation, it would be quite wrong to assume that black British art exists entirely independently of such a framework, or else that this art has a somehow antagonistic relationship to theoretical discourse.

Indeed, it would be fruitless to try to disavow such a relation, even in the course of exposing the shortcomings of the established view. There are contextually justified reasons for discourses on black British art to hold on to their founding critical paradigms, and the sophistication and motivations of their proponents should not be traduced through philosophical examination. Moreover, the discursive category of 'black British art' has helped to accord greater public attention to its artists. This is a wide political economy of contemporary art in which artists have benefitted from the theoretical architecture of the commentary they have attracted, while contributing heavily to forming the perspectives and conclusions carried there. Yet the same artists have also encountered the limits of black cultural theory, and its terms of description have brought mixed results.

The 'phenomenal difference' found in operation through these artworks is a possible way out of this paradox, renewing intellectual interest in black British artworks in a more philosophical register. There has been a stubborn tendency in the academy, and in public art curating and cultural policy, to separate and marginalise artists through the appropriation of the very same analytical categories that black cultural criticism has promulgated. Obviously, black British artists and their commentators have felt unhappy about this convergence, and there is a larger history to be written of their gains and losses as a community, the ways in which they and their works, their historical struggles and their success, have been translated and to an extent circumscribed through public and academic interest. Evidently it is not desirable to see cultural studies and art history as disciplines at odds with one another, therefore, but as capable of occupying shared ground, with opportunities and shortcomings that apply to each in their various attentions to black British art.

Granting attention to the phenomenal presence of black British art is at the same time a step away from the much-furrowed ground of debate on how scholarship can best serve black British artists – questions about how writing may do justice to their history and expand the opportunities or traverse the limits that they face in the wider landscape of contemporary art. Indeed, that phenomenology offers no formal method of writing whatsoever seems to make it distinctive and is its strength. When accounting ontologically for black British art, it is necessary to elucidate how such cultural objects exist as an affective origin, how they are the material foundation for the construction and conveyance of meaning. The phenomenal presence of such art forms the ground for what might follow of their social importance. The effectiveness of black British art as a field of representation – *as significant of* black or diaspora culture – is only possible at all by virtue of its material foundation.

Overall, concerns about effectiveness need to give way more precisely to those regarding affectivity. A range of recent studies in the social sciences have foregrounded the social importance of materiality in a very similar way. Anthropologists such as Elizabeth Edwards have claimed that 'it is materiality, the physical nature of the photograph that allows the representational quality of photographs to function' (Edwards, 2001: 16; Edwards and Lien, 2014). Beyond photography, there is an entire spectrum of vocal utterances, scriptural enunciation, graphic statement and digital communication – a myriad of ways to 'make sense' – which are mutually entwined with the world of the senses. The starting point for my own account of materiality is staked out on that phenomenological territory and is more strictly Merleau-Pontian. It traces the productive possibilities for relations between the phenomenal and the representational while accounting for the materiality of difference through a review of early twentieth-century thought. It is also worth recalling Walter Benjamin's writing on the 'medium of perception' and 'perceptibility', which can be drawn out from his better-known observations on 'the aura'. Benjamin wrote that:

> Experience of the aura … arises from the transposition of a response characteristic of human society to the relationship of the inanimate or nature with human beings. The person we look at, or who feels s/he is being looked at, looks at us in turn. To experience the aura of a phenomenon we look at means to invest it with the ability to look back at us. (1968; see also Hansen, 2008)

Such an insight from Benjamin may help in understanding how foundational philosophies of essence and origin can bear upon more critically engaged accounts of cultural life – how far black British art objects come to have agency through their visual affectivity. Obviously, at a glance, this would seem to recapitulate upon a commonplace idea that is already well known: art objects are phenomenally apparent. But this view ceased to be accepted as soon as theoreticians surveying this field became intent on disentangling and explaining black artists' works as if they were visual texts or linguistic 'signs' alone.

We need to stress anew the primacy of perception in the agency of black artworks, and that social importance always relies on an intimate relationship with perception. Emphasising such features as equivalence, intertwining and the corporeality that they enable should then ensure that the relatedness of seer and seen is conceived to be fundamentally perceptual (Smith, 1993). Relatedness is particularly strongly exemplified in the idea of reversibility, and certain diaspora artists' works meditate upon this directly. 'Reversibility' (Merleau-Ponty, 1968), or the *Fundierung* after Husserl, are terms to describe a reciprocal founding–founded relationship which stems from attention to the notion of figure and ground that characterises Gestalt psychology (Merleau-Ponty, 1968; Dillon, 1988: 52). Merleau-Ponty's thesis of reversibility, with its beginnings in his *Phenomenology of Perception*, suggests that things can be said to 'perceive' me inasmuch as I am perceptible from the positions they occupy. A trace of that view is carried into one of his short essays, 'Eye and Mind', with the claim that there is a metaphorical sense in which the things I see also 'see' me (Merleau-Ponty, 1993b: 167). The philosopher's full thesis on this only emerges with his later idea that 'the seer and the visible reciprocate one another and we no longer know which sees and which is seen' (Merleau-Ponty, 1968: 139).

We have seen how such an insight has relevance for black British artworks, in particular how the idea of reversibility marks an attempt to purge thought of dualistic categories. It recasts the traditional disjunction between perceiver and perceived in an attempt to understand differences between seer and seen within the framework of a genuinely phenomenological ontology. In attempting to point the way for that ontological analysis of artworks in Britain, such works prompt an alternative consideration of the relationship between perceiver and perceived, the body as sensing and the body as sensed, and between the phenomenal body and other worldly phenomena.

The manipulation of visual materials assists black British artists in contributing to the art environment that they share. The notion of articulation, in which distinct elements interact in a moment of temporary unity, or 'conjunction' (Hall, 1980c; 2006; Grossberg, 1996; Du Gay et al., 1997), would seem constructive in showing how this happens through representational practices in a way that is always contingent and contextual.[1] But such an approach only goes so far in explaining

---

1  Hall remarks on articulation: 'In England, the term has a nice double meaning because "articulate" means to utter, to speak forth, to be articulate. It carries that

how artworks allow such acts of articulation, and why art-making is the chosen practice for certain black British individuals in the first place. Where the overlap lies is in the question of how aesthetic concerns have a role in constituting artists as active subjects.

A phenomenological attitude to inquiry comes considerably closer to pinning this down. It elaborates the relationships of intimacy that pertain through this art, drawing together artists, audiences and artworks. Such active articulation through art-making is something like Heidegger's notion of the origin of the artist, who actually appears *in* the work of art, but of course not always in any simply self-referential way (such as through portraiture). Such a view suggests that making works of art is part of the skilled cultural navigation necessary for black British artists to take up positions within the (art) world and its discursive spaces of aesthetic value. In turn, the fundamental situatedness of the art object can be identified through its relationship with the being of its artist. This relationship also always operates in reverse: the being of the artist (Heideggerian 'Being') is characterised by directedness and actions in the world.

This sort of ontological interest in perception can have a bearing on the idea set out by Stuart Hall and others that culture is largely characterised by acts of articulation as social action, leading to variable and contingent outcomes (Hall, 1980c; Grossberg, 1996). Attention to the phenomenal lends definition to Hall's cultural contextualism by enlarging upon the idea of a material ground that offers the context for contingency: the primacy of perceptual and bodily relationships which are existentially open-ended and ambiguous yet always situated in a world. Indeed, a more radical way of thinking about the articulation of subjectivity for black British artists is through the idea of intertwining, since it offers a sense of how the bodies of artists, their objects and those who apprehend them enter into relations primarily through perception.

sense of language-ing, of expressing, etc. But we also speak of an "articulated" lorry (truck): a lorry where the front (cab) and back (trailer) can, but need not necessarily, be connected to one another. The two parts are connected to one another, but through a specific linkage, that can be broken. An articulation is thus the form of a connection that *can* make a unity of two different elements, under certain conditions. It is a linkage which is not necessary, determined, absolute and essential for all time. You have to ask, under what circumstances *can* a connection be forged or made? So the so-called "unity" of discourse is really the articulation of different, distinct elements which can be re-articulated in different ways because they have no necessary "belong-ingness"' (Grossberg, 1996: 141).

Emphasising the phenomenological importance of black artists' objects requires recognition of the inseparability of self and world. We are inserted into the world through the body with its range of perceptual acts, its movements and expressions. The intimate relations of body and world take place in an 'interworld', where body meets lived environment and is confronted by it, as flesh meeting with flesh, as Merleau-Ponty argues (1968). This intimacy and intertwining of 'the flesh of the world' is something that black British artworks urge us to consider as they bring to the fore the entire question of how bodies relate to one another through lived space. Material phenomena are the very fabric of our interaction with the world and the application of the concept of reversibility (Merleau-Ponty, 1968; Dillon, 1988: 52) to black British art throws light on it as a context of visual representation that is always also the setting for reciprocal founding–founded relationships.

## Presence and historicality

It is clear that phenomenology has a particular usefulness for grasping how black British artists' visual representations are grounded and made material. The idea of intertwining brings to light a corporeal relationship with the construction of meaning and representation, and in the process it can elevate our understanding of the agency of artworks and artists. It has been shown that the historicality of these artists can be conceived in terms of the regimes of representation that they develop (Bailey and Hall, 1992b). But it is worth recalling that such regimes have a visuality and tactility, indeed an ontological peculiarity. Aesthetic production both draws on historical materials and offers an origin for phenomenal experiences that exceed the representational. Accordingly, through philosophical analysis we can do away with certain theoretical distinctions that have prefigured and underlain much existing thought on the field of black British art, for example the putative division between visual form and content, between style and subject matter, between material and context. Such a language of distinctions is precisely what a consideration of ideas such as reversibility and intertwining discourages and can ultimately overcome. They promote instead the very fundamental relatedness of seer and seen (Dillon, 1988: 148) and replace the disjunction of subject and object with a relationship of communion and reciprocity.

These are the more layered ways in which artworks assist in intertwining sites of difference, bringing together bodies, materials and the imagination, much as Edouard Glissant has identified in his 'poetics of relation' (1997), yet assisted by perceptual phenomenology. I raise Glissant's contribution here in view of my running discussion about how to parse such a relation between postcolonial identity and the phenomenal world. His thought complicates both critical accounts of black subjectivity and the attempts in anthropology to specify the affectivity of art in the social realm (for instance, the notion of 'enchantment' put forward by Alfred Gell, 1992; cf. Bennett, 2001). As such, he is part of a wider debate on the 'new materialism' in which art objects are neither part of language nor constitute an alternative language (Fuglerud and Wainwright, 2015: 3). Nearly 20 years ago, Gell triggered such interest when he wrote about feeling 'anxious to avoid the slightest imputation that (visual) art is "language-like" and that the relevant forms of semiosis are language-like' (1998: 14). At the same time, Glissant shows the need to attend to the *incorporeal* traits of expression within the cultural legacy of diaspora, for instance reminding us that diaspora subjects continue to negotiate 'the haunting force of slavery and colonization as a memory formation that is not always materially present' (Hantel, 2012: 38).

Such traits underline the urgency of scrutinising the politics of language surrounding art, and to set it in relation to art's phenomenal status. This does not mean that analysis should drop the linguistic altogether (indeed, how could it?), but that we should opt to bring all of these elements together to better understand the presence and historicality of black British art and artists. This would intertwine each of the available approaches, steered by a phenomenological attitude that could help to conceive of the meeting place and meaning of black British art, as we try to appreciate it in all its contingency by opening our analytic senses and sensitivities to aesthetic ambiguity and to art's relational poetics. It is crucial to tackle these various dimensions of black British art simultaneously. Such a philosophical mode of inquiry, alive to the processes of reciprocity at work in this art, can in turn promote awareness of the communion of artists and ourselves as viewers at the place of artworks. This ontology deepens the rendering of black British artworks as belonging to a cultural field, but goes further in specifying philosophically *how* this art is so experientially effective in setting up such a communally intertwined world.

# Chapter 8

# Art and mediation

As any student of visual communication could easily point out, works of art are much like forms of media. They behave like media when they communicate and signify, when their visual status seems simultaneously to be linguistic, textually codifying and representational. In the last decades of the twentieth century, the art made by black British artists was particularly apt to be seen in this way. The view was promoted in stark terms by writers such as Kobena Mercer, who emphasised the meanings 'inscribed in the artistic text of the black diaspora', and employed a vocabulary drawn from the 'philosophy of language' that is shared with the study of media and communications.[1] On that framework, artworks seem to offer evidence of the experience of migration and displacement, the desire and struggle for cultural continuity and community, and the crisis of belonging and of 'exile', which are all associated with conditions of diaspora. All told, choosing to treat this art as a form of media served to locate it centrally in a black and diasporic cultural milieu.

This chapter explores further the implications of seeing black British art within the category of media, the intellectual gamble of doing so being set against the yield brought by cultural identification and more specifically, how a philosophy of this art can make use of 'mediation' as an analytical construct. It is important to understand why images and objects made by black British artists have been regarded as media, and at the same time much can be gained from problematising the claim made for seeing or 'reading' this or any artwork as media.

Art and media show some clearly definable similarities, but they also have differences, so that marrying up the two needs to be done with care, with disclaimers, with qualification. Black British art, indeed, has come

---

1  As Mercer explains: 'The philosophy of language … provides an analytical vocabulary which can be reused for "making sense" of the struggles of the sign inscribed in the artistic text of the black diaspora' (1994: 254–255).

close to being 'de-authorised' through its conflation with the more flatly discursive processes of mediating and codifying the constructs of 'race', ethnicity, identity and cultural difference. There are clear dangers of casting this art as nothing more than a practice or site of mediation for responding to dominant regimes of representation. In the process, black British artists are denied the individuated status so taken for granted by creative artists at large, denied their creative agency and sovereignty. During the 1980s, it was pointed out that the racist discourse that such artists endured tried to associate blackness 'with the derivative and provincial, lacking credibility or status' (Roberts, 1987: 59). There was a search at that time for an appropriate terminology to name black British art, in a debate over its labelling and identification. But there was far less scrutiny of the growing convention to conceptualise such art as a medium in a play of signifiers and visually textual practices that linked blackness and diaspora culture to the wider political economy of representation.

If the habit of applying the same paradigm of mediation to accounts of black British art has persisted into the present, then it is worth perhaps evaluating its implications for philosophy for the first time. While the notion that art is simply another form of media may indeed be a constructive one for the philosophy of language (reminding thinkers in that field not to neglect art), for black British artists in particular it does present some difficulties. Not least of these is that the conventions of talking about black British art in those terms have become so accepted as to seem uncontroversial. Black British artists share with their more progressive peers in the field of contemporary art the motivation to critically question pre-formulated models for making art. After all, that is their basic starting point, if not their right. Yet when black British art is framed by a theory of mediation, a curious exception and indeed an intellectual exclusion seems to have been made on its behalf. The currently prevailing style of thinking about black British art is haunted by that spectre of unspoken intellectual values. In what follows, I will demonstrate why this is so, and how this can become a pressing scene of inquiry and of struggle, to which philosophical work may contribute.

## Showing signs of alienation

How does the concept of 'art as media' trouble contemporary art's potential for transcending the boundaries of culturalist, ethnic and racial classification? A touring exhibition that moved between London, Manchester and Norwich during 2006–07 provided an opportunity to consider this question by showing that art and media are both entwined and at the same time still separable. Entitled *Alien Nation*,[2] the exhibition explored the relationship between the interests of certain artists who were grouped together for the purpose of the display, along with certain images drawn from films. It included clips of sequences from popular movies, and the advertising posters that had accompanied them when they were initially released during the 1950s and 1960s in cinemas across the Anglophone world. In marketing the show, its promoters adapted the original poster used for US distribution of the 1956 film *Invasion of the Body Snatchers* (fig. 41). Styled as a movie billing, it listed the names of the 12 participating artists and three curators against a blood-orange ground on which an aquatint of two figures – a startled couple seen frontally in period dress – were fleeing crowds of crazed, perhaps cannibalistic pursuers.

*Alien Nation* collected examples of film and art in order to take a critical stance on the contribution of image-making to the ways in which outsiders, aliens and racial others have been imagined. By tackling the proximity of visual culture to everyday practices of social and cultural alienation, it offered a transparently provocative case for asking about the historical roots of current global fear and insecurity. The exhibition drew together diverse strands of the filmic and the 'foreign', the visual and the spectral – including sculpture, photography, painting, multimedia installation – in which artists, as described by its curators, 'adopted the figure of the extraterrestrial and the alien(ated) landscape in order to comment upon the fantasies, fears and desires that lie, barely suppressed, beneath the surface of contemporary culture and society' (Gill et al., 2006: 11). To employ a vaguely cinematic metaphor, the exhibition was a sudden jerk out of the comfy seat from which Western subjects have watched ethnic and racial differencing on the silver screen. It seemed designed to make visitors spill the fizzy drinks of critical analysis on to the velour cushions of the hegemonic visual culture. Certainly it helped with thinking through some of the implications for artists of twentieth-century cultural

2   The exhibition *Alien Nation* was curated by John Gill, Jens Hoffmann and Gilane Tawadros for the Institute of Contemporary Arts and Institute of International Visual Art (ICA/Iniva), staged at ICA London, 17 November 2006–14 January 2007, Manchester Art Gallery, 17 March–7 May 2007, and Sainsbury Centre for Visual Arts Norwich, 2 October–9 December 2007. Participating artists included Laylah Ali, Hamad Butt, Ellen Gallagher and Edgar Cleijne, David Huffman, Hew Locke, Marepe, Henna Nadeem, Kori Newkirk, Yinka Shonibare MBE, Eric Wesley and Mario Ybarra Jr.

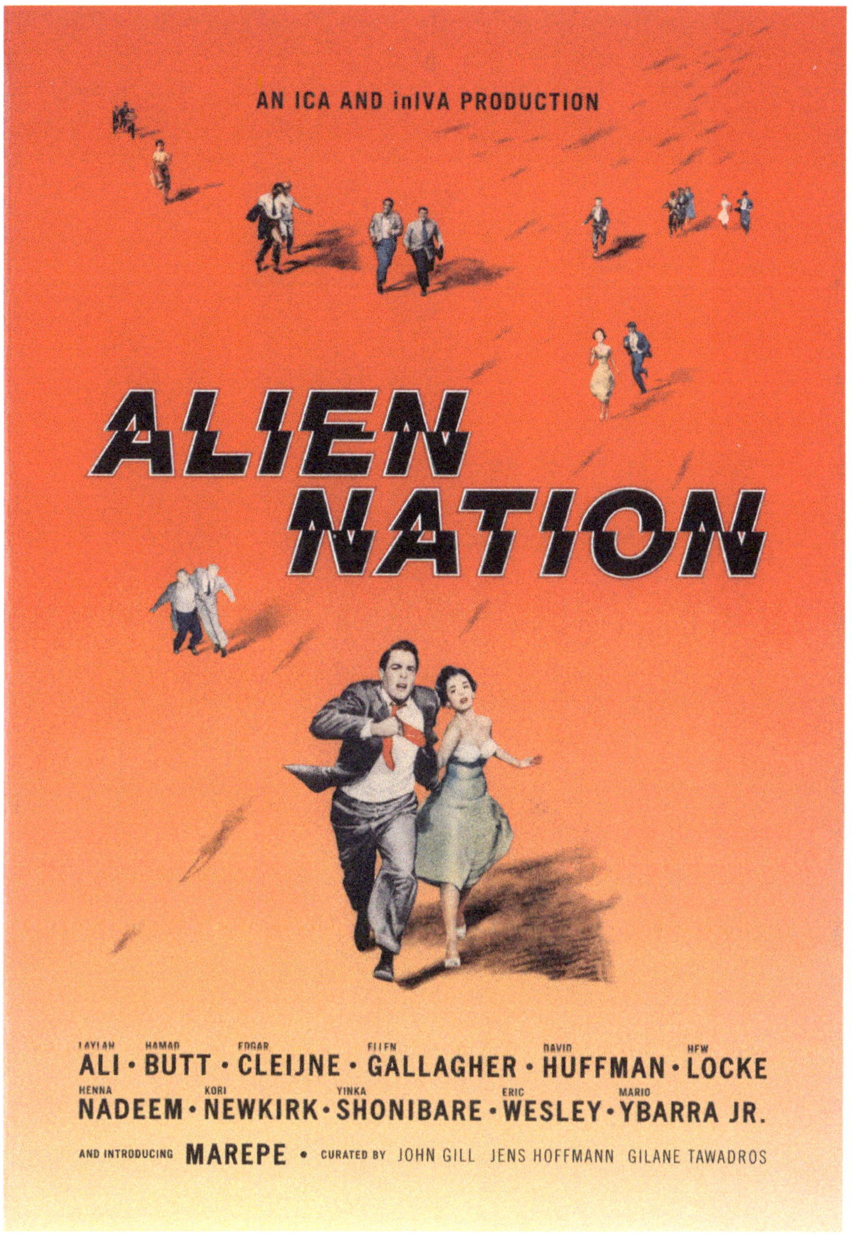


Figure 41: *Alien Nation*, cover of the exhibition catalogue, 2006. ICA/inIVA publication.

narratives and pictorial traditions of differencing, and the way they have evolved into the present.

When looking at the circumstances in which *Alien Nation* was staged, it is worth recalling the historical nature of a widely taken choice to consider art and media as occupying an identical sphere of attention. As touched upon in Chapter 1, notions such as 're-presentation', deliberately hyphenated, announced the processual nature of media practices through an analogy to language:

> Re-presentation is a very different notion from that of reflection. It implies the active work of selecting and presenting, of structuring and shaping; not merely the transmitting of an already-existing meaning, but more the active labour of *making things mean*. (Hall, 1982: 64)

In the context of first- and second-generation African, Asian and Caribbean artists in Britain, during the 1980s moment of considering the politics of identities, many artists appeared to benefit from embracing a notion of art as eminently readable, an understanding that art is much the same as the other cultural texts that are the subject of analysis for media studies. Yet two decades later the exhibition *Alien Nation* pointed to a shift away from that approach. It emphasised the notion of art as media but within the bounds of a markedly different curatorial rationale, and with the complicity of artists from within and without a black British identification.

An artist whose work was given a room of its own in the *Alien Nation* exhibition is Hew Locke. Locke grew up in Guyana, a country that lies in both the Caribbean and South America, and settled in Britain in his late teens, where he began his career as an artist. Focusing on sculpture, his works have often been in temporary or vulnerable forms and on a large scale. At London's Brunei Gallery, at East International, Norwich, and more prominently in the entrance hall of the Victoria and Albert Museum (fig. 42), he worked with cardboard and black-and-white poster paint to create shapes that were specific to their venues.[3] Built on wooden frames that are clearly visible from their basic supports, these sprawled and appeared to sail across the floors of these various spaces, seeming to push apart columns as they went. Such early work by Locke

---

3   These works by Locke first appeared in *Routes: Five Artists from Four Continents* at the Brunei Gallery, London (22 January–26 March, 1999), the Victoria and Albert Museum (1999) and East International, Norwich (2000). See also Marsden and Robinson (2005).

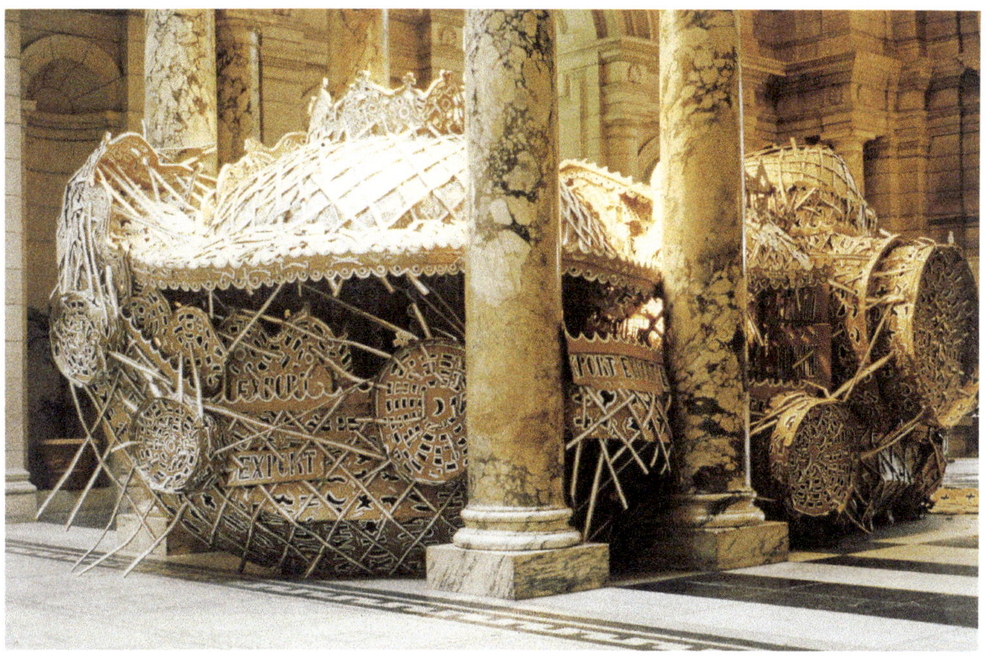

Figure 42: Hew Locke, *Hemmed in Two* (Victoria and Albert Museum version), 2000, cardboard, acrylic, marker pen, wood, found objects, height 4 m, length 7.5 m, width 6 m. Photo by the artist. © Hew Locke. All rights reserved, DACS 2016.

drew attention to a history of transport and travel, and considered the role of ships in communicating across the Atlantic Ocean. Curators would try to explain this focus of interest by way of his upbringing in Guyana, with its long history of plantation slavery. These ship shapes were emblazoned with the single word 'EXPORT' and remembered the human cargo vessels that forcibly transported Africans to the Americas. A further reference was to the production of goods such as sugar, cocoa, tobacco and cotton, carried across the Atlantic for consumption in European and North Atlantic metropolitan markets.

Locke's contribution to *Alien Nation* was an innovation on these hulking cardboard vessels made from discarded materials. His installed works of assemblage exploited the tactics of 're-presenting' found objects: mass-produced plastic toys, dolls and animals, artificial flowers, beads, decorations and so on. With these the artist built up the surface decoration of a fleet of battleships or spaceships entitled *Golden Horde*

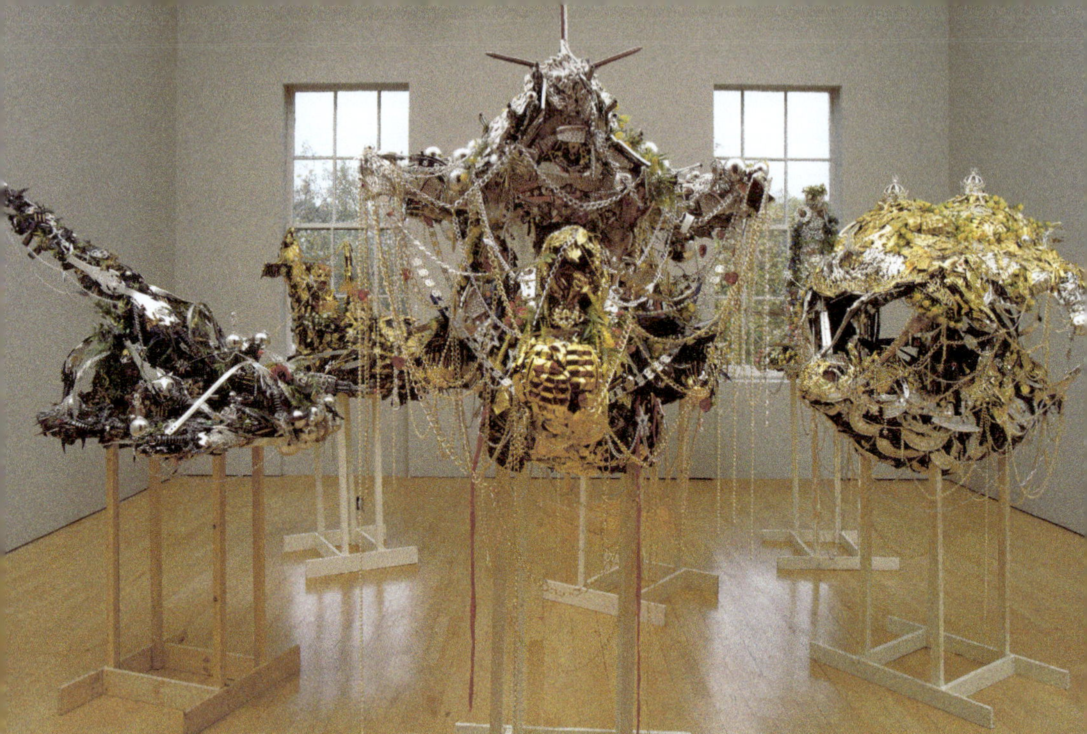

Figure 43: Hew Locke, *Golden Horde*, 2006, mixed media including plastic, metal, textile and wood, maximum height 273 cm, length 253 cm, width 200 cm. Photo: Marcus Leith. © Hew Locke. All rights reserved, DACS 2016.

(fig. 43), in reference to the Mongol forces that dominated much of Central Asia during the mid-thirteenth to fourteenth century. Viewers familiar with his continuing interest in ships can interpret *Golden Horde* as high-tech vessels sent to protect trade, tasked with military incursion and territorial expansion. In contrast with the freight vessels, this work was set on narrow upright pedestals, and elevated as if to suggest flight, appearing to hover against the gallery floors and walls. They seem also to suggest Sir Francis Drake's *Golden Hind* (originally called the *Pelican*), the first British ship to be navigated around the globe, while plundering indigenous and Spanish territories in the Caribbean and South America: 'the Golden Hind returning with her round flanks full of treasure … what greatness had not floated on the ebb of that river … the seed of commonwealth, the germs of empires', Joseph Conrad wrote in 1899 (2007: 5). This connotation is lent weight by the assortment of children's toy weapons and the polished plastic armour that provides a casing or shell for Locke's series of sculptures, suggesting a battalion prepared for attack, armed to the teeth with (albeit harmless) plastic machine guns. A six-piece fleet manned by luminous reptiles and dirty-faced dolls

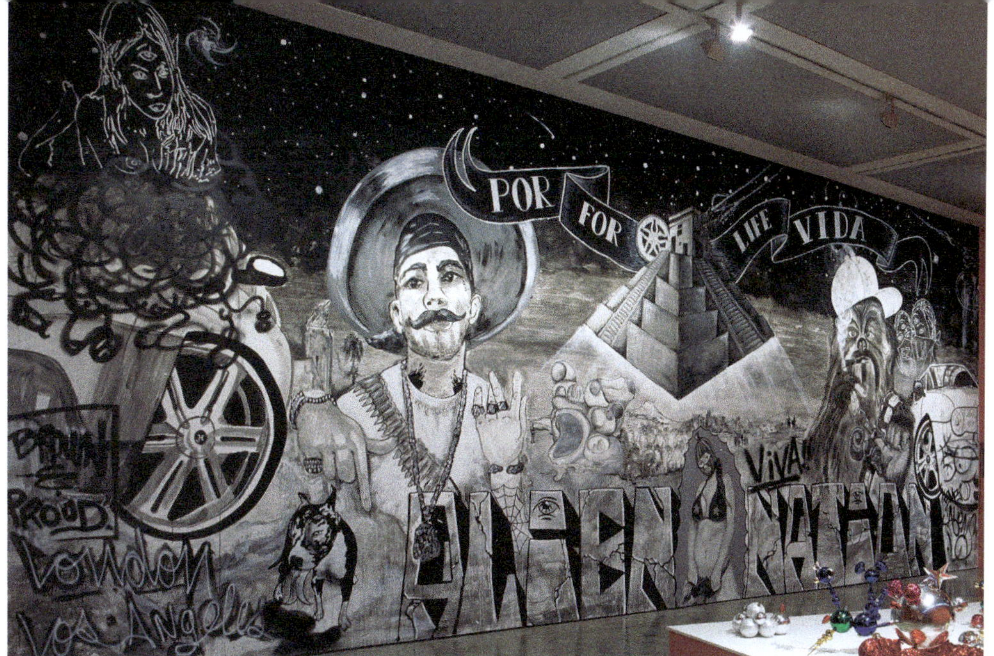


Figure 44: Mario Ybarra Jr, *Brown and Proud*, 2006, mixed media. Photo: Marcus Leith. Image used with permission.

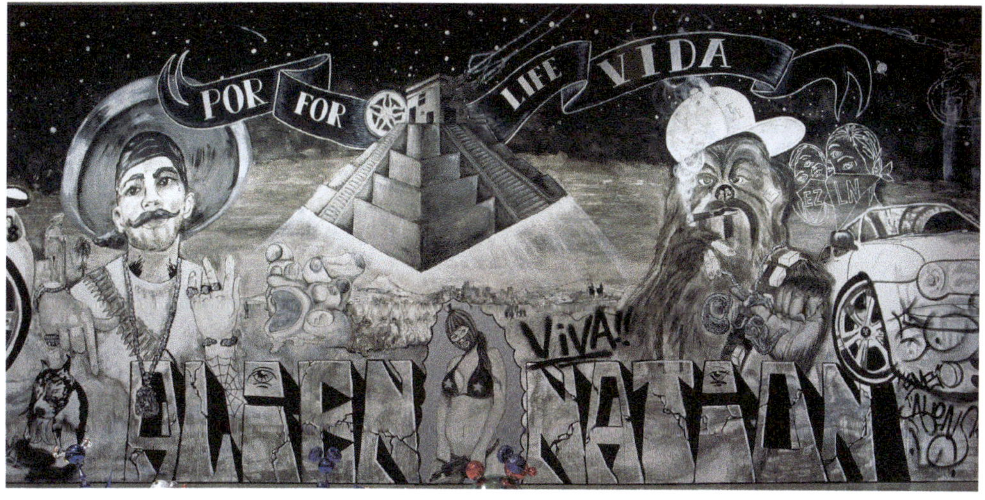


all glue-gunned into place, the results epitomise the artistic labour of 'making things mean'.

Locke's demonstration of the syntax of reuse, the retelling of history, of appropriation, of the notion of artworks as readable references to one another, was enlarged upon by another installed work in *Alien Nation*, a painting on the gallery wall entitled *Brown and Proud* (fig. 44) by Mario

Ybarra Jr. Placed so as to be seen first from the entrance, it featured like a theatrical backdrop. In contrast with the beating technicolour of much of the rest of the exhibition, this was monochromatic, yet on the scale of a film hoarding, and it supported a profusion of larger-than-life-sized figures. Making for an especially 'busy' composition, the painting followed the general theme of otherworldly visitations and the monster-horrors of science fiction. The work featured a leering, simian Chewbacca and a female form loosely resembling Princess Leia of *Star Wars*, yet Ybarra's rendering of the fleshy contents of a push-up bra was a camp allusion to the same galactic bawdiness as in Mel Brooks's film spoof *Spaceballs*.

That figurative painting was flanked by the more modestly scaled *Merk* by Kori Newkirk (fig. 45), a veil of luminescent glass 'pony' beads tacked to the bare gallery wall. The beads were ingeniously strung on artificial hair extensions to depict a column of bright celestial light that divided a scene of suburban housing. Houses are pictured at night time, when curtains are drawn and all are asleep. The suggestion is one of various roots of alienation: homeowners cherishing their privacy and property but screening themselves off from contact with their neighbours; the domestic setting as a refuge from public space and the working day; and a reminder that popular home entertainment such as television has served as the principal site of encounter with science fiction narratives. This ideal image of orderly and tended buildings, boundary walls, fences and garden plots has frequently been used to hysterically alarmist ends, and it points to the fear of what might be lost through 'swamping' by immigrants or those seeking asylum. It is the ideological background to the image of an uninvited flying saucer above the rooftops of every 'respectable' neighbourhood. An extraterrestrial glow from Newkirk's beads is a sinister presence – beaming down as from a *Star Trek* teleporter among retirement bungalows and their tidy, moon-kissed lawns.

In each of these works, the intermedial potential of visual meaning to be transferred among film, television, photography, painting, sculpture and so on is what supplies the running thread. These are sites of artistic 're-presentation' since they indicate the appropriation of forms and associations from sites of display – genres of cinema, or historical documents and memories of slavery – translated into the milieu of the white cube. The transposition is extended by many of the artworks choosing to reassign threatening emotions such as fear and anxiety to the realm of humour, diffusing sobriety through sublimation, punning, irony. In art-making, as much as in film, the comfortable position of the

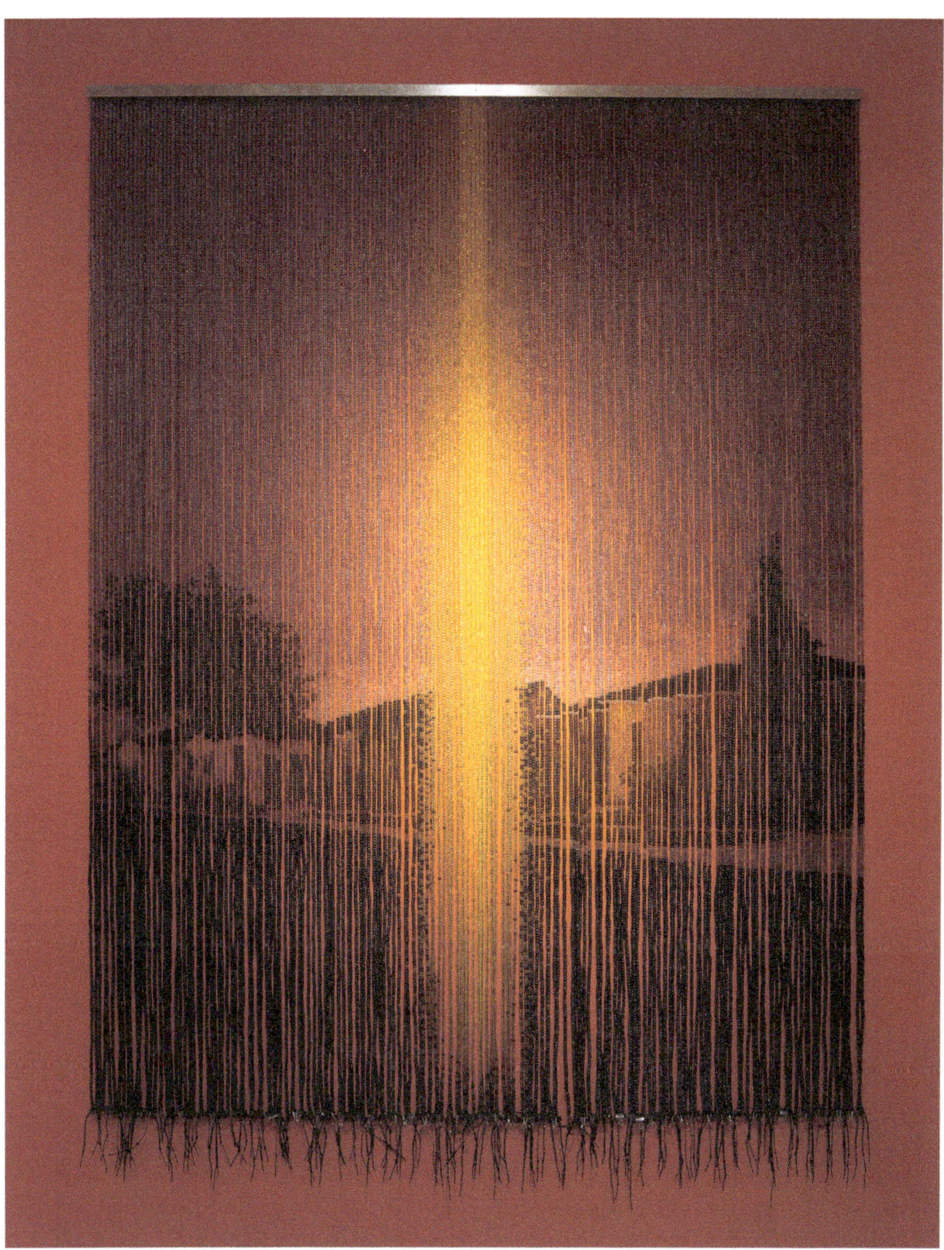

Figure 45: Kori Newkirk, *Merk*, 2006, pony beads, artificial hair extensions, aluminium and dye, approx. 239 x 183 x 3 cm. Courtesy of the artist. Photo: Marcus Leith.

entertained can be reached by disassociating from the outsider position and by marking out the fantastical basis of a community's 'aliens'.

## Sanguinity and defamiliarisation

That *Alien Nation* explored the histories and geographies of practices of Othering, by focusing frequently on Britain, was the exhibition's signature theme. The cut-and-mix photography of Henna Nadeem, in works such as *People*, made in 2006 (fig. 46), settled on the status of a timeless folk fantasy of English women enjoying one another's company in a picturesque landscape. It is unclear from the obscured pictorial surface of *People* whether they are glorying in some wholesome celebration of spring, and what the picture does not disclose is left to the imagination. Lace-makers in the temperate North of England are garlanded above their cotton skirts and pinafores, perhaps joining hands around the maypole, or clapping to the tambourine. It is a fractured image – an interlacing of subjects overlain upon one another – that serves centrally in Nadeem's practice. She writes:

> My early experiences as a British Muslim growing up in semi-rural Yorkshire determined the cultural and stylistic motivation of my practice. Nature and landscape formed the backdrop to my childhood, but it was nature viewed through a window rather than experienced directly. Experiencing life indoors and through a window manifested itself in an obsessive collecting of ephemera … culled from magazines, papers and general stuff bought and found. A marked incongruity about my collection has been the absence of figurative imagery (Islam discourages figurative representation) and my collection reflects that through an emphasis on pattern and landscape. (quoted in Gill et al., 2006: 37)

The artist is ironic about a taste for ornamented surfaces once transposed to picturesque outdoor scenes. Her choice of the term 'semi-rural' implies a halfway house for the countryside, an inauthentic status for Yorkshire that disavows its popular description as the quintessence of rural England, as 'God's own county'. Her statement about having first-hand knowledge of that space corroborates Nadeem's further claims that notions of rural tradition in this country are forever being reified. Tradition for this artist is continually reinvented through modes of picturing, such as photography; tradition can only ever be spied through a window, framed forever by representation.

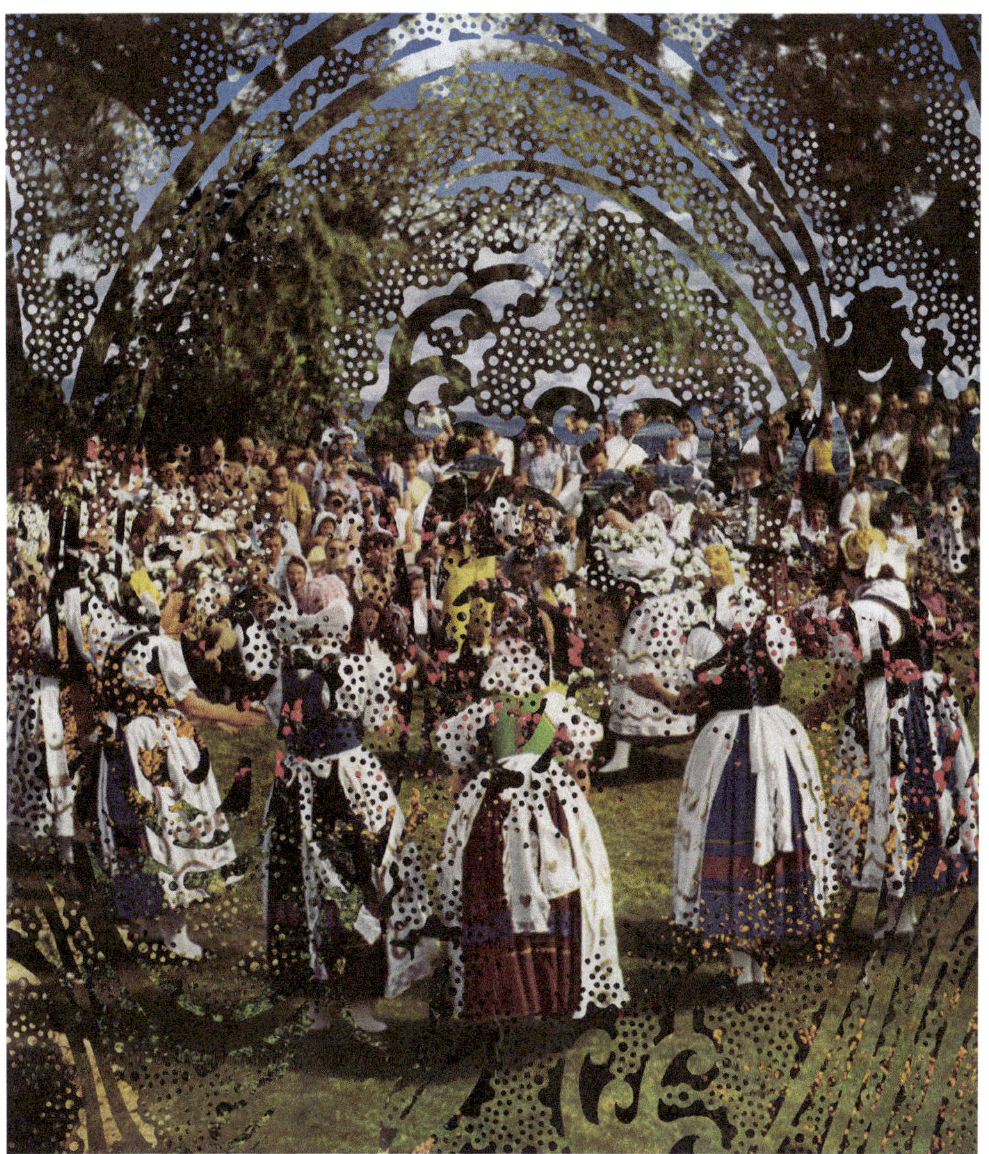

Figure 46: Henna Nadeem, *People*, 2006, digital montage, 32 x 36 cm. Courtesy of the artist.

Nadeem's sense of the role of photographs in triggering nostalgia and in celebrating the mythic timelessness of the British landscape was extensively treated in a commission by the Brighton-based agency Photoworks, which resulted in a richly illustrated publication.[4] Taking a randomly discovered 1966 edition of *Country Life's Picture Book of London*, the artist modified its pages through cutting and pasting, complemented by digital techniques. The popular series of *Picture Books of Britain*, published from 1937 until the late 1980s, spanned a period of intense social change, and its growing success after the Second World War can be understood as a palliative for Britain's shell-shock, the grinding effort of reconstruction, the food shortages. When Nadeem approaches these already schizophrenic images – selected to reassure their viewers of stability in the face of such upheaval – she emphasises the ambivalence and confusion over what should and should not be pictured as British. Benedict Burbridge and David Chandler wrote in a prefatory essay to the work that 'In these collages 1960s Britain seems in the grip of parallel realities, not just an unstable, evolving place but one going through a gradual and at times nightmarish metamorphosis' (2006: n.pag.). Their response raises the question of just whose nightmare these photographs signal. For Nadeem, these found objects become the raw material for a delicate pictorial stitching and an overlay of templates derived from linear principles in Islamic and North African traditions. The resulting series of works interposes extraordinary patterns with a superb tactic of defamiliarisation. Continuous images, they are more kaleidoscopic than fractured, and seen as though through a second lens. A carefully designed pictorial space is created from a harmonious assemblage of photographic surfaces, cut and combined so as to embellish its chosen subject matter. With all of this, Nadeem creates a position from which to look as an ostensible 'outsider' that suggests an embroidered and plainly dystopian vision of Britain's sanguine and manufactured self-image.

## Countering reductionism

*Alien Nation* recalled the parallel rise of fear and delectation around the filmic image, alongside the other projections and complexes directed at the trickle and then the influx of settlers to Britain as its empire

---

4   The exhibition *Henna Nadeem: A Picture Book of Britain* was staged at Charleston Farmhouse, Sussex, 6–29 October 2006, in association with the Brighton Photo Biennial.

dwindled. The curators succeeded in emphasising some of the routes by which today's romance with cultural difference arrived at a cinema near you. If strangers and aliens are perpetually the bogeymen of our made-up nation stories, *Alien Nation* returned, as it were, to the forbidden planet of the drivers and consequences of those everyday fantasy images. The exhibition showcased artists who took the stuff of movie posters and translated them into the digital, photographic, painted and sculptural round. Consequently, it achieved more than simply melding the big screen to the blockbuster artist. It pinpointed various nation-based techniques of visualising and emphasised how artists have responded with their own counter-calls and materialisations. Above all, it suggested that art-making can gesture beyond a repeating vocabulary of marginalisation from the nation, even as it suggests a condition of alienation from the terms of counter-hegemonic struggle.

There was indeed something strange in the neighbourhoods of the northern metropole when cinema screens were first chilled by the pulsating light of 'alien invasions' and terror at 'outsiders'. A leading manifestation of 'outsider' identity, which has been discussed widely in cultural theory, is the notion of the diaspora subject. It is notable that many of the artists featured in *Alien Nation*, when participating in other exhibitions, have been described by way of the diaspora theme. And, as I have been hinting, it is even more significant that science fiction in particular was employed for its framing context.

*Alien Nation* took this same approach of representing ways in which diasporic subjects are seen as alien outsiders and how this status is sedimented in popular imaging. The emphasis on science fiction showed how apparently innocuous sources of visual entertainment serve to underwrite the expectations of belonging and unbelonging that are embedded in ideologies of the nation state, with lingering and adverse outcomes for diasporic experience. The exhibition was in some ways typical in approaching art as a 'visual index' of the politics of identity and difference, of art as a 'signifier' of diaspora and diversity. Its focus on parodying and questioning science brought it forcefully into the orbit of that interpretative framework.

At the same time, the exhibition marked the beginning of the end of a historical 'moment', a break from the past: by focusing on science itself as a fiction, the art on display urged consideration of the wider context of interpreting black diaspora visual culture. It signalled some recent developments in the uses of the terms 'cultural difference', 'national community' and the 'exotic', and their value for critical commentators and black British artists who had tired of marginality, racial exclusion and 'invisibility'. But therein lies a *Tale of the Unexpected* for our times. In art criticism and historiography, curating and arts programming, and with the complicity of many artists themselves, like Klingons with Federation dollars, it would seem that the arts began trading in the commodity of difference – embracing 'diversity' with as much enthusiasm as audiences sought those little green men of yesteryear's Cold War movies.

Exhibitions like *Alien Nation* disclosed some of the operational language and the complexities of Britain's politics of multiculturalism. By 2007, in arts programming and the art market, the taste for black British art was dwindling. The exhibition called upon artists to present a visual commentary on the historical architecture and the legacies of exclusion and marginalisation in the hegemonic spaces of art and film. Even though they were not asked to foreground or embody 'race' so much as to highlight and undermine racism, this only devolved responsibility on to the artist to mediate race relations. It was an encumbrance on their art to be the medium for sorting out differences, after the critiques of exhibitions and institutional histories had made it institutionally unthinkable not to give space and resources for the enunciation of blackness.

An establishment appetite for difference in Britain has in part been catered to by the application of the paradigm of media to black British art. Evidently such an adverse outcome cannot be rectified by the simple substitution of yet another intellectual paradigm, and it is consequently hard to see how to reassert the sovereignty of art in the otherwise overdetermined landscapes of visual meaning that black British artists have come to inhabit. The only ground remaining for the *Alien Nation* artists was one of irony, exposing the conditions of art's circulation by turning on its head the binary of 'alien' and 'insider'. Locke's series of sculptural pieces *Golden Horde* invited a humorous dismissal of current fears about organised 'incursions' from the East, recalling the deeper history of European maritime expansionism. Ybarra took the same tone, indicating how to undermine science-fiction xenophobia through a poetics of camp. Newkirk's presentations located a kind of group paranoia within orderly domesticity, while the photographic assemblages of Henna Nadeem transparently confronted nationally embedded nostalgias.

Each of these artworks certainly operates in a common mediascape. They subvert the hegemonic terms of difference by borrowing and resisting dominant codifications of 'race' and ethnicity. But the surrounding discursive pressures weigh in so heavily on them that the ambition to be an affective presence is threatened with suffocation. Additionally, it has come to be subjected to what the historian of philosophy Martin Dillon (1995) has named the 'semiological reductionism' that is practised in the field of cultural analysis. The same conceptual positioning of black British artists has been attempted from a number of directions: from cultural studies and the wider humanities; from public institutions and art policies; continually from curators and indeed from among artists themselves. They converge and condense from seemingly opposed quarters. The art of black Britain is much abused by the expectations of its status as the high cultural medium for constructing identity and ethnicised difference. It plays the troubled role of brokering public 'race' relations in the safely sublimated field of the visual arts. Identifying a critical thread in black British art is nowadays a task of remembrance for how reaching intellectual consensus about its value seemed to coincide with the end of the era of identity politics.

Most of all, black British art has become a token in a game of institutional cultural 'inclusion'. No matter that multiculturalism was declared to be over by the 2000s, well before the time of the *Alien Nation* exhibition and the major arts funding 'austerity' measures that were applied to the public sector after the economic crisis of 2008. Such art is still all of those things that theories of culture and media have confirmed to be in evidence: it is textual, linguistic, signifying, representational, mediating, connective, codifying, context-producing. But the acceptance of such a status also makes it prone to excision and special treatment outside the mainstream of contemporary cultural achievement; as the terminologies but not the principles of critical theory come to filter outward, the danger of reductionism grows. Artists are having to try to counter this effect and stay clear of reactionary forces. And yet it seems unfair to ask that they should sustain such pressures as never arise for their white counterparts.

It is commendable in the circumstances that black British artists have not evacuated from their art the component of phenomenal affectivity, the drive to maintain a perceptual efficacy that artworks seem to command. Their art is all the more fascinating for enfolding if not embodying the representational and discursive, asserting the right to differentiate itself from its surrounding conditions. And while it is not always easy to see how it does so, philosophy can still show how black British art *makes a phenomenal difference* in ways that a site of mediation cannot.

## Beyond mediation

Recent discussion among phenomenologists of art has conveyed some of this same sense of a division between social and embodied experience.[5] A similar outlook has formed in the humanities more generally, with social interaction and human perception being accounted for somewhat separately. Art history, for instance, moved marginally away from its positivistic relation to looking by allowing visual culture and literary studies to propose that 'vision' ought to be treated as a physical operation, in contradistinction to 'visuality', or sight as a social fact, before proposing to bring these fields together (Mitchell, 1996; Foster, 1988; Jay, 1988). It might be argued that this sort of procedure can be greatly extended by attention to the importance of perception and the cultural in the phenomenological tradition, following avenues of thought set out in this book. All such efforts need to be sharpened by a sense of phenomenology's deeper relation with the very discursive traditions that it would sometimes seem to mistrust.

Merleau-Ponty is a precursor in the work of unseating the idea that many social visualities comprise one essential vision, or order them into a natural hierarchy of sight. As I have explored, what characterises this attitude in the philosopher is a commitment to a ground of experience that is possible only through our presence as bodies in the world. For the study of contemporary black British art, adopting this attitude bears certain results, and taking a phenomenological outlook represents a sea change in our existing understanding. It serves to unfix the primacy hitherto held by cultural theories of art, loosening their analytic handle on art as an index of diaspora community and as a site of identification.

An ontology of black British art is only possible by untangling and separating off such concerns, by the use of bracketing, the phenomeno-logical *epoché*. But the preliminary nature of that bracket needs to be emphasised. Attendant upon identifying the phenomenal character of art in the setting of black Britain is a responsibility and the interpretative issue of what to do with the themes of difference so prevalently cast in its artworks. That will require some thinking on how to appropriate

---

5  This is carried on in the anthology of *Art and Phenomenology*, which states, 'Our approach to art is to treat it as a kind of phenomenology – which is not to say that art can be reduced to a discursive content, but rather that art can function as a way of directing us to important phenomena and helping us to understand them in their own terms' (Parry and Wrathall, 2011: 1).

the historiography of these individuals in such a way as to appreciate their struggles to transcend the status of excluded 'others'. Alongside the technique of phenomenological bracketing is that of keeping in view how aesthetic discourse not only delineates human relationships with perception but also, more crucially, produces them. If there is such a thing as a 'diaspora aesthetic', then phenomenology can unravel what might be promised as well as withheld by that term, and develop an alternative relationship to artworks that reflects upon perception.

## Post-critical ontology

I have dealt with the question of why it might be significant to point to the phenomenological possibilities of black British art, but what has been said of this kind of interest could equally apply to many other contemporary artists without a black or diaspora identification. Indeed, the interest in art and ontology being shown by philosophers is well repaid in the contemporary art environment at large. Artists themselves, in a manner perhaps peculiar to the past two decades, have engaged a sort of 'research-practice' in which ontologies of creativity, originality and expression – those features seen to be generic to modernist fine art practice – have been taken up afresh with the aim of fragmenting the very psychic, institutional and ideological conditions and assumptions that have allowed them to persist, and in an attempt to introduce 'thing theory and affect discourse' into the world of art in an effort to be 'post-critical' (Foster, 2015: 120–122).

Among the strongest challenges to this tradition is the ontology of the materiality of the artwork, and a growing sense of how this might support artistic authorship in changing conventions of display and cultural exchange. Black British artists were part of that larger sphere of activity during the period of the 1980s and early 1990s. Epistemologies of belonging, location and ethnicity became central preoccupations, linked to a critically disruptive attitude towards racialised and hegemonic forms of visually representing the nation and 'nationhood'. Such outlooks engendered the need for self-definition and an open engagement with composite, 'intersectional' identities structured through differences of many kinds, extending well beyond ethnicity and gender.

These complexities can be historicised more closely by recalling the intellectual climate of Britain's art schools in the early 1980s and the wide respect for 'dematerialising' the art object and post-conceptualism, such as associated with the British grouping Art and Language. For all the differences between figureheads of black British art – such as Sonia Boyce and Eddie Chambers – in their views on how best to construct an art of 'blackness', their respective art practices share that institutional legacy. This is not the place for a genealogy of black British art which may point to the strictures surrounding attention to blackness, diaspora and so on, nor to assess the extent to which the development of black British art has been steered by its market location, the response of public cultural policy, funding initiatives and so on. What can be said on the evidence of a philosophical survey is that its rich mix of intellectual procedures and aesthetic traditions have become hollowed out, if not homogenised, in the retrospective glance of the current historicisation.

Clearly there is more to explore empirically in the trajectories of personal and professional contact and interaction during the first years of 'black art' in Britain (Hylton, 2013), and the achievements of such artists in shaping an artistic 'canon' or 'counter-canon'. But to do so without the requisite perceptual analysis of the actual works of art that emerged from the hands of such individuals, the 'work between us' as Fisher put it in 1997, would impoverish our understanding. At the same time, the 'archival impulse' (Hall, 2001a; 2001b), which is felt in response to a sense of losing black British art to the past, to social amnesia, needs to be cross-checked with a symptomology of all such motivations to recover history. Greater self-examination of the particular hope and nostalgia that condenses around the need for an 'unfinished conversation'[6] with the history of black British art can be guided by a philosophy of art's own capacities for remembrance – what I called art's modes of 'visual historiography' in Chapter 3.

## No more culturalism

During the 1980s the black British project or art movement found affinity with black nationalist aesthetics from across the Atlantic (Bailey et al., 2005), and awareness has developed subsequently of how certain African American artists and thinkers are confronting certain paradoxes in their national history of art, with its 'standpoint-driven subject of

---

6  The allusion here, of course, is as much to director John Akomfrah's three-screen installation film (*The Unfinished Conversation*, 2013, United Kingdom, 103 minutes; part of The Stuart Hall Project) as to psychoanalytic critiques of historiography (Fanon, 1986), the historiographic drive at large and the overtones of melancholia in postcolonial thought.

identity politics' (English, 2007: 287). In parallel, black British artists have contrived to localise, personalise and embody some important global currents in the politics of 'race' and representation, and in other cases they have taken a far more contrary view of the relevance of such politics. Whatever the approach, there is a greater incidence of active interest in art's affective relations. Such art is deliberate in projecting an uneasy fit with the dominant social imaginary of difference, as was always the case for black British creativity. It has also reserved the right to diverge from the paths taken in larger national contexts such as the United States, with its putatively 'post-black' discourse. Often it pushes the opinion that a critical problematic on difference has little or no place in the visual arts, as if such issues are beneath or behind us. At one extreme, this stance finds comfort in a reprise of modernism's 'internalist' theory of the aesthetic service performed by an artwork, which was always in play, even during the emergence of the black British art discourses of the 1980s (see Bhabha, 1998, on the sculptor Anish Kapoor, for instance).

Appreciating such a diversity of approaches among black British artists in part depends on seeing how these conservative and progressive forces have set no uniform agenda for how people of diaspora backgrounds will choose to engage with visual creativity. In fact, the historical development of black British art has stalled at those times when a consensus seemed to be forming. At the height of the identity politics and 'black art' of the twentieth century, there were clearly dissimilar, discrepant currents apparently flowing away from the very issues of representation that have come to seem so representative of that time. This added usefully to the mix as an impetus for change. Artists' ontologies of sexuality, gender and desire (Pivin and Sealy, 1996), of illness and pain (see, for instance, Hylton, 2003), had a vividly corporeal dimension that can hardly be summed up as so many readable signs of identitarian resistance to exclusion and marginalisation. Such artworks may indeed carry an index of the 'multiaccentual properties of blackness [that] can be pushed and pulled into many antagonistic and competing discourses' (Mercer, 2009: 77). Still, the materiality of art exceeds the expectation placed upon it to serve as a discursive field per se.

Reviewing this art's historical development can also show up the extent to which black British artists carry diverse phenomenal concerns with subjective being that are shared with creative practitioners from other historical and geographical contexts. The closest comparisons are certainly elsewhere in the Atlantic world, perhaps in the Caribbean and its wide diaspora (Wainwright, 2011; Wainwright and Zijlmans, 2017), or in other settings such as the African diaspora, where even the phenomenon of light has been shown to have a 'visual economy' (Thompson, 2015). Conversely, we must keep open the possibility that there are artists who have operated in contexts with no such links to contemporary Britain, and yet whose art it is instructive to consider. At the extreme opposite to the cultural contextualism of critical writing on black British art is an intellectual position on art, visuality, subjectivity and so on that shows how we may dispense altogether with the need to provide evidence of art's historical contingencies, how to do away with finding 'conjunctions' in the field of culture. Davis (2011), for example, seems to recommend this turn, asking that we kick the methodological habit of such comparativism and reflect more seriously on the proclivity towards evidencing art's value by way of culturalism.

Such an intervention does give pause for thought. It could be the aperture for liberating black British art from the need to try to link or map the apparent peculiarities of that art to other formations, whether past or present. Just as usefully, it could also transcend the racialising parochialisms that pop up and hamper progress in understanding black British art and waste so much scholarly time. Certainly investigation of what black British artists have achieved in their works can reward historical study. But that must reckon with how and why their reservoir of critical tactics and identifications with and without difference, blackness or diaspora is also filled with discrete experiences of tactility, light and vision that form art's material ground. Perception itself has a foundational role to play in ensuring that black British artworks extend beyond historical and cultural articulation, beyond mediation.

# Conclusion:
## The phenomenal as practice

In a conversation that took place in the 1940s between two celebrated authors, the African American Richard Wright and the Trinidad-born C. L. R. James, Wright reportedly claimed an 'intuitive foreknowledge' of the ideas of Nietzsche, Kierkegaard, Heidegger and Husserl before he had actually read their works (James, 1984). Paul Gilroy has suggested that this conversation provides the basis for the proposition that 'non-European expressive traditions have refused the caesura which Western high culture would introduce between art and life', and that 'the insights of Wright and James can … be read as an implicit questioning of the idea that occidental aesthetics and philosophy are best understood as cohesive yet autonomous projects' (1988b: 39). Now, while I am uncertain about such a 'caesura … between art and life' in 'Western high culture', I am even less sure that it helps to try to draw lines between the 'non-European' or the 'non-West' at all, after centuries of migration and diaspora have surely falsified those clear distinctions. But that may be entirely beside the point. Phenomenological thought strongly questions the notion that 'the everyday' and art-making or aesthetics are indeed so radically separated.[1] And if black British art is among those 'expressive traditions' that have interwoven and reconciled art and the everyday, then phenomenological study is well suited to bringing such processes to light.

---

1  See, for instance, Desjarlais on a phenomenology of the aesthetics of the everyday: 'anthropology of experience might profit from an analysis not only of the contours and boundaries of "selves" as they are culturally constructed, but of the way in which social actors compose, manage and evaluate their actions and those of others in everyday social contexts … As human interactions are based on a series of "doings and undoings", tensions and resolutions, so processes of aesthetic balance, harmony and completion are by nature grounded in the rhythms of ordinary experience. The creation and perception of art forms are simply more perfected fulfilments of, and commentaries on, these experiences' (1992: 66–67).

This debate between Wright and James, and the black British return to it, helps in part to clarify this book's general interest, and in part to extend my remarks on how to release this art from some rather circular discussions about its value. Focusing on the origins of the phenomenological concerns of diaspora artists has not meant attributing them to any distinctively Asian, African or Caribbean tradition or set of traditions, nor for that matter any European ones. If black cultural practices do prove themselves to have 'spontaneously arrived at insights which appear in European traditions as the exclusive results of lengthy and lofty philosophical speculation' (Gilroy, 1988b: 39), then this rhetoric of spontaneity could furnish a foregoing conclusion that phenomeno-logical approaches are the principal or sole means of studying black British art. That may be going a step too far, however, confusing a concrete, existential and foundational philosophy with a prescriptive sort of 'foundationalism' (cf. Mercer, 1994: 246) that would encumber this cultural field by insisting on its own authority.

Instead, philosophical inquiry needs to maintain an attitude of openness and sensitivity towards the processual dimensions of creativity, to the fluidity of relations between artist, artwork and viewer(s)/audience(s), and to the very 'matter' of meaning. Black artists' works are the outcome of the manipulation of visual materials, according to conventions of doing so that identify such activities as the procedural processes of the work of an artist. They convey a sense of wonder, fascination and perceptual complexity, but for all that, they are no less contingent on their conditions of production and the surrounding expectations for art practices, whether local or global. No philosophy should try to remove them from their historical settings – let us not name them 'spontaneous' in that sense – but should become receptive to their particularities. The historical dimensions are not obscured through ontological study. As Howard Morphy has noted: 'People act in relation to objects as a part of a history of relating to objects, a history that is supra-individual yet reproduced through individual action' (2009: 20). Indeed, the knowledge, interpretations and experiences that people bring to bear on art objects (whether images, material manifestations, gestures, performances, acts, etc.) cannot be reduced to individual agency, nor can they be thought of as contained in the objects themselves. Black British art is embedded in relationships of visuality as well as of vision.[2]

---

2 Fred Moten has written insightfully, if elliptically, on this issue, disputing the distance between ontological understandings of performance and the 'economy of

Many artists have taken up at length with their social contingencies, addressing these to and from an aesthetic realm. At the level of phenomenological analysis, such practices may be actively de-linked from received notions of what a canon of Western art should look like, diversified by difference or not. The entire debate about canonicity has proved to be a confusing mix of liberating and stultifying (Wainwright, 2006). Where black British art has remained encumbered by those contestations with hegemonic cultural canons, it has rendered anachronistic any attempt to posit a place in the world on its behalf, governed by perceptions of contemporary culture as divisible into the achievements of 'the West' versus its 'Others'. Philosophy offers the licence to put aside such rehearsals and contentions about the value and structures of art canons. Endeavouring to understand this art's place in a phenomenal world has little to do with dilemmas over the cultural categorisation of black British art. Whether this art should be called black or/and British, how it should be located within the cultural politics of 'race', nation and representation, and so on – these are not strictly philosophical questions. Trying to answer them does not deepen our understanding of how black British art discloses its importance on the basis of accepting the primacy of perception. These are the arguments I have made throughout this book, and I have clarified the possibilities for introducing philosophy to this field, that is, what happens when black British artworks are brought together with phenomenology, what bearing do they have on perception?

But what if, as I do in this closing chapter, we turn this question around and ask: to what extent should phenomenal analysis of this art leave behind a political interest? Why should we avoid seeing such analysis

reproduction' (2003: 4) in an ongoing dispute with Peggy Phelan (1993). Moten notes that 'blackness is always a disruptive surprise moving in the rich nonfullness of every term it modifies. Such mediation suspends neither the question of identity nor the question of essence. Rather, blackness, in its irreducible relation to the structuring force of radicalism and the graphic, montagic configurings of tradition, and, perhaps most importantly, in its very manifestations as the inscriptional events of a set of performances, requires another thinking of identity and essence. This thinking converges with the re-emergent question of the human that self-critical articulation demands. Such articulation implies and enacts an unorthodox essentialism wherein essence and performance are not mutually exclusive' (2003: 255). He also reminds us of the relation between Heideggerian thought and that of the black American writer Amiri Baraka ('But Baraka's work is much more than either a repetition or an overturning of Heidegger's'; Moten, 2003: 143), in a way that extends Gilroy's remarks on Wright and James in their stance on European philosophy.

as an end in itself? More plainly: what remains *after* a phenomenology of black British art?

## Intertwining experience and signification

I want to answer this group of questions by coming from a slightly oblique angle. In the *Alien Nation* exhibition there were many artworks that seemed averse to the exploration of affective relations, and by contrast performed distinctively *conceptual* manoeuvres, or took an ironic distance from the seriousness that often accompanies discussion of art and cultural difference. But the foundation on which such choices and practices are made and achieved is always and inescapably a material one. Such artworks may be suitably framed upon the ground of perception, since it is through *aesthetic* practices, after all, that artists introduce a conceptual dimension to unsettle the values and perceptions of viewers. Rather than probing such intentions, it is preferable to assume that all black British art shares this fact of perceptual presence, and to take the view that there is much to gain by exploring the *outcomes* of such a presence for its audiences. The point cannot be overstressed that any meaningful exploration of art's affective relations will always be grounded in perception. Whether black British artists embrace the creative potential of affectivity or, at the opposite extreme, attempt to displace it, any commentary that sets out to understand such differences must reckon closely with the facticity of the phenomenal.

There is a broad parallel here with the intertwining of perception and discourse, pointed out by some thinkers on deconstruction. If we want to disrupt the way in which something is inscribed in written language, we tend to do so upon a ground of representation that is always an economy of perceptual concerns that demands an ontological analysis. For instance, Jean-François Lyotard has written about this phenomenological commitment to perception, showing that 'an articulated, discontinuist, active, logical conception of meaning and space could not but miss the datum or rather the donation of the visible' (1993: 312). His point aptly clarifies the argument that all such 'articulated, discontinuist' conceptions of black British art have also to contend with the perceptual world.

What, then, is really at stake in recognising black British art through philosophy? A philosophy of attitudes to vision, the body, the material world and so on, which may be explored with the assistance of black British art, does not somehow disaffirm the utility of a post-structuralist understanding of experience – as if phenomenology were some sort of methodology, poised to replace another. The two do not equate or even separate in that way: the critical analyses of cultural studies and post-structuralist attitudes to culture-as-text on the one hand, and (post-)formalist art historical theories and the (post-)humanities, with their curiosity about the 'new materialism', on the other (summarised in Fuglerud and Wainwright, 2015). What others have taken to be a methodological difference and a division of political values and commitments is a misreading of these currents and genealogies of contemporary thought.

Underscoring this point, Lawrence Grossberg, in his essay on cultural studies, 'Signification, Experience and Reality', characterised post-structuralist deconstruction in related terms:

> The deconstruction of texts is, in some way, the mirror image of the phenomenological reading of experience … Any semiotic theory concerned with describing structures and contexts of signification is located within a transcendental framework of experience. Post structuralism is not condemned to find phenomenological traces within its discourse; rather it should seek ways to more effectively understand and utilize the mirror provided by the discourse of experience. (1997: 102)

The admission among post-structuralists that phenomenological experience is mediated through its discourse should embolden any attempt to recognise the differences between these approaches, certainly; but more so it helps us to draw comparisons and to spot the imbrication or 'intertwining' of one with the other. A project of phenomenal analysis which is sensitive to the creative drives of black British artists needs to be able to cope with the social basis for such aesthetic complexities. There is no denying that artists have explored the issues of representation that commentators have modelled on a post-structuralist frame. For a time, black British artists seemed to practise by the metaphors of cultural studies, while its discourse has contrived to grant their works a sociological and historical value. Much of that visual work sharply indexes a range of themes that focus on the constructedness of cultural identities and the fluidity of meaning, reflecting on the role of 'the unconscious in desire, fantasy and memory' (Bailey and Hall, 1992b: 20). Conversely, the very heterogeneity of artists' 'positions' in the world is also an index of the diversity of their existential experience, and this breadth of complexity demands a requisitely fluid and open sort of analysis. Developing my discussion through what I have long regarded to be a 'strategic phenomenology' of black British art (Wainwright, 2003), dynamic relationships among such artworks are disclosed, implying the need for attention to the primacy of perceptual experience in a field of action which is always social.

Most academic discussion around art of the black diaspora has avoided phenomenological modes of inquiry, perhaps assuming that attention to the phenomenal would distract from art's social nexus and its critical potential for political change. This is unfortunate both for phenomenology (hardly giving it its due) *and* for understanding of the social and the political, which is also by consequence oversimplified. At a time when scholarship on black visual culture was first facing the need to respond with such openness – during the 1990s when the convergence became obvious between the terms of black cultural criticism and the semiological reductionism that framed the hegemonies of multicultural vision in public art policy, curating and museology – the view was that ontological concerns were ineffective for the production of a discourse on the role of marginalised cultures in staging counter-hegemonic struggle (see, for example, Baucom, 1998). This dismissal, however, was made far too hastily. It has furnished a mood of intellectual conformism through a slew of writing whose mode of theorisation, it was wrongly supposed, could somehow withstand the test of time.

All such outlooks on ontology by implication also render their own preferred approach – post-structuralism – in a far too basic light. It would be inaccurate to say that during the 1990s, when critical theory still held sway in the academy, there was not also in evidence an ontologically expanded view of culture. Some of the more sophisticated post-structuralists explained their proximity to the phenomenological tradition and embraced that complexity. Laclau and Mouffe, for instance, while similar to Stuart Hall in showing that meaning is context-oriented and constituted in action ('in our terminology, every identity or discursive object is constituted in the context of an action'; Laclau, 1990: 103), looked in detail at the philosophical basis for politically engaged intellectual work. Suggesting that 'the discursive character of an object does not, by any means, imply putting its *existence* into question' (Laclau, 1990: 100), they recognised that an object's positioning in discursive practices is exactly what presses it further into existential being (see also Culler, 1988; Derrida, 1973; 1981; 1982).

This is a short step away from Heidegger's use of the hammer, in his example of intricate contexts of meaning for which *things* come to reveal their being. In our everyday dealings with tools, things reveal their 'truth' (*alētheia*) in a manner of becoming-present that in sundry ways typifies being as such. In this fundamental but unobtrusive manner, human interaction, with objects as well as one another, produces being in contexts of meaning that constitute a 'world' (Heidegger, 1996: §26; Krell, 1996: 19–20). More notably, the enumeration given by Foucault of various 'technologies of the self'[3] translates quite well to the field of black British art, since it can encapsulate the field's existential dimension along with the historical contingencies of artworks. Of course, in actual practice the ontological work of trying to understand the range of 'technologies' operating in this field of relations has not been undertaken. Black cultural studies has tended to settle for a purchase on the patently critical dimensions of selfhood rather than contending more ambitiously with the breadth of Foucault's categories and their foundation of existential being.

## A theory of practice

In other words, by bridging this shortfall, phenomenology can offer a theory of practice (praxis) and, most importantly, it can do so without contradicting the value of art's technological status in fields of discourse and representation. I have taken it to be a valuable means of pointing to how black British art achieves its material realisation, and have expressed this in terms of the Heideggerian 'worlds' or 'horizons' of such art objects, emphasising our corporeal involvement with them. Five chapters of this book were dedicated to these themes: Chapter 3 took up the idea of situated visual practices (in terms of the objects that succeed in 'setting up' a world); chapters 4 and 5 worked through the nature of our bodily pact with their material settings and the 'equivalence' of perceptual registers; and chapters 6 and 7 explored the interworld or 'flesh of the world' which emerges from this intertwining. Such a turn towards phenomenal and ontological interests is a way of grounding and augmenting the common understanding of black British art practice. The

---

3 Foucault lists them as follows: '(1) Technologies of production, which permit us to produce, transform or manipulate things; (2) technologies of sign systems, which permit us to use signs, meanings, symbols, or signification; (3) technologies of power, which determine the conduct of individuals and submit them to certain ends or domination ...; (4) technologies of the self, which permit individuals to effect by their own means or with the help of others a certain number of operations on their own bodies and souls, thoughts, conduct, and way of being, so as to transform themselves in order to attain a certain state of happiness, purity, wisdom, perfection or immortality' (1988: 18).

status of these phenomenological moves – as a theory of practice – rests largely on the idea of the merging of horizons, a form of interaction that may be traced out in terms of corporeal contact, in the tactile and the visual encounters that can be had with black British art. Merging takes place following any such perceptual encounter; the horizons that merge are those of the artist, the artwork and the wider world, including the art world and ourselves as diverse audiences. As I suggested in Chapter 3 on visual historiography:

> Considering the spatial metaphor of horizon brings to the fore a conception of artworks as places, not only as *expressive* places, or places of articulation (for the *placing* of ideas) but as materially present, 'place worthy' and ostensive, an instance of what David Summers has called 'place-making' ... Artworks are visual places when they form a meeting point for artist, spectator/reader and idea(s); the work of art expands the possibilities of such elements coming to experience one another.

What remains important is that nothing of this event is guaranteed in advance, and this leaves open an ambiguous, contingent space. This distinctly phenomenological direction – taking up ideas of corporeality, perception and so on from Merleau-Ponty, his attention to ambiguity (see Merleau-Ponty, 1962; 1968), and world and horizon from Heidegger – has through its emphasis on contingency, a recursive bearing on the post-structuralist ideas infusing black cultural studies, in which I share a regard for what Laclau had called the political necessity of contingency. At the same time I would broaden the sense that contingency is required only as the source of radical democracy. I underline its value for understanding how relations in the wider phenomenal world can never be predetermined, and therein are the foundations of difference.

Parsing these phenomenal and political philosophies, we still need to borrow something from deconstructionism, perhaps something like Derrida's notion of *différance*, in order to understand how the 'other', which any society requires in order to shape itself, can cease to be regarded as such, indeed as 'outside' in any absolute sense, since it is an integral part of that same shaping process. In traditional phenomenological thought, political dialogue can also be conceived as a merging of horizons – as negotiation, conflict or agreement – which distinguishes the situatedness of being as an area of practice. By considering an individual's relation to his or her own context as another such merging of horizons of sorts, we can also show up the phenomenal aspects of social

life and make judgements about whether individuals feel that their needs
are met or provided for.

The sociological work on this matter of provision is also pertinent to
the field of representation, and how it overlaps with the emotions in the
black British setting. If an individual's needs are not met (for instance,
in the existing public infrastructure for the arts, in arts funding, arts
education, the curating and display of art and so on), then the inevitable
result is alienation, or a 'privatisation' of interests, as Bauman (1999)
reminds us. This process can help to sharpen a view of the identity
politics within the black British art milieu as shaped by the perception
of whether one's needs within a social or cultural horizon are being
catered for. Especially during the 1980s, for black artists, feelings of
exclusion and marginalisation suggested that those needs were not met
– circumstances that precipitated such individuals banding together as a
group, and some frustrating outcomes.[4] In the present day, those feelings
have not abated entirely, even if the institutional and critical landscape
has undergone transition and certain black British artists are subject to
the 'predicament of "hypervisibility"' largely through increased public
attention (Fisher, 1996: 35; Mercer, 1999: 56; cf. Chambers, 2012).[5]

In those social formations characterised by artists continuing to
group together, the shared political conviction that once galvanised
their practices has lately given way to a more generalised belief in the
need for basic historical work on black British art. Scholarship can
indeed reward curiosity about the decisive developments that brought
a generation of black British artists together in the first place so many
years ago. But the normativity of the historiographic drive has not been
fully grasped among those who would excavate this past. An assumption
about historical study being the route to social justice has been left to
stand somewhat precariously, without qualification, and it deserves the

---

4   The situation drew keen analysis at the time. Paul Gilroy wrote: 'The most unwholesome
    ideas of ethnic absolutism hold sway and they have been incorporated into the
    structures of the political economy of funding black arts. The tokenism, patronage
    and nepotism that have become intrinsic to the commodification of black culture
    rely absolutely on an absolute sense of ethnic difference. This variety of absolutism is
    strongest and most theoretically coherent in non-vernacular cultural forms. It is most
    eloquent where white audiences are not simply assumed but actively sought out and
    where the glamour of ambivalent ethnicity borrows most heavily from the devious,
    rhetorical excesses of literary poststructuralism' (1988b: 42).

5   Mercer described, in the late 1990s, 'a scenario in which the longstanding metaphor of
    minority "invisibility" has given way to a new and wholly unanticipated predicament
    of "hypervisibility"' (2009: 56).

support of a more robust philosophical approach to black British art that can harness its intellectual inheritance more effectively.

## Identification after multiculturalism

The perils of identification through difference are exemplified in those cases where individuals are encouraged to see identification as black or diasporic as a moral responsibility. Identification can become binding for the cultural field of visual creativity and the transformative potential of social relations when it is the sole currency of exchange. The definition and maintenance of categories of difference can prompt creative responses but can also become a drain on creative resources. There are no guarantees of achieving agency under the rubric of difference when the process of identification presses upon artists as their chief motivation to collect as a group or to make meaningful art. What seems to secure an ameliorating outcome for cultural identification, when it is at its most effective, is appreciation of a larger purpose for it: that identification may be simply a means to an end, a way station towards deeper social changes that will allow us in time to dispense with terms that had previously objectified the value of artworks under the moral pressure for their artists to affiliate.

Highlighting such possibilities, it helps to consider the specific scalar issues of space and place. At the time of writing, the coming together of black British artists in order to try to solve shared problems happens on a notably circumscribed scale, as compared to the movement of artists of preceding decades around the closing of the twentieth century. These circles of association are noticeably diminishing as Britain's historical conviction in the effectiveness of a black and diaspora identification through the arts recedes.

Scalar issues show up most clearly in the relationships between this present-day grouping of artists and the structuring ideas – policies and practices – of multiculturalism, which have also come under attack and suffered crisis. One line of debate on multiculturalism urges us to regard it as being prevalently to do with the reifying of 'others' by institutions and authorities, granting them space as a measure of control. For Rasheed Araeen, this is 'the benevolence of dominant culture, creating a space in which the "other" is accommodated in a spectacle that produces an illusion of equality' (1989b: 4).[6] I note that the operative word here is

6  Araeen developed this view in a later essay: 'in the West, [multiculturalism] has been
   used as a cultural tool to ethnicise its non-white population in order to administer and

'spectacle'. The power of such representations – the 'illusion of equality' – derives from spectators coming to view their condition according to the metaphor of distance between themselves and the 'dominant culture'. Power is never totalising or exclusively located, and the considerable critical force wielded by commentary and scholarship on black British art implies that a more 'emancipated' role is actually more within the reach of artists and critics than has commonly been imagined. Such an observation can be reached following Rancière (2010), whose thinking has been formative when drawing my overall conclusions. This analysis builds on the more common refrain of criticism towards multiculturalism: that the term is a false notion since it implies that there are cultures that can be defined as coherent wholes. The metaphor of distance is false given the degree of intermixing, yet the illusion or the 'semblance of harmony', through and not despite difference, denies the actual inequalities that remain (Žižek, 1997).

At the same time, multicultural thinking is unable to reckon with the ordinary social processes that do not fall within the boundaries of bureaucratic or marketised multiculturalism, processes resembling the sort of 'conviviality' that Gilroy observes in everyday Britain (2004). Here are diachronic social developments that ensue through an extended duration of coexistence against a deep historical background of migration, empire and decolonisation. What seems required is an understanding of Britain's virtuously unruly moral and political economy of commensality, with reference to a time-based dimension of Heideggerian 'dwelling'. More specifically, this would take into account the important distinctions between instances of cultural practice such as art and the 'everydayness' – Heidegger's *Alltäglichkeit* – of more ordinary social interactions. Critical thought on black and diaspora culture during the final decades of the twentieth century had set out to parse the relationship between the cultural and the social. Yet black British artists have faced 'the union *and* the tension of instituting society and of instituted society, of history made and of history in the making', to borrow a phrase from Castoriadis (1987: 108) that may better describe the uneasy relation between the imagination of such artists

control its aspirations for equality. It also serves as a smokescreen to hide the contradictions of a white society unable or unwilling to relinquish its imperial legacies. It is in this context that we should understand the fascination and celebration of cultural difference' (1994: 9). And, commenting on the 1989 exhibition *Magiciens de la Terre* (Musée National d'Art Moderne, Paris), he urged that 'the paternalism of power must constantly be questioned if we are not to be imprisoned by its benevolence' (1989b: 7).

('individual intentionality') and the imaginary of multiculturalism ('social institutionalisation').

Ultimately, the continuing identification with blackness among certain artists in Britain, and the disengagement from identification among others, can be appreciated as a phenomenal matter of the horizons of experience. Philosophy must now play a role in showing how these horizons merge – however messily – with one another through black British art's materialising processes. Black British artists, caught in the 'frictions', 'the awkward, unequal, unstable, and creative qualities of interconnection across difference' (Tsing, 2005: 4), seem left to contemplate the problems of organising political resistance more generally under the timeworn rubric of 'black British art'. Once difference is commoditised under conditions of multinational capitalism, identifications through difference have nowhere else to go but follow narrowing, reductionist lines. Any simple sense of boundedness – of where lines of difference should be drawn – is also made uncertain by lived experience. In its place are more conservative political affiliations that tend to furnish self-interest.

While critical theory has announced, and then re-announced, 'the end of the essential black subject' and the advent of 'new ethnicities' (Hall, 1988; 2006: 20), the wider social reality by contrast shows the continuing embrace of what may be called 'new essentialisms', fixed categories of difference that adhere even after so much institution-based deconstructionism, assimilation and integration. Certainly the fruitful conviviality of an actually existing multicultural Britain is at odds with the bureaucratic measures and market forces that try to reify difference, glossing over the conjunctive forces and developments that give rise to politically decisive 'moments', or the genealogically located 'problem-spaces' (Scott, 2004) that have challenged reductive configurations of 'race' and nationhood. New essentialisms emerge in a worrying trend: individuals forming into small, bounded groups and privatising their interests. Within these small units of affiliation, the prospect of facing up to the wider pressures – the forces that prompt the creation of such boundaries in the first instance – is diminished. Social energies are instead displaced and reflected in anxieties about 'strangers', as Bauman reminds us, in a taking of power which results in all differences being reinscribed as 'other' to one another: altogether a failed and compromised sort of equality.

To a degree, current thought on black British art is similarly afflicted. It is encumbered by a sense of the 'chaos' of 'strange' ideas threatened by the freshly interventionist work that could reconnect this art's local social contexts to broader global currents and to emerging political philosophies more generally. I have tempered my criticism of it, rather than trying to prise open the carapace of intellectual conservativism on the matter of difference. (I note a recent journalistic example that attempted its polemic by contradictorily appealing to *generational* difference.)[7] What is needed is a compassionate response that tries to explain where and when things went so awry, in the hope of staving off any future re-entrenchment. The political and scholarly legacy of cultural studies in its address to black British art must be gauged by the slow waning of the linguistic turn in the academic world that began in the 1970s. Influential thinkers such as Latour see the liberating potential of such deconstructionism in general to be ebbing: that 'critique has run out of steam' (Latour, 2004). Reflecting on what I have described, it would be wrong to conclude that such a paradigm is about to utterly outplay its role, since the social distances and differences that precipitated the 'epistemological revolution' (Mercer, 2009: 76) of critical work on black British art have not entirely collapsed nor evaporated. What has emerged as a problem in itself is all the false expectation about the yield of post-structuralism, evidenced in a scramble for 'ownership' of that discourse. Here is critical thinking somehow emptied of its revolutionary portent and quicksilver pliability, unable to reckon with the historical change that has taken place since its inception.

## Art and hierarchy

Philosophy can be a fulcrum for promoting scholarly dialogue on black British art, and one that exceeds the boundaries of one or other theoretical approach by giving up on an 'either this/or that' style of reasoning. A readership that marginalises the black British field by consigning its significance to the past developments of the humanities – employing the politics of time (Wainwright, 2011) – needs to know that those who still have a stake in the discursive category of 'black British art' are part of a broader global field of interest in art's affective relations and historical consciousness that philosophical thought can address head-on, and successfully, through problems of aesthetics and corporeality.

7 'The shortsightedness of the second postcolonial generation here in the UK has been its inability to see how the representations it authored and supported, to challenge repressive institutions responsible for perpetuating states of otherness, may themselves become repressive for later generations they presume to speak for, and may be co-opted by the very same forces they were meant to combat' (Quaintance, 2013: 4).

A focus on the horizons of phenomenal difference is the basis of such a wide appeal: the idea of interaction between individuals made possible through contact of a perceptual and bodily nature with certain special objects, the artworks of diaspora artists in Britain. The need to understand what is possible through the spaces, the worlds 'set up' by those works, in terms of the experiences they affect should steer our descriptions. It may in turn elaborate on the contemporary scholarship around art and visuality which accepts that 'Objects are active participants in the performance of analysis in that they enable reflection and speculation … and thus constitute a theoretical object with philosophical relevance' (Bal, 2003: 24).

This sphere of phenomenal importance retains an emphasis on different horizons. Indeed, it keeps in view encounters with and among social and ontological horizons. Ultimately, a phenomenal analysis can develop flexibly and ethically to shine light on black British art as a field that breaks from circularity, away from having to contend perpetually with the pressure to set differences within a hierarchy of cultural categories. The distribution of the phenomenal world into critical sites of difference is a feature of everyday life that should be highlighted with a view to changing it. As I have shown, the dilemmas presented by black British art require dialogic events of perceptual encounter that bring about a hermeneutic merging of horizons. The real alternative that such art anticipates is certainly one that blurs the boundaries between disciplines, but more so, that makes sure that the customary acknowledgement of difference that characterises our era is reminded insistently that equality and community should be our very starting point.

Viewers of black British art need to be their own active interpreters and cultural practitioners, capable of collapsing the distance between artworks and their audiences so that the interpretations which form within a gamut of emotions are imbued with perceptual wonder about art. The guidance for doing so is there in the trajectory that I have plotted, from art-making as a way of placing the past to the poetics of corporeality, from the patterns of equivalence to chiasmic intertwining. Quietly insistent in its repeating message, philosophy can bring that phenomenal difference to a general theory of practice for black British art.

# Bibliography


Abraham, Julia, 2012, 'Transformation and Defiance in the Art Establishment',
    unpublished MPhil thesis, University of Birmingham.
Alexander, Meena, 2001, 'Post-Colonial Theatre of Sense: The Art of Chila Kumari
    Burman', *n.paradoxa*, 14, pp. 4–13.
Araeen, Rasheed, 1984, *Making Myself Visible*, London: Kala Press.
Araeen, Rasheed, 1988a, *The Essential Black Art*, London: Kala Press.
Araeen, Rasheed, 1988b, 'Conversation with Avinash Chandra', *Third Text*, 2.3/4,
    pp. 69–96.
Araeen, Rasheed (ed.), 1989a, *The Other Story: Afro-Asian Artists in Post-War Britain*,
    London: Hayward Gallery.
Araeen, Rasheed, 1989b, 'Our Bauhaus, Others' Mud House', *Third Text*, 3.6, pp. 3–14.
Araeen, Rasheed, 1991, 'From Primitivism to Ethnic Art', in Susan Hiller (ed.), *The
    Myth of Primitivism*, London: Routledge, pp. 132–152.
Araeen, Rasheed, 1994, 'New Internationalism, or the Multiculturalism of Global
    Bantustans', in Fisher 1994, pp. 3–11.
Araeen, Rasheed, 2000a, 'A New Beginning: Beyond Postcolonial Cultural Theory
    and Identity Politics', *Third Text*, 14.50, pp. 3–20.
Araeen, Rasheed, 2000b, 'The Art of Benevolent Racism', *Third Text*, 14.51,
    pp. 57–64.
Araeen, Rasheed, 2001, 'Rewriting History: Another Story', *Art Monthly*, 247, p. 52.
Araeen, Rasheed, 2004, 'The Success and Failure of Black Art', *Third Text*, 18.2,
    pp. 135–52.
Araeen, Rasheed, and Chambers, Eddie, 1988, 'Black Art: A Discussion', *Third
    Text*, 5, pp. 51–77.
Arana, R. Victoria, 2009, *'Black' British Aesthetics Today*, 2nd ed., Newcastle:
    Cambridge Scholars Publishing.
Archer, Michael, Brett, Guy, and de Zegher, Catherine (eds), 1997, *Mona Hatoum*,
    London: Phaidon.
Armstrong, Philip, Lisbon, Laura, and Melville, Stephen (eds), 2001, *As Painting:
    Division and Displacement*, Cambridge, MA: MIT Press and the Wexner Center.
Ashcroft, Bill, Griffiths, Gareth, and Tiffin, Helen (eds), 1989, *The Empire Writes
    Back: Theory and Practice in Post-Colonial Literatures*, London: Routledge.
Bacci, Francesca, and Melcher, David (eds), 2011, *Art and the Senses*, Oxford: Oxford
    University Press.

Bachelard, Gaston, 1994, *The Poetics of Space*, Boston, MA: Beacon Press.

Bachelard, Gaston, 2000, *The Dialectic of Duration*, trans. Mary McAllester Jones, London: Clinamen Press.

Bailey, David A., and Hall, Stuart (eds), 1992a, *Ten.8*, 2.3, special issue, 'Critical Decade: Black British Photography in the 1980s'.

Bailey, David A., and Hall, Stuart, 1992b, 'The Vertigo of Displacement: Shifts within Black Documentary Practices', in Bailey and Hall, 1992a, pp. 14–23.

Bailey, David A., Baucom, Ian, and Boyce, Sonia (eds), 2005, *Shades of Black: Assembling the 8os. Black Arts in Post-War Britain*, Durham, NC and London: Duke University Press and Institute of International Visual Arts.

Bailey, David A., and Mercer, Kobena (eds), 1995, *Mirage: Enigmas of Race, Difference and Desire*, London: Institute of Contemporary Art and Institute of International Visual Arts.

Baker, Houston A., Diawara, Manthia, and Lindeborg, Ruth A. (eds), 1996, *Black British Cultural Studies: A Reader*, Chicago, IL: University of Chicago Press.

Baker, Jennifer M., 2009, *The Tactile Eye: Touch and the Cinematic Experience*, Berkeley, CA: University of California Press.

Baker, Jennifer M., 2011, 'Touch and the Cinematic Experience', in Bacci and Melcher, 2011, pp. 149–160.

Bakhtin, Mikhail, 1981, *The Dialogic Imagination: Four Essays*, Austin, TX: University of Texas Press.

Bal, Mieke, 2003, 'Visual Essentialism and the Object of Visual Culture', *Journal of Visual Culture*, 2.1, pp. 5–32.

Bal, Mieke, and Bryson, Norman, 1991, 'Semiotics and Art History', *The Art Bulletin*, 73.2, pp. 174–208.

Barad, Karen, 2007, *Meeting the Universe Halfway: Quantum Physics and the Entanglement of Matter and Meaning*, Durham, NC: Duke University Press.

Barraclough, Jon, Chan, Deborah, and Leung, Wing-Fai (eds), 2002, *Ten Thousand Li: Chinese Infusion in Contemporary British Culture*, Liverpool: Liverpool School of Art and Design and the Centre for Art International Research.

Barson, Tanya, and Gorschlüter, Peter (eds), 2010, *Afro Modern: Journeys through the Black Atlantic*, Liverpool and London: Tate Publications.

Barthes, Roland, 1977, *Image-Music-Text*, London: Fontana.

Baucom, Ian, 1998, *The Unmapped Body: Three Black British Artists*, New Haven, CT: Yale University Press.

Baucom, Ian, et al. (eds), 2004, *Sutapa Biswas*, London: Institute of International Visual Arts in collaboration with the Douglas F. Colley Memorial Art Gallery, Reed College, Portland, Oregon.

Bauman, Zygmunt, 1997, *Postmodernity and its Discontents*, Cambridge: Polity Press.

Bauman, Zygmunt, 1999, *In Search of Politics*, London: Polity Press.

Belting, Hans, 1994, *Likeness and Presence: A History of the Image Before the Era of Art*, trans. Edmund Jephcott, Chicago, IL: University of Chicago Press.

Belting, Hans, 2002, *An Anthropology of Images: Picture, Medium, Body*, trans. Thomas Dunlap, Princeton, NJ: Princeton University Press.

Benjamin, Andrew, 2012, 'Matter and Movement's Presence: Notes on Heidegger, Francesco Mosca and Bernini', *Research in Phenomenology*, 42, pp. 343–373.

Benjamin, Walter, 1968 [1939], 'The Work of Art in the Age of Its Technological Reproducibility' (third version), in *Illuminations*, ed. Hannah Arendt, trans. Harry Zohn, New York: Harcourt, Brace and World.

Bennett, Jane, 2001, *The Enchantment of Modern Life: Attachments, Crossings and Ethics*, Princeton, NJ: Princeton University Press.

Bennett, Jane, 2010, *Vibrant Matter: A Political Ecology of Things*, Durham, NC: Duke University Press.

Berger, Maurice, 1997, *Minimal Politics: Performativity and Minimalism in Recent American Art*, University of Maryland, Baltimore County, Fine Arts Gallery.

Bernier, Marie-Celeste, and Durkin, Hannah (eds), 2016, *Visualising Slavery: Art across the African Diaspora*, Liverpool: Liverpool University Press.

Bernstein, Jay, 2003, 'Wax, Brick and Bread: Apotheoses of Matter and Meaning in Seventeenth Century Philosophy and Painting', in Dana Arnold and Margaret Iversen (eds), *Art and Thought*, Oxford: Blackwell, pp. 28–50.

Bhabha, Homi K., 1994, *The Location of Culture*, London: Routledge.

Bhabha, Homi K., 1998, 'Anish Kapoor: Making Emptiness', in South Bank Centre, *Anish Kapoor*, London and Berkeley, CA: Hayward Gallery and University of California Press, pp. 11–41.

Bhimji, Zarina, 1990, 'Live for Sharam and Die for Izzat', in Rutherford, 1990, pp. 127–156.

Blackman, Lisa, and Walkerdine, Valerie, 2001, *Mass Hysteria: Critical Psychology and Media Studies*, Basingstoke: Palgrave.

Boetzkes, Amanda, 2010, 'Phenomenology and Interpretation Beyond the Flesh', in Dana Arnold (ed.), *Art History: Contemporary Practices on Method*, Oxford: Blackwell, pp. 34–55.

Boetzkes, Amanda, and Vinegar, Aron (eds), 2014, *Heidegger and the Work of Art History*, Farnham: Ashgate.

Bontekoe, Ronald, 1996, *Dimensions of the Hermeneutic Circle*, Amherst, NY: Humanity Books.

Boyce, Sonia, 2000, 'Sisters Are Doing it for Themselves', in Jean Fisher (ed.), *Reverberations: Tactics of Resistance, Forms of Agency in Trans/cultural Practices*, Maastricht: Jan van Eyck Akademie.

Bradley, Jyll, 1993, 'An Audience unto Herself: Jyll Bradley Profiles Zarina Bhimji', *Women's Art Magazine*, 51, pp. 23–24.

Brunei Gallery, 1999, *Routes: Thou Shalt Not Covet Thy Neighbour's Idols*, London: The Brunei Gallery.

Bryson, Norman, 1983, *Vision and Painting: The Logic of the Gaze*, New Haven, CT: Yale University Press.

Burbridge, Benedict, and Chandler, David (eds), 2006, *Henna Nadeem: A Picture Book of Britain*, Brighton: Photoworks.

Burman, Chila, and Hunjan, Bhajan, 1987, 'Mash it Up', in Roszika Parker and Griselda Pollock (eds), *Framing Feminism: Art and the Women's Movement 1970–1985*, London: Pandora, pp. 326–330.

Butler, Judith, 1989, 'Sexual Ideology and Phenomenal Description: A Feminist Critique of Merleau-Ponty's Phenomenology of Perception', in Jeffner Allen and Iris Marion Young (eds), *The Thinking Muse: Feminism and Modern French Philosophy*, Bloomington, IN: Indiana University Press, pp. 85–100.

Caldwell, Paulette M., 1991, 'A Hair Piece: Perspectives on the Intersection of Race and Gender', *Duke Law Journal*, 40.2, pp. 365–396.

Casey, Edward S., 1997, *The Fate of Place: A Philosophical History*, London and Berkeley, CA: University of California Press.

Castoriadis, Cornelius, 1987, *The Imaginary Institution of Society*, Cambridge: Polity Press.

Caygill, Howard, 1998, *Walter Benjamin: The Colour of Experience*, London: Routledge.

Chakrabarty, Dipesh, 2001, 'Postcoloniality and the Artifice of History', in Salah Hassan and Iftikhar Dadi (eds), *Unpacking Europe: Towards a Critical Reading*, Museum Boijmans Van Beuningen, Rotterdam: Museum Boijmans Van Beuningen, pp. 178–195.

Chambers, Eddie, 1991, *Four x 4: Installations by Sixteen Artists in Four Gallery Spaces*, exhibition catalogue, Bristol: Arnolfini Gallery.

Chambers, Eddie, 1998, 'The Emergence and Development of Black Visual Arts Activity in England between 1981 and 1986: Press and Public Responses', unpublished PhD thesis, Goldsmiths College, University of London.

Chambers, Eddie, 2012, *Things Done Change: The Cultural Politics of Recent Black Artists in Britain*, Amsterdam and New York: Rodopi.

Chambers, Eddie, 2014, *Black Artists in British Art: A History since the 1950s*, London: I. B. Tauris.

Chandler, David (ed.), 1997, *Keith Piper: Relocating the Remains*, London: Institute of International Visual Arts and the Royal College of Art.

Clark, T. J., 2001, 'Phenomenality and Materiality in Cézanne', in Tom Cohen, Barbara Cohen, J. Hillis Miller and Andrzej Warminski (eds), *Material Events: Paul de Man and the Afterlife of Theory*, Minneapolis, MN: University of Minnesota Press, pp. 93–114.

Clarke, Victoria, and Tawadros, Gilane (eds), 1999, *Run Through the Jungle: Selected Writings by Eddie Chambers*, London: Institute of International Visual Arts.

Clifford, James, 1997, *Routes*, Cambridge, MA: Harvard University Press.

Conrad, Joseph, 2007 [1899], *Heart of Darkness*, London: Penguin.

Copeland, Huey, 2013, *Bound to Appear: Art, Slavery, and the Site of Blackness in Multicultural America*, Chicago, IL: University of Chicago Press.

Crapanzano, Vincent, 1986, 'Hermes' Dilemma: The Masking of Subversion in Ethnographic Description', in James Clifford and George Marcus (eds), *Writing Culture: The Poetics and Politics of Ethnography*, London and Berkeley, CA: University of California Press, pp. 51–76.

Creation for Liberation, 1985, *Creation for Liberation Open Exhibition: Art by Black Artists*, London: Creation for Liberation.

Csordas, Thomas J., 1994, *Embodiment and Experience: The Existential Ground of Culture and Self*, Cambridge: Cambridge University Press.

Cubitt, Sean, 1999, 'Keith Piper: After Resistance, Beyond Destiny', *Third Text*, 47, pp. 77–86.

Culler, Jonathan, 1988, *Framing the Sign: Criticism and its Institutions*, Norman, OK: University of Oklahoma Press.

D'Alleva, Anne, 2001, 'Metaphor and Metonymy in Tahitian Tamau', in Christopher Pinney and Nicholas Thomas (eds), *Beyond Aesthetics: Art and the Technologies of Enchantment*, London: Berg.

Danto, Arthur, 1988, 'Art and Artifact', in Susan Vogel (ed.), *ART/Artifact: African Art in Anthropology Collections*, New York: Center for African Art, pp. 18–33.

Davis, Whitney, 2011, *A General Theory of Visual Culture*, Princeton, NJ: Princeton University Press.

Demos, T. J., 2012, 'Zarina Bhimji: Cinema of Affect', in *Zarina Bhimji*, exhibition catalogue, London: Ridinghouse, pp. 11–29.

Demos, T. J., 2013, *Return to the Postcolony: Spectres of Colonialism in Contemporary Art*, Berlin: Sternberg Press.

Dempsey, Andrew, Tawadros, Gilane, and Williams, Maridowa (eds), 1998, *Aubrey Williams*, London: Institute of International Visual Arts and the Whitechapel Gallery.

Derrida, Jacques, 1973, *Speech and Phenomena and Other Essays on Husserl's Theory of Signs*, trans. David B. Allison, Evanston, IL: Northwestern University Press.

Derrida, Jacques, 1981, *Positions*, trans. A. Bass, London: Athlone Press.

Derrida, Jacques, 1982, *Margins of Philosophy*, trans. Alan Bass, Brighton: Harvester.

Desjarlais, Robert, 1992, *Body and Emotion: The Aesthetics of Illness and Healing in the Nepal Himalayas*, Philadelphia, PA: University of Philadelphia Press.

Dillon, Martin C., 1988, *Merleau-Ponty's Ontology*, Bloomington, IN: Indiana University Press.

Dillon, Martin C., 1995, *Semiological Reductionism: A Critique of the Deconstructionist Movement in Postmodern Thought*, New York: State University of New York Press.

Doy, Gen, 2000, *Black Visual Culture: Modernity and Postmodernity*, London: I.B. Tauris.

Du Gay, Paul, Hall, Stuart, Janes, Linda, Mackay, Hugh, and Negus, Keith, 1997, *Doing Cultural Studies: The Story of the Sony Walkman*, London: Sage and The Open University.

Edwards, Elizabeth, 2001, *Raw Histories: Photographs, Anthropology and Museums*, Oxford: Berg.

Edwards, Elizabeth, and Lien, Sigrid (eds), 2014, *Uncertain Images: Museums and the Work of Photographs*, Farnham: Ashgate.

Egan, Gregory Mark, 1997, *Diaspora*, London: Millennium/Orion Press.

Elkins, James, 2008, 'On Some Limits of Materiality in Art History', *31: Das Magazin des Instituts für Theorie* [Zürich], 12, pp. 25–30, special issue *Taktilität: Sinneserfahrung als Grenzerfahrung*, edited by Stefan Neuner and Julia Gelshorn.

English, Darby, 2007, *How to See a Work of Art in Total Darkness*, Cambridge, MA: MIT Press.

Fanon, Frantz, 1986, *Black Skin, White Masks*, trans. Charles Lam Markmann, London: Pluto Press.

Ferguson, Leland, 1992, *Uncommon Ground: Archaeology and Early African America, 1650–1800*, London and Washington, DC: Smithsonian Institution Press.

Fisher, Jean (ed.), 1994, *Global Visions: Towards a New Internationalism in the Visual Arts*, London: Kala Press.

Fisher, Jean, 1996, 'The Syncretic Turn: Cross-Cultural Practices in the Age of Multiculturalism', in Milena Kalinovska, Lia Gangitano and Steven Nelson (eds), *New Histories*, Boston, MA: The Institute of Contemporary Art, pp. 32–38.

Fisher, Jean, 1997, 'The Work Between Us', in Okwui Enwezor (ed.), *Trade Routes: History and Geography*, biennial catalogue, Johannesburg: Greater Johannesburg Metropolitan Council and the Prince Claus Fund for Culture and Development, pp. 20–22.

Fisher, Jean, 2003, *Vampire in the Text*, London: Institute of International Visual Arts.

Fisher, Jean, 2008, 'Diaspora, Trauma and the Poetics of Remembrance', in Mercer, 2008, pp. 190–212.

Foster, Hal (ed.), 1988, *Vision and Visuality*, Seattle, WA: Bay Press.

Foster, Hal, 1994, 'The Artist as Ethnographer?', in Fisher, 1994, pp. 12–19.

Foster, Hal, 2015, *Bad New Days*, London: Verso.

Fóti, Véronique M., 1993, 'The Dimension of Colour', in Johnson and Smith, 1993, pp. 293–308.

Foucault, Michel, 1988, 'Technologies of the Self', in Luther H. Martin, Huck Gutman Gutman and Patrick H. Hutton (eds), *Technologies of the Self: A Seminar with Michel Foucault*, Amherst, MA: University of Massachusetts Press, pp. 16–49.

Freedberg, David, 1989, *The Power of Images: Studies in the History and Theory of Response*, Chicago, IL: University of Chicago Press.

Fried, Michael, 1998, *Art and Objecthood: Essays and Reviews*, Chicago, IL: University of Chicago Press.

Fuglerud, Øivind, and Wainwright, Leon (eds), 2015, *Objects and Imagination: Perspectives on Materialization and Meaning*, New York and Oxford: Berghahn.

Gadamer, Hans-Georg, 1979, *Truth and Method*, trans. Sabine Wilke and Richard Gray, Minneapolis, MN: University of Minnesota Press.

Gallopp, Jane, 1988, *Thinking Through the Body*, New York: Columbia University Press.

Garrison, Len, 1990, 'The Black Historical Past in British Education', in Peter Stone and Robert MacKenzie (eds), *The Excluded Past*, London: Routledge, pp. 231–244.

Gates Jr, Henry Louis, 2010, *Tradition and the Black Atlantic: Critical Theory in the African Diaspora*, New York: Basic Civitas.

Geertz, Clifford, 1973, 'Deep Play: Notes on the Balinese Cockfight', in *The Interpretation of Cultures: Selected Essays by Clifford Geertz*, New York: Basic Books, pp. 412–454.

Gell, Alfred, 1992, 'The Technology of Enchantment and the Enchantment of Technology', in Jeremy Coote and Anthony Shelton (eds), *Anthropology, Art and Aesthetics*, Oxford: Clarendon Press, pp. 40–63.

Gell, Alfred, 1998, *Art and Agency: An Anthropological Theory*, Oxford: Oxford University Press.

Gibbons, Joan, 2007, *Contemporary Art and Memory: Images of Recollection and Remembrance*, London and New York: I. B. Tauris.

Gill, John, Hoffmann, Jens, and Tawadros, Gilane (eds), 2006, *Alien Nation*, London/Ostfildern: Institute of Contemporary Arts and the Institute of International Visual Arts/Hatje Cantz Verlag.

Gilroy, Paul, 1987, *'There Ain't No Black in the Union Jack': The Cultural Politics of 'Race' and Nation*, London: Hutchinson.

Gilroy, Paul, 1988a, 'Nothing But Sweat Inside My Hand: Diaspora Aesthetics and Black Arts in Britain', in Mercer, 1988, pp. 44–46.

Gilroy, Paul, 1988b, 'Cruciality and the Frog's Perspective: An Agenda of Difficulties for the Black Art's Movement in Britain', *Third Text*, 2.5, pp. 33–44.

Gilroy, Paul, 1993a, *The Black Atlantic: Modernity and Double Consciousness*, London: Verso.

Gilroy, Paul, 1993b, *Small Acts: Thoughts on the Politics of Black Cultures*, London: Serpent's Tail.

Gilroy, Paul, 2004, *After Empire: Melancholia or Convivial Culture*, London: Routledge.

Glissant, Edouard, 1997, *Poetics of Relation*, trans. Betsy Wing, Ann Arbor, MI: Michigan University Press.

Greater London Council, 1985, *Anti-Racist Mural Project*, London: GLC Race Equality Unit.

Grossberg, Lawrence, 1996, 'On Postmodernism and Articulation: An Interview with Stuart Hall', in Morley and Chen, 1996, pp. 131–150.

Grossberg, Lawrence, 1997, 'Experience, Signification and Reality: The Boundaries of Cultural Semiotics', in Lawrence Grossberg, *Bringing it all Back Home: Essays on Cultural Studies*, Durham, NC: Duke University Press, pp. 70–102.

Gupta, Sunil, 1995, *Joy Gregory: Monograph*, London: Autograph, ABP.

Hadreas, Peter, 1986, *In Place of the Flawed Diamond: An Investigation of Merleau-Ponty's Philosophy*, New York: Peter Lang.

Hagen, Margaret, 1986, *Varieties of Realism: Geometries of Representational Art*, Cambridge: Cambridge University Press.

Hall, Stuart, 1980a, 'Cultural Studies and the Centre: Some Problematics and Problems', in Stuart Hall et al. (eds), *Culture, Media, Language: Working Papers in Cultural Studies, 1972–1979*, London: Routledge in association with the Centre for Contemporary Cultural Studies, pp. 2–35.

Hall, Stuart, 1980b, 'Encoding/Decoding', in Stuart Hall et al. (eds), *Culture, Media, Language: Working Papers in Cultural Studies, 1972–1979*, London: Routledge in association with the Centre for Contemporary Cultural Studies, pp. 117–127.

Hall, Stuart, 1980c, 'Race, Articulation and Societies Structured in Dominance', in *Sociological Theories: Race and Colonialism*, Paris: UNESCO Publishing, pp. 305–345.

Hall, Stuart, 1982, 'The Rediscovery of "Ideology": Return of the Repressed in Media Studies', in Tony Bennett, James Curran, Michael Gurevitch and Janet Woollacott (eds), *Culture, Society and the Media*, London: Methuen, pp. 56–90.

Hall, Stuart, 1988, 'New Ethnicities', in Mercer, 1988, pp. 27–31.

Hall, Stuart, 1990, 'Cultural Identity and Diaspora', in Rutherford, 1990, pp. 222–237.

Hall, Stuart, 1992a, 'What is this "Black" in Black Popular Culture?', in Gina Dent (ed.), *Black Popular Culture: A Project by Michele Wallace*, Seattle, WA: Bay Press, pp. 20–33.

Hall, Stuart, 1992b, 'Reconstruction Work', in Bailey and Hall, 1992a, pp. 106–113.

Hall, Stuart, 1996a, 'When was "the Post-Colonial?" Thinking at the Limit', in Iain Chambers and Lidia Curti (eds), *The Post-Colonial Question: Common Skies, Divided Horizons*, London and New York: Routledge, pp. 242–260.

Hall, Stuart, 1996b, 'The After-Life of Frantz Fanon', in Alan Read (ed.), *The Fact of Blackness: Frantz Fanon and Visual Representation*, London: Institute of Contemporary Arts, pp. 12–37.

Hall, Stuart, 1996c, 'Cultural Identity and Cinematic Representation', in Baker, Diawara and Lindeborg, 1996, pp. 210–222.

Hall, Stuart, 1996d, 'Who Needs Identity?', in Hall and du Gay, 1996, pp. 1–17.

Hall, Stuart (ed.), 1997, *Representation: Cultural Representations and Signifying Practices*, London: Sage and The Open University.

Hall, Stuart, 2001a, 'Constituting an Archive', *Third Text*, 54, pp. 89–92.

Hall, Stuart, 2001b, 'Museums of Modern Art and the End of History', in Sarah Campbell and Gilane Tawadros (eds), *Stuart Hall and Sarat Maharaj: Modernity and Difference*, London: Institute of International Visual Arts, pp. 8–23.

Hall, Stuart, 2006, 'Black Diaspora Artists in Britain: Three "Moments" in Post-War History', *History Workshop Journal*, 61.1, pp. 1–24.

Hall, Stuart, and du Gay, Paul (eds), 1996, *Questions of Cultural Identity*, London: Sage.

Hall, Stuart, and Maharaj, Sarat, 2001, 'Modernity and Difference: A Conversation between Stuart Hall and Sarat Maharaj', in Sarah Campbell and Gilane Tawadros (eds), *Stuart Hall and Sarat Maharaj: Modernity and Difference*, London: Institute of International Visual Arts, pp. 36–56.

Hall, Stuart, and Sealy, Mark, 2001, *Different: A Historical Context: Contemporary Photographers and Black Identity*, London: Phaidon.

Hanna, Heather, 2012, 'Women Framing Hair: Serial Strategies in Contemporary Art', unpublished Phd thesis, The Open University.

Hansen, Miriam Bratu, 2008, 'Benjamin's Aura', *Critical Inquiry*, 34, pp. 336–375.

Hantel, Max, 2012, 'Errant Notes on a Caribbean Rhizome', *Rhizomes*, 24, http://www.rhizomes.net/issue24/hantel.html (accessed 1 January 2016).

Heidegger, Martin, 1978, 'The Origin of the Work of Art', in David Farrell Krell (ed.), *Martin Heidegger: Basic Writings*, London: Routledge, Kegan and Paul, pp. 139–212.

Heidegger, Martin, 1996, *Being and Time*, trans. Joan Stambaugh, Albany, NY: SUNY Press.

Hemmings, Clare, 2005, 'Invoking Affect: Cultural Theory and the Ontological Turn', *Cultural Studies*, 19.5, pp. 548–567.

Herbert Art Gallery, 1983, *The Pan-Afrikan Connection: An Exhibition of Work by Young Black Artists*, exhibition catalogue, Coventry: Herbert Art Gallery and Museum.

Hiro, Dilip, 1992, *Black British, White British: A History of Race Relations*, London: Paladin.

Hobart, Mark, 2000, *After Culture: Anthropology as Radical Metaphysical Critique*, Yogyakarta: Duta Wacana University Press.

Hylton, Richard (ed.), 2003, *Donald Rodney: Doublethink*, London: Autograph ABP.

Hylton, Richard, 2007, *The Nature of the Beast: Cultural Diversity and the Visual Arts Sector – A Study of Policies, Initiatives and Attitudes 1976–2006*, Bath: The Institute of Contemporary Interdisciplinary Arts, University of Bath.

Hylton, Richard, 2013, 'Keeping Up Appearances: Black Artists, State Patronage and the Politics of Visibility', *Critical Interventions: Journal of African Art History and Visual Culture*, 7.2, pp. 37–57.

Irvine, Jaki, 1993, 'Zarina Bhimji: I Will Always Be Here', *Third Text*, 7.22, pp. 107–110.

James, C. L. R., 1984, 'Black Studies and the Contemporary Student', in C. L. R. James, *At the Rendezvous of Victory: Selected Writings*, London: Allison and Busby, pp. 186–201.

Jay, Martin, 1988, 'Scopic Regimes of Modernity', in Foster, 1988, pp. 3–28.

Jay, Martin, 1995, 'Photo-Unrealism: The Contribution of the Camera to the Crisis of Ocularcentrism', in Stephen Melville and Bill Readings (eds), *Vision and Textuality*, Basingstoke: Macmillan, pp. 344–360.

Jim, Alice Ming Wai, 2014, '20 Years of Departure Lounge Art: Airplanes, Airports and Visa Centres in Contemporary Art', in Beccy Kennedy, Alnoor Mitha and Leon Wainwright (eds), *Triennial City: Localising Asian Art*, Manchester: Cornerhouse, pp. 40–62.

Johnson, Galen A. (ed.), and Smith, Michael B. (trans. and ed.), 1993, *The Merleau-Ponty Aesthetics Reader: Philosophy and Painting*, Evanston, IL: Northwestern University Press.

Jones, Amelia, 2003a, 'Body', in Robert Nelson and Richard Shiff (eds), *Critical Terms for Art History*, Chicago, IL: University of Chicago Press, pp. 251–266.

Jones, Amelia, 2003b, 'Meaning, Identity, Embodiment: The Uses of Merleau-Ponty's Phenomenology in Art History', in Dana Arnold and Margaret Iversen (eds), *Art and Thought*, Oxford: Blackwell, pp. 71–90.

Jones, Caroline, 2006, *Eyesight Alone: Clement Greenberg's Modernism and the Bureaucratization of the Senses*, Chicago, IL: University of Chicago Press.

Julien, Isaac, and Mercer, Kobena, 1988, 'De Margin and De Centre. The Last "Special Issue" on Race?', *Screen*, 29.4, pp. 2–11.

Keen, Melanie, and Ward, Elizabeth, 1996, *Recordings: A Select Bibliography of Contemporary African, Afro-Caribbean and Asian British Art*, London: Institute of International Visual Arts and Chelsea College of Art and Design.

Krell, David Farrell (ed.), 1996, *Martin Heidegger: Basic Writings*, London: Routledge.

La Fontaine, Jean S., 1985, 'Person and Individual: Some Anthropological Reflections', in Michael Carrithers, Steven Collins and Steven Lukes (eds), *The Category of the Person: Anthropology, Philosophy, History*, Cambridge: Cambridge University Press, pp. 123–140.

Laclau, Ernesto, 1990, *New Reflections on the Revolution of our Time*, London: Verso.

Latour, Bruno, 2004, 'Why Has Critique Run Out of Steam? From Matters of Fact to Matters of Concern', *Critical Inquiry*, 30, pp. 225–248.

Leder, Drew, 1990, *The Absent Body*, Chicago, IL: University of Chicago Press.

Leicester City Art Gallery, 1992, *Crossing Black Waters*, exhibition catalogue, London: Working Press.

Leys, Ruth, 2011, 'The Turn to Affect: A Critique', *Critical Inquiry*, 37.3, pp. 434–472.

Lyotard, Jean-François, 1993, 'Discours, figure', in Johnson and Smith, 1993, pp. 309–322.

McClintock, Derrick, 1986, 'Colour', *Ten.8*, 22, p. 4.

MacCormack, Carol. P., and Strathern, Marilyn, (eds), 1980, *Nature, Culture and Gender*, Cambridge: Cambridge University Press.

McGuire, Randall H., and Paynter, Robert (eds), 1991, *The Archaeology of Inequality*, London: Blackwell.

Malik, Rohini, 1998, *Dave Lewis: Monograph*, London: Autograph.

Maniura, Robert, and Shepherd, Rupert (eds), 2006, *Presence: The Inherence of the Prototype within Images and Other Objects*, Aldershot: Ashgate.

Marks, Laura U., 2000, *The Skin of the Film: Intercultural Cinema, Embodiment, and the Senses*, Durham, NC: Duke University Press.

Marks, Laura U., 2002, *Touch: Sensuous Theory and Multisensory Media*, Minneapolis, MN: University of Minnesota Press.

Marsden, Emily, and Robinson, Deborah (eds), 2005, *Hew Locke*, Walsall: The New Art Gallery.

Melville, Stephen, 1998, 'Phenomenology and the Limits of Hermeneutics', in Mark A. Cheetham, Michael Ann Holly and Keith Moxey (eds), *The Subjects of Art History: Historical Objects in Contemporary Perspectives*, Cambridge: Cambridge University Press, pp. 143–154.

Mercer, Kobena (ed.), 1988, *Black Film/British Cinema, ICA Documents 7*, London: Institute of Contemporary Arts and the British Film Institute.

Mercer, Kobena, 1992, 'Engendered Species', *ArtForum*, Summer, pp. 74–77.

Mercer, Kobena, 1994, *Welcome to the Jungle: New Positions in Black Cultural Studies*, London: Routledge.

Mercer, Kobena, 1997, 'Witness at the Crossroads: An Artist's Journey in Postcolonial Space', in Chandler, 1997, pp. 13–19.

Mercer, Kobena, 1999, 'Ethnicity and Internationality: New British Art and Diaspora-Based Blackness', *Third Text*, 13.49, pp. 51–62.

Mercer, Kobena, 2000, 'A Sociography of Diaspora', in Paul Gilroy, Lawrence Grossberg and Angela McRobbie (eds), *Without Guarantees: In Honour of Stuart Hall*, London: Verso, pp. 233–245.

Mercer, Kobena, 2005, 'Iconography after Identity', in Bailey, Baucom and Boyce, pp. 49–53.

Mercer, Kobena (ed.), 2008, *Exiles, Diasporas and Strangers*, London: Institute of International Visual Arts.

Mercer, Kobena, 2009, '"Diaspora Didn't Happen in a Day": Reflections on Aesthetics and Time', in Arana, 2009, pp. 66–78.

Mercer, Kobena, 2016, *Travel and See: Black Diaspora Art Practices Since the 1980s*, Durham, NC: Duke University Press.

Merleau-Ponty, Maurice, 1962, *Phenomenology of Perception*, trans. Colin Smith, London: Routledge and Kegan Paul.

Merleau-Ponty, Maurice, 1964a, *The Primacy of Perception and Other Essays*, ed. Edie, James, Evanston, IL: Northwestern University Press.

Merleau-Ponty, Maurice, 1964b, *Signs*, trans. Richard C. McCleary, Evanston, IL: Northwestern University Press.

Merleau-Ponty, Maurice, 1964c, *Le Visible et l'invisible*, Paris: Gallimard.

Merleau-Ponty, Maurice, 1968, *The Visible and the Invisible*, trans. Alphonso Lingis, Evanston, IL: Northwestern University Press.

Merleau-Ponty, Maurice, 1993a, 'Cézanne's Doubt', in Johnson and Smith, 1993, pp. 59–75.

Merleau-Ponty, Maurice, 1993b, 'Eye and Mind', in Johnson and Smith, 1993, pp. 121–149.

Merleau-Ponty, Maurice, 1998, 'The Philosophy of Existence', in Jon Stewart (ed.), *The Debate Between Sartre and Merleau-Ponty*, Evanston, IL: Northwestern University Press, pp. 492–503.

Meskimmon, Marsha, 2013, 'The Precarious Ecologies of Cosmopolitanism', *Open Arts Journal*, 1, pp. 15–25.

Mirza, Munira (ed.), 2006, *Culture Vultures: Is UK Arts Policy Damaging the Arts?*, London: Policy Exchange.

Mirzoeff, Nicholas, 2000, *Diaspora and Visual Culture: Representing Africans and Jews*, London: Routledge.

Mitchell, W. J. T., 1996, 'What Do Pictures *Really* Want?', *October*, 77, pp. 71–82.

Moran, Dermot, 2000, *Introduction to Phenomenology*, London: Routledge.

Morley, David, and Chen, Kuan-Hsing (eds), 1996, *Stuart Hall: Critical Dialogues in Cultural Studies*, London: Routledge.

Morphy, Howard, 2009, 'Art as a Mode of Action: Some Problems with Gell's Art and Agency', *Journal of Material Culture*, 14.1, pp. 5–27.

Moten, Fred, 2003, *In the Break: The Aesthetics of the Black Radical Tradition*, Minneapolis, MN: University of Minnesota Press.

Naguib, Saphinaz-Amal, 2015, 'Materializing Islam and the Imaginary of Sacred Space', in Øivind Fuglerud and Leon Wainwright (eds), *Objects and Imagination: Perspectives on Materialization and Meaning*, New York and Oxford: Berghahn, pp. 64–78.

Nead, Lynda, 1995, *Chila Kumari Burman: Between Two Cultures*, London: Kala Press.

Nicodemus, Everlyn, 1999, 'Routes to Independence', in The Brunei Gallery, *Routes: Thou Shalt Not Covet Thy Neighbour's Idols*, exhibition catalogue, London: The Brunei Gallery.

Oguibe, Olu, 1999, 'In the "Heart of Darkness"', in Olu Oguibe and Okwui Enwezor (eds), *Reading the Contemporary: African Art from Theory to the Marketplace*, London: Institute of International Visual Arts, pp. 320–327.

Owusu, Kwesi (ed.), 1988, *Storms of the Heart: An Anthology of Black Arts and Culture*, London: Camden Press.

Panofsky, Erwin, 1955, *Meaning in the Visual Arts: Papers in and on Art History*, Garden City, NY: Doubleday.

Panofsky, Erwin, 1972, *Studies in Iconology: Humanistic Themes in the Art of the Renaissance*, New York and London: Harper and Row.

Papastergiadis, Nikos, 1995, *The Complicities of Culture: Hybridity and 'New Internationalism'*, Manchester: Cornerhouse.

Parry, Joseph D., and Wrathall, Mark, 2011, 'Introduction', in Joseph D. Parry (ed.), *Art and Phenomenology*, London and New York: Routledge, pp. 1–8.

Perry, Grayson, 2007, 'Positive Discrimination Patronizes Black Artists', *The Times*, 30 May, p. 16.

Phelan, Peggy, 1993, *Unmarked: The Politics of Performance*, London: Routledge.

Picton, John, 1999, 'In Vogue, or the Flavour of the Month: The New Way to Wear Black', in Olu Oguibe and Okwui Enwezor (eds), *Reading the Contemporary: African Art from Theory to the Marketplace*, London: Institute of International Visual Arts, pp. 115–126.

Picton, John, 2001, 'Yinka Shonibare: Undressing Ethnicity', *African Arts*, 34.3, pp. 66–73.

Piper, Keith, 1991, *A Ship Called Jesus*, exhibition catalogue, Birmingham: Ikon Gallery.

Pivin, Jean Loup, and Sealy, Mark, 1996, *Rotimi Fani-Kayode and Alex Hirst*, London: Autograph ABP.

Preziosi, Donald, 1998, *The Art of Art History: A Critical Anthology*, Oxford and New York: Oxford University Press.

Quaintance, Morgan, 2013, 'Post-Racialism: Morgan Quaintance Looks beyond Identity Constructs', *Art Monthly*, October, pp. 1–4.

Radcliffe-Brown, Alfred R., 1940, *Structure and Function in Primitive Society*, London: Cohen and West.

Rancière, Jacques, 2010, *The Emancipated Spectator*, London: Verso.

Ratnam, Niru, 1999a, 'Run through the Jungle: Selected Writings by Eddie Chambers', *Third Text*, 13.46, pp. 104–107.

Ratnam, Niru, 1999b, 'Chris Ofili and the Limits of Hybridity', *New Left Review*, 235, pp. 153–159.

Ricoeur, Paul, 1981, *Hermeneutics and the Human Sciences*, trans. and ed. John B. Thompson, Cambridge: Cambridge University Press.

Roberts, John, 1987, 'Interview with Sonia Boyce', *Third Text*, 1, pp. 55–64.

Roberts, John, 1990, *Postmodernism, Politics and Art*, Manchester: Manchester University Press.

Roberts, John, 1994, 'Indian Art, Identity and the Avant-Garde', *Third Text*, 27, pp. 31–37.

Rodowick, David N., 2001, *Reading the Figural, or, Philosophy After the New Media*, Durham, NC: Duke University Press.

Rutherford, Jonathan (ed.), 1990, *Identity: Community, Culture, Difference*, London: Lawrence and Wishart.

Rycroft, Daniel J., 2013, 'Co-existence and Art Historical Apprehensions', in Daniel J. Rycroft (ed.), *World Art and the Legacies of Colonial Violence*, Farnham: Ashgate, pp. 231–252.

Scarry, Elaine, 1985, *The Body in Pain: The Making and Unmaking of the World*, Oxford: Oxford University Press.

Schmidt, Barbara U., 1999, 'What Sense Do the Senses Make? Aspects of Corporeality in the Works of Miriam Cahn and Maureen Connor', in Amelia Jones and Andrew Stephenson (eds), *Performing the Body: Performing the Text*, London and New York: Routledge, pp. 283–293.

Scott, David, 2004, *Conscripts of Modernity: The Tragedy of Colonial Enlightenment*, Durham, NC: Duke University Press.

Sealy, Mark (ed.), 1993, *Vanley Burke: A Retrospective*, London: Lawrence and Wishart.

Shilling, Chris, 1993, *The Body and Social Theory*, London: Sage.

Smith, Michael B., 1993, 'Merleau-Ponty's Aesthetics', in Johnson and Smith, 1993, pp. 192–211.

Sobchack, Vivian, 1992, *The Address of the Eye: A Phenomenology of Film Experience*, Princeton, NJ: Princeton University Press.

Stafford, Barbara Maria, 1995, *Good Looking: Essays on the Virtues of Images*, Cambridge, MA: MIT Press.

Stewart, Jon (ed.), 1998, *The Debate Between Sartre and Merleau-Ponty*, Evanston, IL: Northwestern University Press.

Stoller, Sylvia, 2000, 'Comment on Shannon Sullivan's "Domination and Dialogue in Merleau-Ponty's Phenomenology of Perception"', *Hypatia*, 15.1, pp. 175–182.

Summers, David, 1996, 'Representation', in Robert S. Nelson and Richard Shiff (eds), *Critical Terms for Art History*, Chicago, IL: University of Chicago Press.

Summers, David, 2003, *Real Spaces: World Art History and the Rise of Western Modernism*, London and New York: Phaidon.

Tawadros, Gilane, 1995, 'The Sphinx Contemplating Napoleon: Black Women Artists in Britain', in Katy Deepwell (ed.), *New Feminist Art Criticism: Critical Strategies*, Manchester: Manchester University Press, pp. 25–30.

Tawadros, Gilane, 1996, 'Beyond the Boundary: The Work of Three Black Women Artists', in Baker, Diawara and Lindeborg, 1996, pp. 240–277.

Tawadros, Gilane, 1997, *Sonia Boyce: Speaking in Tongues*, London: Kala Press.

Taylor, Paul C., 2016, *Black is Beautiful: A Philosophy of Black Aesthetics*, Oxford: Wiley Blackwell.

Theophilus, Jeremy, 1994, 'Expressing the Essential: Ahmed Moustafa', *The Scribe: Journal of the Society of Scribes and Illuminators*, 62, pp. 6–7.

Thompson, Krista, 2015, *Shine: The Visual Economy of Light in African Diasporic Aesthetic Practice*, Durham, NC: Duke University Press.

Ticineto Clough, Patricia, and Halley, Jean (eds), 2007, *The Affective Turn: Theorizing the Social*, Durham, NC: Duke University Press.

Tsing, Anna, L., 2005, *Friction: An Ethnography of Global Connection*, Princeton, NJ: Princeton University Press.

Turner, Bryan S., 1984, *The Body and Society: Explorations in Social Theory*, Oxford: Blackwell.

Van Campen, Cretian, 2011, 'Visual Music and Musical Paintings: The Quest for Synaesthesia in the Arts', in Bacci and Melcher, 2011, pp. 495–512.

Vasseleu, Cathryn, 1998, *Textures of Light: Vision and Touch in Irigaray, Levinas and Merleau-Ponty*, London: Routledge.

Venn, Couze, 2009, 'Identity, Diasporas and Subjective Change: The Role of Affect, the Relation to the Other, and the Aesthetic', *Subjectivity*, 26.1, pp. 3–28.

Vlach, John Michael, 1990, *The Afro-American Tradition in Decorative Arts*, Athens, GA: Brown Thrasher Books.

Wainwright, Leon, 2000a, 'History as a Topic for Visual Thinking: British Art of the Caribbean Diaspora', *Wadabagei: A Journal of the Caribbean and its Diaspora*, 1.4, pp. 44–76.

Wainwright, Leon, 2000b, 'A Phenomenology of Origins: Artist Sonia Khurana', in *Sonia Khurana: Lone Women Don't Lie*, exhibition catalogue, New Delhi: The British Council.

Wainwright, Leon, 2003, 'Perception and Presence in British Art of the African, Asian and Caribbean Diasporas', unpublished PhD thesis, School of Oriental and African Studies, University of London.

Wainwright, Leon, 2005, 'Assembling Sources: An Annotated Bibliography', in Bailey, Baucom and Boyce, 2005, pp. 307–318.

Wainwright, Leon, 2006, 'Canon Questions on the Art of Black Britain', in Gail Low and Marion Wynne-Davies (eds), *A Black British Canon?*, Basingstoke: Palgrave Macmillan, pp. 143–167.

Wainwright, Leon, 2010, 'Art (School) Education and Art History', in Richard Appignanesi (ed.), *Beyond Cultural Diversity: The Case for Creativity (A Third Text Report)*, London: Third Text Publications, pp. 93–103.

Wainwright, Leon, 2011, *Timed Out: Art and the Transnational Caribbean*, Manchester: Manchester University Press.

Wainwright, Leon (ed.), 2017, *Disturbing Pasts: Memories, Controversies and Creativity*, Manchester: Manchester University Press.

Wainwright, Leon, and Zijlmans, Kitty (eds), 2017, *Sustainable Art Communities: Contemporary Creativity and Policy in the Transnational Caribbean*, Manchester: Manchester University Press.

Walmsley, Anne (ed.), 1990, *Guyana Dreaming: The Art of Aubrey Williams*, Coventry: Dangeroo Press.

Warner, Marina, 1995, *From the Beast to the Blonde: On Fairy Tales and Their Tellers*, London: Vintage.

West, Cornel, 1990, 'The New Cultural Politics of Difference', *October*, 53, pp. 93–109.

Wetherell, Margaret, 2012, *Affect and Emotion: A New Social Science Understanding*, London: Sage.

Williams, Glenn, 2000, 'Translating Music into Visual Form: The Influence of Music in the Work of Bertram Brooker', *Revue d'Art Canadienne / Canadian Art Review*, 37.1–2, pp. 111–122.

Wolff, Janet, 2012, 'After Cultural Theory: The Power of Images, the Lure of Immediacy', *Journal of Visual Culture*, 11.1, pp. 3–19.

Wölfflin, Heinrich, 1932, *Principles in Art History*, trans. and ed. M. D. Hottinger, New York: Henry Holt.

Wollheim, Richard, 1991, 'What the Spectator Sees', in Norman Bryson, Michael

Ann Holly and Keith Moxey (eds), *Visual Theory*, Oxford: Polity Press, pp. 101–150.

Wolverhampton Art Gallery, 1981, *Black Art an' Done: An Exhibition of Work by Young Black Artists*, exhibition catalogue, Wolverhampton: Wolverhampton Art Gallery.

Yeh, Diana, 2000, 'Ethnicities on the Move: "British-Chinese" Art: Identity, Subjectivity, Politics and Beyond', *Critical Quarterly*, 42.2, pp. 65–91.

Žižek, Slavoj, 1997, 'Multiculturalism, or, the Cultural Logic of Multinational Capitalism', *New Left Review*, 225, pp. 28–51.

# Index

Numbers in italics refer to illustrations.

Adrus, Said, *Trespassing* 79–81
agency and reversibility 132–157
Akomfrah, John, *The Unfinished Conversation* 190n6
Alexander, Meena 133
Ali, Laylah 174n2
*Alien Nation* exhibition 173–182, 185–186, 196
Ames, Ali Omar 113
animism 136–138, 155–156
Araeen, Rasheed 47–48, 113, 202–203
    *Green Painting* 113n1
Arif, Salim 111
art *see* Asian art; black British art
art and mediation 172–192
Asian art 110–131
    feminism and language 114–117
    food and sensory response to art 120–122
    intersectional with black arts movement 110–131, 133
    language-based engagement 110–111, 113, 119–120

Bachelard, Gaston 61, 115, 146
Bakhtin, Mikhail 28, 50
Barad, Karen 144
Barthes, Roland 153–155
Bauman, Zygmunt 201, 204
Belting, Hans 71–72, 160
Benjamin, Walter 43–44, 167

Berger, Maurice 39
Bhimji, Zarina 43, 101–102, 114–117, 118–119, 126
    *Charing Cross* series 121, 127
    *I Will Always Be Here* 114, 116–117
    *Live for Sharam, Die for Izzat* 114–116, 118–119
    *Vulnerable and Sticky* 98–99
Biard, François-Auguste, *The Slave Trade* 66
Biswas, Sutapa 86n12, 111
black British art
    animism of art objects 136–138, 155–156
    art and mediation 172–192
    'burden of representation' 26–27, 42, 136, 172–173, 197–198, 202–205
    countering reductionism 184–187, 195
    critical decade 31–33
    cultural representation 19–36, 37–38, 53, 172–173, 191–192, 197–198, 202–205
    disciplinary specificity 29–31, 35, 166
    efficacy of representation 45–46, 166–167
    equivalence of experience 109–131, 158
    fetishising of 'difference' 34–35, 42–43, 47, 173
    intertwining 158–171, 196–199
    locus of remembrance 53–69
    minimalism 39–40

multiculturalism 37, 186–187, 202–205
perceptual primacy 41–44, 49–51,
  70–71, 123–126, 191–192, 196–199
phenomenological approach 9–10,
  53–69, 70–108, 110–111, 130–131,
  152–155, 188–189, 193–206
post-critical ontology 189–190,
  199–200
're-presentation' 40–42, 44–45,
  180–181
reversibility of perceptual encounters
  132–157, 158
right of artist to self-identification
  34–35, 173
situatedness 46–49
state 'inclusionist' art policies 37–38,
  118
*see also* Asian art
Boyce, Sonia 54, 57, 67, 70, 126, 127,
  189–190
  *Afro Blanket* 105–106
  *Big Women's Talk* 57, 58, 60–61
  *Bringing Up Babies* 57, 61
  *Conversational Piece* 57, 61
  *Do You Want To Touch?* 105
  *She Ain't Holding Them Up* 57–60
  *Talking Presence* 162–163
Bradley, Jyll 117
Bruegel, Pieter 74
Bryson, Norman 78
Burbridge, Benedict 184
'burden of representation' 26–27, 42, 136,
  172–173, 197–198, 202–205
Burke, Vanley 82–86
  *Church meeting 84*
  *Outside George Street Church 82*
  *Portrait of a Woman 85*
  *The March 83*
Burman, Chila Kumari 86n12, 133–136
  *For Tune 133–135*
Butler, Judith 72–73n3
Butt, Hamad 174n2

Castoriadis, Cornelius 203–204
Chakrabarty, Dipesh 35

Chambers, Eddie 26–27, 80n11, 189–190
Chandler, David 184
Chuhan, Jagjit 86n12
Cleijne, Edgar 174n2
Clifford, James 127–128
colonialisation *see* diaspora
cultural representation 19–36, 37–38, 53,
  107–108, 172–173, 191–192, 197–198,
  202–205

da Vinci, Leonardo, *Battle of Anghiari* 75
D'Alleva, Anne 75
de Gheyn, Jacob 74
Demos, T.J. 43
Derrida, Jacques 200
diaspora
  aesthetic and interpretation 23–25,
    27–29, 30–31, 35–36, 43–44, 51–52,
    130–131, 164–165, 172, 193–194
  critical decade 31–33
  state 'inclusion' art policies 37–38
Dillon, Martin 187
disciplinary specificity 29–31, 35, 166
Dong, Song 128
Doy, Gen 27

Edge, Nina 86n12
Edwards, Elizabeth 167
efficacy of representation 45–46, 166–167
Elkins, James 72–73n3
English, Darby 128n11
equivalence 109–131, 158

feminism, Asian art 114–117
Fisher, Jean 35, 36n9, 44, 47–48n3, 190
Foster, Hal 107–108
Foucault, Michel 199

Gallagher, Ellen 174n2
Geertz, Clifford 48–49
Gell, Alfred 46, 75, 136–138, 154–155, 171
Gill, John 174n2
Gilroy, Paul 26, 28, 193, 201n4, 203
Glissant, Édouard 170–171
Grossberg, Lawrence 197

Haacke, Hans 39
Hagen, Margaret 78
Hall, Stuart 25n3, 28, 30–31, 39–40, 42,
    44, 47–48, 165, 169, 198
    'reconstruction' of black Britain 51
Hatoum, Mona 125, 126, 127
    *Baid Ghanam* 99–101
    *Corps étranger* 96–98
    *Jardin Public* 160–161
    *Kroush* 100–101
    *Measures of Distance 112*, 113
    *Recollection* 102–105
    *Rous Ghanam 100*–101
Heidegger, Martin 56, 67, 136, 156, 193,
    198–199, 200, 203
hermeneutics 151–152
historiography, visual 54–57
Hoffmann, Jens 174n2
Huffman, David 174n2
human body
    hair and touch 102–106
    'incarnate subjectivity' 71–74
    as locus of experience 93–95, 107–108,
      125–127
    perceptual analysis 71–74, 93–95
    phenomenology of the 95–98,
      107–108
Hunjan, Bhajan, *Trespassing 79–81*
Husserl, Edmund 56, 71, 124, 142, 168,
    193

'incarnate subjectivity' 71–74
intertwining, black British art 158–171,
    196–199
Irvine, Jaki 116–117

James, C.L.R. 193–194
Jay, Martin 78n7
Jordaens, Jacob 74

Kaur, Permindar 29, 86
    *Arrival* 20–23, 29
Kelly, Mary 39
Key, Anthony 128
Khanna, Balraj 111

Khurana, Sonia 139–151
    *Anhad: The 'Original' Sound 146–147*
    *Breath 140*, 141, 142
    *I'm Tied to My Mother's Womb with a*
      *Very Long Chord* 141–142, *143*
    *Lone Women Don't Lie* 144, *145*
    manipulation of time 146–151
    *The Waters, Forgotten of the Foot*
      147–149
    *Zoetrope 150*–151
Kierkegaard, Søren 193
Klee, Paul 159

Lacan, Jacques 41
Laclau, Ernesto 42, 198, 200
Lamba, Juginder 111
    *Local Marriage 90–91*
    *Pod Four 89–90*
    *The Cry 86–93*
    *Tree 91–92*
Lamba, Manjeet 29, 86
    *Arrival 19–20*, 29
language-based engagement, Asian art
    110–111, 113, 119–120
Latour, Bruno 205
Locke, Hew 174n2, 176–179
    *Golden Horde 177–178*, 186
    *Hemmed in Two 176–177*
Lyotard, Jean-François 71, 164, 196

McQueen, Steve 32n5
Manet, Édouard 74
Marchand, André 159
Marepe 174n2
mediation 172–192
    *Alien Nation* exhibition 173–182, 196
memorialisation
    artistic representation 53–69
    visual historiography 54–57
Mercer, Kobena 25–27, 28, 30, 32, 36,
    46–48n2, 172, 201n5
Merleau-Ponty, Maurice 41, 44, 46, 71,
    72
    objectivity and perception 93–95, 101,
      123–125, 129, 137–138, 142, 153, 200

*Phenomenology of Perception* 123–125,
    158, 168
  reversibility 158–160, 162, 168, 188–189
  *The Visible and the Invisible* 158
Meskimmon, Marsha 51
migration *see* diaspora
minimalism 39–40
Mistry, Dhruva 111
Mo, Yeu-Lai 120–*122*, 126, 127–128
  *Food Jars* series 120–122
modernity, perspective of diaspora 24–25
Morphy, Howard 194
Morris, Robert 39
Mouffe, Chantal 198
multiculturalism 202–205
  policies of 37, 186–187
Mustafa, Ahmed 113

Nadeem, Henna 174n2, 182–184, 186
  *A Picture Book of Britain* 184
  *People* 182, *183*
Newkirk, Kori 174n2, 180, 186
  *Merk* 180–*181*
Nietzsche, Friedrich 193

Ofili, Chris 32n5
Oguibe, Olu 42

Panchal, Shanti 111
perceptual primacy 41–44, 49–51, 70–71,
    123–126, 191–192, 196–199
phenomenological approach 9–10,
    53–69, 70–108, 107–108, 110–111,
    130–131, 152–155, 188–189, 193–206,
    205–206
Phokela, Johannes 74–77, 78, 140
  *Mortal Diptych Surmounted by Cameo
    Emblems* 74–77
Picton, John 32
Piper, Adrian 39
Piper, Keith 54, 57, 67, 70, 125, 127
  *A Ship Called Jesus* 62–66
  *The Fictions of Science* series 93–94
  *UnRecorded* 66
post-critical ontology 189–190, 199–200

Rancière, Jacques 203
're-presentation' 40–42, 44–45, 180–181
reductionism 184–187, 195
  countering of 184–187
'representation', burden of 26–27, 42, 136,
    172–173, 197–198, 202–205
reversibility 132–157, 158
  of perceptual encounters 132–157
Roberts, John 113
Rodowick, David 164
Rubens, Peter Paul 74
  *The Consequences of War* 75
  *The Rape of the Daughters of Leucippus*
    75

Shilling, Chris 72n2
Shonibare, Yinka 174n2
signification 27–29, 29–31, 35–36, 41–44
  *see also* Asian art; black British art
Sikand, Gurminder 86n12
situatedness 46–49
Spender, Dale, *Man Made Language* 119
Spinoza, Baruch 156
Summers, David 56

Tawadros, Gilane 174n2
Thomas, Shanti, *The Traveller* 86–87
Titian, *Bacchanal of the Andrians* 75
Turner Prize 32n5

visual historiography, notion of place
    54–57

Warner, Marina 102
Wesley, Eric 174n2
Wetherell, Margaret 156
Williams, Aubrey
  *Olmec-Maya* series 78
  *Quetzlcoatl* 77–78
  *Symphonies* series 78–79
Wollheim, Richard 48
Wright, Richard 193–194

Ybarra Jr, Mario 174n2, 186
  *Brown and Proud* 179–*180*